Resistance and Collaboration in Hitler's Empire

Studies in European History Series

Series Editors: Julian Jackson, Peter Wilson and Sarah Badcock

Catherine Baker	*The Yugoslav Wars of the 1990s*
Jeremy Black	*A Military Revolution? Military Change and European Society, 1550–1800*
T.C.W. Blanning	*The French Revolution: Class War or Culture Clash?* (2nd edn)
John Breuilly	*The Formation of the First German Nation-State, 1800–1871*
Peter Burke	*The Renaissance* (2nd edn)
Markus Cerman	*Villagers and Lords in Eastern Europe, 1300–1800*
Michael L. Dockrill & Michael F. Hopkins	*The Cold War 1945–1991* (2nd edn)
William Doyle	*The Ancien Régime* (2nd edn)
William Doyle	*Jansenism*
Vesna Drapac & Gareth Pritchard	*Resistance and Collaboration in Hitler's Empire*
Andy Durgan	*The Spanish Civil War*
Geoffrey Ellis	*The Napoleonic Empire* (2nd edn)
Donald A. Filtzer	*The Khrushchev Era*
Karin Friedrich	*Brandenburg-Prussia, 1466–1806*
Mary Fulbrook	*Interpretations of the Two Germanies, 1945–1990* (2nd edn)
André Gerrits	*Nationalism in Europe since 1945*
Graeme Gill	*Stalinism* (2nd edn)
Hugh Gough	*The Terror in the French Revolution* (2nd edn)
Peter Grieder	*The German Democratic Republic*
John Henry	*The Scientific Revolution and the Origins of Modern Science* (3rd edn)
Stefan-Ludwig Hoffmann	*Civil Society, 1750–1914*
Henry Kamen	*Golden Age Spain* (2nd edn)
Beat Kümin	*The Communal Age in Western Europe, c.1100–1800*
Richard Mackenney	*The City-State, 1500–1700*
Spencer Mawby	*The Transformation and Decline of the British Empire*
Andrew Porter	*European Imperialism, 1860–1914*
Roy Porter	*The Enlightenment* (2nd edn)
Roger Price	*The Revolutions of 1848*
James Retallack	*Germany in the Age of Kaiser Wilhelm II*
Richard Sakwa	*Communism in Russia*
Geoffrey Scarre & John Callow	*Witchcraft and Magic in 16th- and 17th-Century Europe* (2nd edn)
R.W. Scribner & C. Scott Dixon	*The German Reformation* (2nd edn)
Robert Service	*The Russian Revolution, 1900–1927* (4th edn)
Jeremy Smith	*The Fall of Soviet Communism, 1985–1991*
David Stevenson	*The Outbreak of the First World War*
Peter H. Wilson	*The Holy Roman Empire, 1495–1806* (2nd edn)
Oliver Zimmer	*Nationalism in Europe, 1890–1940*

Resistance and Collaboration in Hitler's Empire

Vesna Drapac & Gareth Pritchard

© Vesna Drapac and Gareth Pritchard, under exclusive licence to Springer Nature Limited 2017

All rights reserved. No reproduction, copy or transmission of this publication may be made without written permission.

No portion of this publication may be reproduced, copied or transmitted save with written permission or in accordance with the provisions of the Copyright, Designs and Patents Act 1988, or under the terms of any licence permitting limited copying issued by the Copyright Licensing Agency, Saffron House, 6–10 Kirby Street, London EC1N 8TS.

Any person who does any unauthorised act in relation to this publication may be liable to criminal prosecution and civil claims for damages.

The authors have asserted their right to be identified as the authors of this work in accordance with the Copyright, Designs and Patents Act 1988.

First published 2017 by
RED GLOBE PRESS

Red Globe Press in the UK is an imprint of Springer Nature Limited, registered in England, company number 785998, of 4 Crinan Street, London, N1 9XW.

Red Globe Press® is a registered trademark in the United States, the United Kingdom, Europe and other countries.

ISBN 978–1–137–38534–5 paperback

This book is printed on paper suitable for recycling and made from fully managed and sustained forest sources. Logging, pulping and manufacturing processes are expected to conform to the environmental regulations of the country of origin.

A catalogue record for this book is available from the British Library.

A catalog record for this book is available from the Library of Congress.

Contents

Acknowledgements	vii
A note on names and terms	viii
Glossary	ix
Maps	x
Introduction	xv

1 Hitler's Empire	**1**
The administration of Hitler's empire	1
Everyday life in Hitler's empire	9
Popular responses to Nazi rule	14
Conclusion	22

2 The Evolution of the Historiography	**23**
The emergence of the terminology of resistance and collaboration	24
Western Europe	28
Communist and post-Communist states	32
Problems of definition	37
Conceptual and methodological problems	45
Conclusion	49

3 Armed Resistance and Collaboration	**50**
The development of armed resistance	50
Armed collaboration	55
Paramilitarisation as social process	61
Conclusion	72

4 Resistance and Collaboration in Everyday Life	**74**
Conceptualising daily-life resistance and collaboration	74
Social control, social agency, social revolution	79

'Measuring' daily-life resistance and collaboration	88
Conclusion	103
5 Genocide and Rescue	**105**
The fate of Jews in Hitler's empire	105
The historiography and the question of responsibility	108
The Holocaust and the resistance/collaboration paradigm	115
Conclusion	131
6 Beyond Resistance and Collaboration	**132**
Seven maxims	132
Towards a 'social history of politics' in Hitler's empire	135
The Catholic Church in Hitler's empire	138
Conclusion	161
7 Resistance and Collaboration in Official and Public Memory	**163**
World War II and the 'memory boom'	163
The *lieux de mémoire* of resistance and collaboration	165
Resistance and collaboration in cinema	172
The memory of resistance and collaboration in contemporary Europe	181
Conclusion	186
Conclusion	**187**
Suggestions for further reading	191
Index	194

Acknowledgements

The authors would like to thank those who contributed in some way to the writing of this book. Vesna would like to thank her mother and her brother, Goran, for their encouragement. She is especially grateful to her husband, Brendan Moran, and their two sons, Thomas and David, for their enthusiasm for the project and for their patience. They have listened to, engaged with, and asked difficult questions about our study of resistance and collaboration as it evolved. Gareth would like to thank his wife, Olga, who provided him with moral support and helped him to improve his Russian. Both Vesna and Gareth are indebted to their colleagues at the University of Adelaide, and in particular to William Woods (who helped to finalise the manuscript) and Margaret Hosking (our wonderful history librarian). We would also like to acknowledge our students, Tamika Glouftsis and Matthew Traeger, who helped us to synthesise some of the literature in the course of their summer research scholarship in 2015.

A note on names and terms

How to represent non-English names and terms in a text of this nature, which covers many countries and languages, is tricky. We use the versions of names and terms that students are most likely to encounter in the Anglophone literature. We have used the term 'fascist' in a generic sense to describe extreme, right-wing nationalist movements. In the case of Italy, however, we capitalise the word Fascist because the Italian Fascists were members of a Fascist Party and called themselves Fascists. Similarly, we have capitalised the term Communist because Communists almost always called themselves that and were members of Communist parties. We mostly use the term 'partisans' in a generic sense to describe guerrilla fighters. In the case of Yugoslavia, however, we capitalise the term Partisans because members of Tito's People's Liberation Army (NOV) referred to themselves as Partisans.

Glossary

AK	Home Army (Poland)
Chetniks	Serbian partisan movement
Einsatzgruppen	SS mobile killing units
ELAS	Greek People's Liberation Army
Hilfswillige (Hiwis)	Soviet citizens who served as auxiliary troops in the Wehrmacht
Hitler Jugend	Hitler Youth
Judenrat	Jewish Council
Milice	French collaborationist militia
NDH	Independent State of Croatia
NOV	People's Liberation Army (Yugoslavia)
OSS	Office of Strategic Services (USA)
Osttruppen	Non-German 'Eastern Troops' in the Wehrmacht
OUN	Organisation of Ukrainian Nationalists
PCI	Communist Party of Italy
Schutzmannschaften	Auxiliary police battalions
SS	Schutzstaffel
SOE	Special Operations Executive (UK)
STO	Service du Travail Obligatoire
UPA	Ukrainian Insurgent Army
Ustaše	Croatian collaborationist militia
Waffen-SS	Military wing of the SS
Wehrmacht	German armed forces

Maps

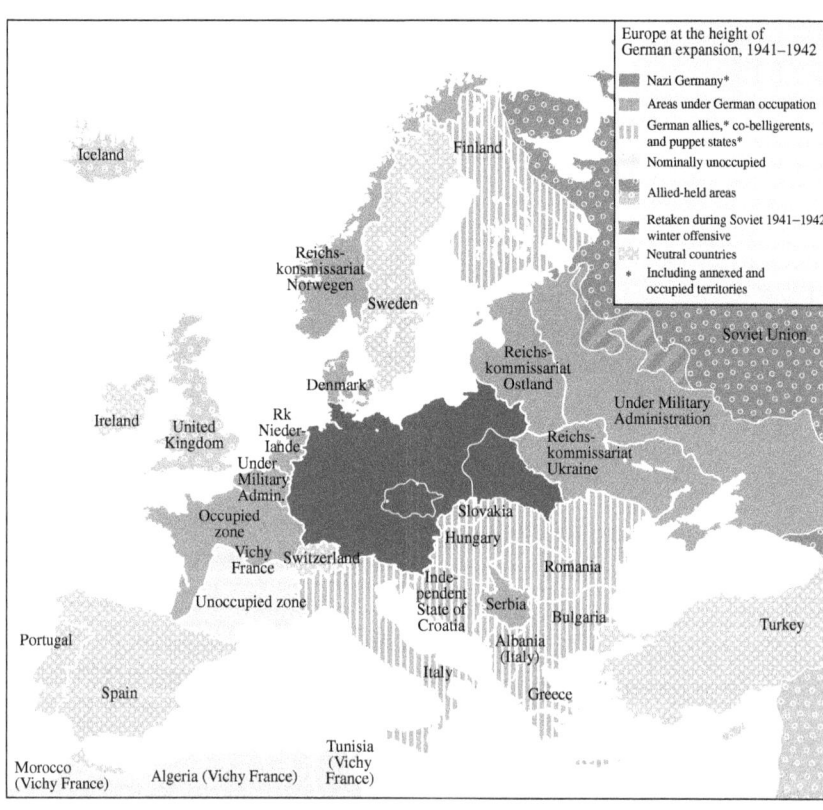

Map 1 The Nazi empire in October 1942.

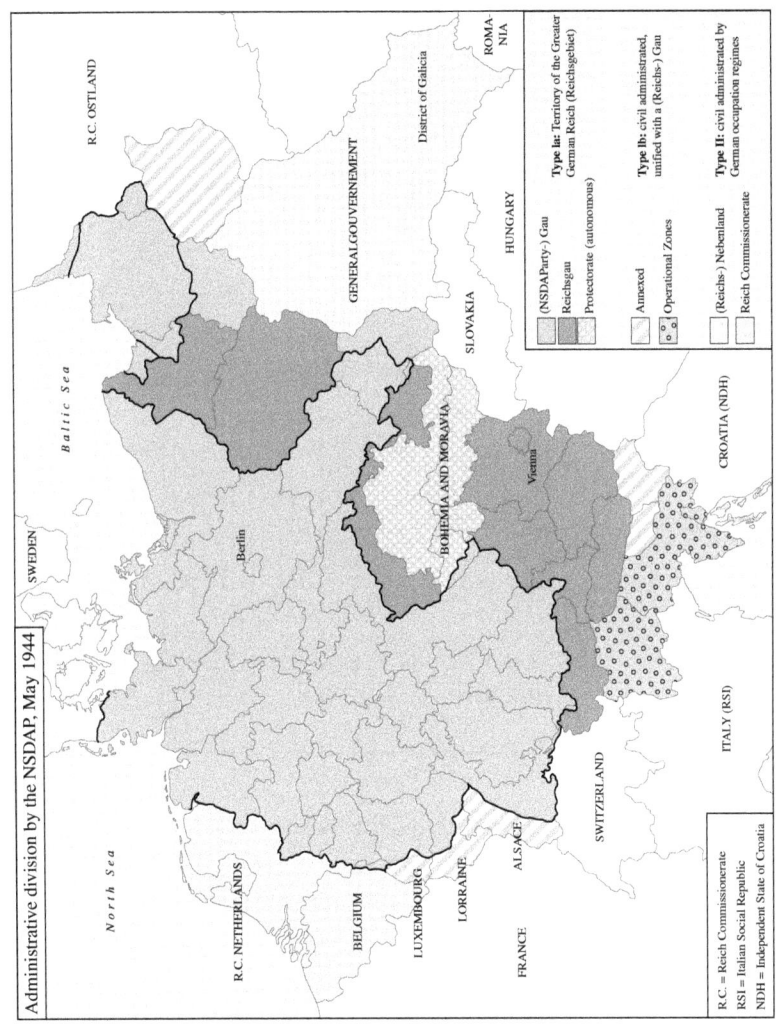

Map 2 The Gaue of the Greater German Reich in 1944.

Maps

	Annexed to Germany		Reichskommissariat Ukraine
	Attached to the Generalgouvernement		Under German Military Government
	Administered by Romania		
	Reichskommissariat Ostland		Not shown: the Caucasus, under German Military Government

Map 3   The German occupation of the USSR, c. November 1942.

Adapted from Timothy Patrick Mulligan, *The Politics of Illusion and Empire: German Occupation Policy in the Soviet Union, 1942–1943* (New York: Praeger, 1988), 25.

Maps

Map 4 France under German occupation, 1940–44.

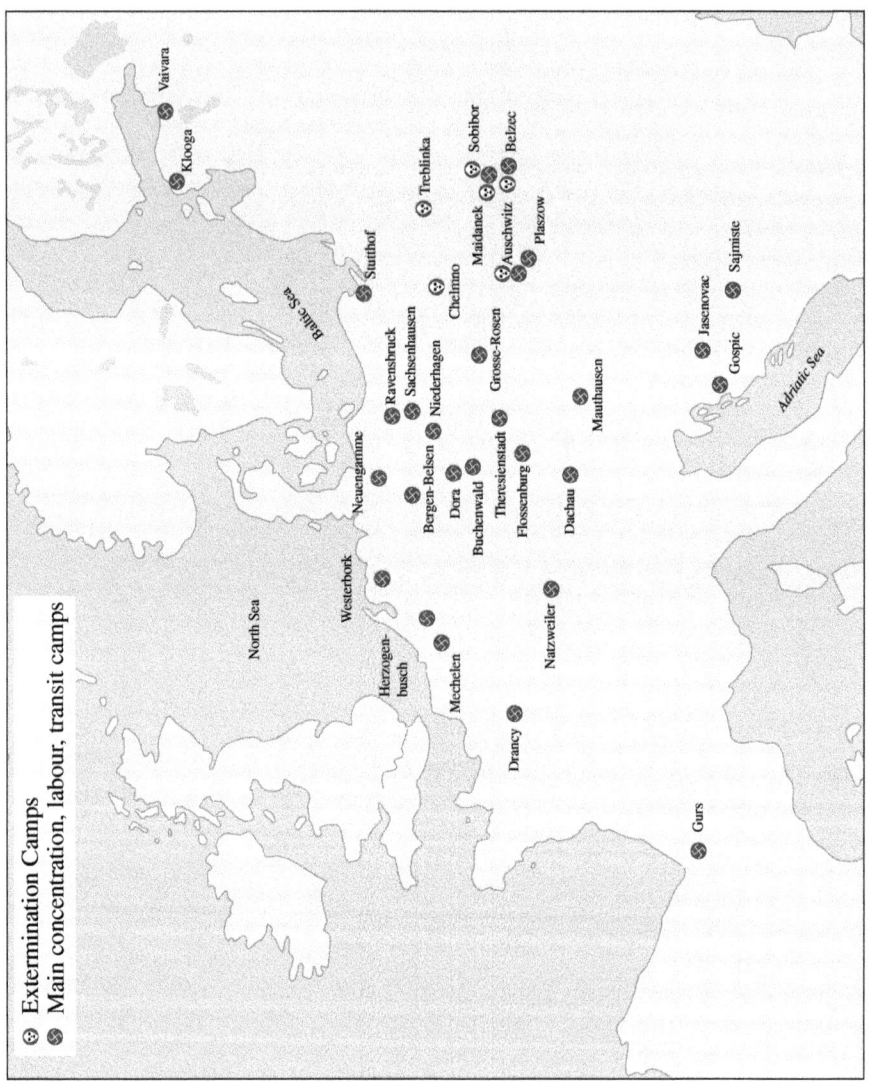

Map 5 Main concentration/labour/transit camps and Extermination Camps.
Source: friends-partners.org/partners/beyond-the-pale/images/58-1.gif

Introduction

This is a book about the ways in which the concepts of resistance and collaboration in Hitler's empire have been described, debated, applied, and politicised. Our purpose was to synthesise the vast literature on resistance and collaboration and to explain how and why it has evolved in the decades since World War II. We have not assumed extensive prior knowledge on the part of the reader, and we have tried to write a book that will be accessible to students, their teachers, and the general public. But we also hope that our critique of the existing literature, and our suggestions for alternative approaches, will be of interest to historians.

There are four basic principles underpinning the rationale of this book. Firstly, we have chosen to deal with resistance and collaboration together, rather than treating them as separate phenomena. In our view, both resistance and collaboration were shaped by the same social processes and they cannot be understood in isolation from each other. Moreover, the concepts of resistance and collaboration are entangled in the minds of almost all those who have written about World War II. Though the meaning of the two concepts has changed significantly over time, most historians still locate people's responses to Nazi rule on a scale between outright resistance at one pole and active collaboration at the other. Resistance and collaboration thus exist in a binary relationship with each other, which is why we refer in this book to the 'resistance/collaboration paradigm'. Our main conclusion is that, although there is no need to discard the paradigm, we do need to be able to transcend it.

The second principle underlying this book is that resistance and collaboration are best understood if they are placed in the context of Hitler's empire as a whole. In this respect, we differ from most other historians, who focus on specific localities, countries, or regions. In our view, Hitler's empire was transnational in character, as was the war which

Introduction

he unleashed. What happened in one part of the empire had repercussions elsewhere, both in terms of Nazi policies and in terms of people's behaviour. Therefore, we have conceptualised this book in a way that addresses some of the problems of historiographical insularity and fragmentation that have resulted from nationally derived explanations of resistance and collaboration.

Thirdly, we reject the linear and teleological framework in which the resistance/collaboration paradigm is embedded. The years 1939 and 1945 bookend most writing about Hitler's empire. But there were different 'starting points' and, for a large area of Europe, May 1945 did not signify a victory but the prospect of incorporation into another repressive empire. The normal chronology of the war from the Western Allies' perspective – as a series of lows, highs, and 'turning points' culminating in Allied victory in 1945 – does not accurately represent the way in which the war was experienced by the majority of Europeans. Just as terms like 'the inter-war period', 'pre-war' and 'post-war' are constructs of the post-1945 world, so, too, is the usual periodisation of the war itself. The notion of something occurring 'as early as' 1940, or 'as late as' 1944 only has meaning from a particular (Western and Allied) vantage point. To judge and label people's behaviour as either resistance or collaboration in so far as it can be made retrospectively to dovetail with this vantage point is an invidious and generally unacknowledged tendency in the historiography. We have tried to buck this trend by discussing resistance and collaboration from the perspective of people who lived the war.

Our fourth principle is that, because resistance and collaboration were processes that were rooted in society as a whole, it is necessary to incorporate gender at every level of our analysis. In most traditional studies of Hitler's empire, the role of women (and the role of relationships between women and men) is either ignored or discussed as a parallel paradigm (for example, a book on resistance in which women are dealt with in a separate chapter). Though there is a growing literature that looks specifically at women, its findings have not been assimilated into the wider historiography. Most importantly, the conceptual assumptions that underpin the resistance/collaboration paradigm are based on a double standard: historians' understandings of collaboration have been broadened and thereby 'feminised' whereas their understandings of resistance have not. By 'feminised' we mean that the concept of collaboration has been coded

Introduction

as feminine and extended to include activities in social domains that were traditionally feminine. The same has not happened to concepts of resistance. In our view, this has always been and remains one of the most serious problems with the way that historians write about European society under Nazi rule.

While we have aimed for broad coverage, space has not allowed for equal treatment of every part of Hitler's empire. Nor has it been possible to discuss in detail the experiences of all the various social and ethnic groups who fell under Nazi rule. Instead, we have focused on case studies, drawn from across the empire, which clearly illustrate the points that we are trying to make. In choosing these examples, we have prioritised the historiographical debates that have engaged historians of Central and Western Europe. Directly and indirectly, many of the main works in these historiographical traditions – especially those on dissent and complicity in the Third Reich – have become models for the study of resistance and collaboration in Europe as a whole. Moreover, since Nazi rule was 'made in Germany' and then exported by force, we felt that any study of Nazi Europe would be incomplete without some reference to developments in Germany itself.

We have also focused on case studies which continue to have relevance in contemporary Europe. For this reason, we have placed emphasis on those regions where debates about the nature of resistance and collaboration have engaged politicians and popular opinion since the collapse of Communism. Our discussion of recent scholarship on post-Communist Europe also reflects the fact that, in the decades since 1989, the centre of gravity of the scholarship has drifted eastwards.

Academic writing on resistance and collaboration is complex and sometimes confusing. There have been many changes in the points of focus and the historical methods applied. Historians have also located their arguments within a range of approaches: political, military, philosophical, social, psychological, sociological, moral, and cultural. Furthermore, the history of resistance and collaboration overlaps with other historiographies which are also substantial. For example, the literature on the Holocaust, which is growing at an exponential rate, frames debates about resistance and collaboration. Making sense of this prodigious literature in a work of this length is, to say the least, a challenge. By organising the book thematically, rather than chronologically or geographically, we have attempted to address that challenge.

A number of concepts that we use have been the subject of some debate among historians, and require a little explanation. For instance, historians frequently use the terms 'top down' and 'bottom up'. Therefore, when we summarise the views of other historians, we are obliged to use them as well. In our view, however, the concepts of 'centre' and 'periphery' are more useful when analysing an empire. Moreover, it should always be borne in mind that the relationship between the two was dialectical. Similarly, we have used the phrase 'total war' because it crops up so frequently in the literature. We prefer the term 'totalising war' because it emphasises the fact that World War II was a dynamic process that was cumulatively radicalising. The word 'totalitarian' is particularly controversial because it implies that Nazi Germany shared fundamental similarities to other 'totalitarian' regimes such as Fascist Italy and the Soviet Union, and because it suggests that the Nazis (and the Fascists and Communists) gained 'total' control of society. Today, many historians try to avoid using the word 'totalitarian' altogether. But whatever view one takes in this ongoing debate, the fact remains that the concept of 'totalitarianism' has been one of the most important ideas in the evolution of the historiography. This is the context in which we use the term and explain its significance.

Historians who read this book will notice that most of the secondary texts to which we refer were either written in English or have been translated into English. The reason for this is pragmatic. Since the purpose of the book is to provide an introduction for Anglophone students and general readers, the function of the references is to direct those who want to know more about a specific topic towards sources that are accessible to them. We have not undertaken any statistical research but we draw our numbers from the work of reputable historians. The reader should bear in mind that it is difficult to arrive at precise numbers regarding issues such as the size of resistance movements, the scale of Nazi and collaborationist atrocities, and the level of rations.

Although we discuss many recent publications on resistance and collaboration, our goal is not just to give an overview of the current literature. Rather, our primary concern is to chart the evolution of the historiography of resistance and collaboration from World War II to the present. We have attempted to explain the underlying conceptual frameworks which have governed – and sometimes impeded - general understandings of resistance and collaboration, and which continue to shape the work of historians today.

Introduction

The structure of the book reflects our goals and priorities. In Chapter 1, we provide contextual information about the administration of Hitler's empire, the nature of Nazi occupation policies, and their impact on the lives of Europeans. In Chapter 2, our focus shifts from the history of Hitler's empire to the historiography. In particular, we analyse the evolution of the definitions of resistance and collaboration and we interrogate the premises on which these definitions are based. Chapters 3–5 look at various kinds of resistance and collaboration, and how historians have discussed them. Since we could not cover every type of resistance and collaboration, we have focused on the case studies that are most paradigmatic in the historiography. Thus, Chapter 3 looks at armed resistance and armed collaboration because these are the most written-about by historians and the most iconic in the public imagination. Chapter 4 discusses resistance and collaboration in everyday life. Chapter 5 explores how ascribing responsibility for the Holocaust has become fundamental to the ways in which historians think about resistance and collaboration. In Chapter 6, we bring the threads of our analysis together and outline a possible new approach to the social history of Hitler's empire, which we call the 'social history of politics'. We then apply a 'social history of politics' approach to the analysis of a specific case study: the Catholic Church. Finally, in Chapter 7, we provide an overview of the social, cultural, and political context in which narratives of resistance and collaboration have been, and still are, contested in the public sphere.

There are some topics which we wanted to discuss in greater depth but which we have omitted because we did not have the space to do them justice. Most obviously, we have not included a chapter on political parties and movements that either resisted or collaborated (or both). Though we do touch occasionally on this important matter, we chose to concentrate more on the social history of Hitler's empire. Central to our analysis is our belief that politics and political choices in the 1940s can best be understood from the perspective of the wider social context created by the changing circumstances of the war. For this reason, we have placed the experiences of 'ordinary' people – rather than those of political elites – at the centre of our analysis.

The last point that we want to make by way of introduction concerns the title that we have chosen for our book. As we have already noted, most historians who have written about European society in World War II have focused on developments at a local, regional, or national level. We believe

Introduction

that this has resulted in an underestimation of the importance of power relations between the centre and the periphery. Describing Nazi Europe as an empire helps us to think about transnational connections as well as the fundamental importance of the ideological drive from the centre. Hitler himself conceptualised his project in imperial terms and, when discussing his policies, he frequently invoked precedents drawn from the history of other empires, including the British Empire. Moreover, the structures of Nazi rule in Europe in the 1940s are compatible with the definitions of empire that have been provided by other historians. Douglas Northrop, for example, explains empires as:

> no more than a particular way of organizing political and social relationships. In some ways they resemble any other powerful government or state, as an entity that exerts sovereign authority over a large number of people and an extensive territory. Unlike other kinds of states, though, empires are characterized by a distinctive pattern of internal and external relationships. These relationships combine three crucial factors: distance, difference, and domination.[1]

Nazi rule in Europe was imposed over a large geographical area and a diverse population, and was held together by various forms of direct and indirect domination. By Northrop's definition, it was therefore clearly a kind of empire, albeit one of unusual brevity and unparalleled brutality.

---

[1] Douglas Northrop, *An Imperial World: Empires and Colonies since 1750* (Boston, MA: Pearson, 2013), 12.

1 Hitler's Empire

Because both resistance and collaboration were shaped by the nature of Nazi rule, we begin by discussing three key issues which pertained to people's experiences of living in Hitler's empire. Firstly, we outline the methods used by the Nazis to administer and govern the territories that fell under their control. Secondly, we look at the impact of Nazi rule on the everyday lives of Hitler's subjects. Finally, we explore the terminology and concepts that are used by academics who write about the social history of World War II.

The administration of Hitler's empire

By the end of 1941, Hitler's empire stretched from the Atlantic coast of France to the gates of Moscow, and from the Arctic Circle in Norway to the deserts of North Africa (see Map 1). At its height, some 244 million Europeans lived under its sway, 90 million of whom were ethnic Germans.[1] How these people experienced Nazi rule varied considerably. One reason for this was the complexity of the administrative arrangements that were made by the Nazis for ruling their empire. For analytical purposes, we can divide the territories that made up Hitler's empire into four categories.

The first category comprised the lands which were governed directly from Berlin and which the Nazis regarded as the 'Greater German Reich'. The core of this territory was made up of Germany within the borders established in 1919 by the Treaty of Versailles. Between 1938 and 1942, the Nazis extended these borders through the piecemeal annexation of neighbouring lands. These included Austria (annexed in March 1938),

[1] Mark Mazower, *Hitler's Empire: Nazi Rule in Occupied Europe* (London: Allen Lane, 2008), 245.

the Sudetenland (taken from Czechoslovakia in October 1938), western Poland (October 1939), the French territory of Alsace-Lorraine (June 1940), the Belgian district of Eupen-Malmédy (June 1940), northern Slovenia (April 1941), and Luxembourg (August 1942).

The second category in Hitler's empire consisted of lands under direct German occupation. By the autumn of 1942, the German armed forces (Wehrmacht) had occupied much of Europe, including northern France, Belgium and Denmark, as well as large parts of Yugoslavia, Greece and the Soviet Union. Other territories were placed under the control of Nazi civilian governors (*Reichskommissare*), who had been hand-picked by Hitler. The most important were Josef Terboven (Norway), Arthur Seyss-Inquart (the Netherlands), Hinrich Lohse (the Baltic states and parts of Belorussia), and Erich Koch (parts of Ukraine). A rump of Polish territory called the Generalgouvernement was ruled as a private fiefdom by Hans Frank. The Czech lands of Bohemia and Moravia were incorporated into the Greater Reich but run by Nazi-appointed governors, the best known of whom was Reinhard Heydrich. Throughout occupied Europe, military commandants and Nazi governors enjoyed considerable autonomy. This led to variations in how they approached their task. Koch was hostile to any degree of local self-administration beyond what was unavoidable. Lohse, by contrast, was willing to tolerate a degree of self-governance by agents of the local population. Military commandants generally adopted a more pragmatic approach to ruling subject populations than the *Reichskommissare*.[2]

A third category of territory consisted of client states which were created in the wake of German military action. These states were notionally independent, but they only existed on German sufferance and were subject to increasing German domination. The most important of these were the Slovak Republic (established in 1939), the Vichy regime in France (1940), the Independent State of Croatia (NDH) and the Government of National Salvation in Serbia (both 1941), the Italian Social Republic (1943), and Hungary after the fascist coup of 1944. The politicians at the apex of these client states were either leaders of local fascist parties, who collaborated out of ideological conviction, or authoritarian conservatives, who collaborated because they thought that it was in the national

---

[2] Timothy Mulligan, *The Politics of Illusion and Empire: German Occupation Policy in the Soviet Union, 1942–1943* (New York: Praeger, 1988).

interest. Frequently referred to by historians as 'puppets', these satellite regimes were more than lifeless marionettes. Though attached to Berlin by numerous strings, the puppets had agendas of their own and a degree of autonomy. Historians normally describe these client regimes as having engaged in 'state collaboration'. The names, dates and political orientation of these regimes are summarised in Table 1.

The fourth category of territory comprised those independent states which aligned themselves with the Third Reich and which fought on its side during the war: Italy (up to 1943, when the Fascist regime collapsed), Bulgaria, Romania, Hungary, and Finland (up to 1944). In 1940 Mussolini

Table 1 Sample of client regimes of Nazi Germany.

Client regime	Dates and seat of government	Leader	Political orientation[3]
Slovak Republic	March 1939 to April 1945: Bratislava	Jozef Tiso	Authoritarian conservative
French State	July 1940 to August 1944: Vichy	Philippe Pétain	Authoritarian conservative
Independent State of Croatia (NDH)	April 1941 to May 1945: Zagreb	Ante Pavelić	Extreme Croatian nationalist
Government of National Salvation	August 1941 to October 1944: Belgrade	Milan Nedić	Authoritarian Serb nationalist
Italian Social Republic	September 1943 to April 1945: Salò	Benito Mussolini	Italian Fascist
Government of National Unity	October 1944 to May 1945: Budapest	Ferenc Szálasi	Hungarian fascist

---

[3] These regimes were often more fluid and complex than it is possible to portray in a table. What we have tried to do here is to demonstrate how they have been perceived both at the time and subsequently.

entered the war on the side of the Germans. However, as a result of the inadequacy of the Italian armies, he became ever more reliant on German support. In 1941 Bulgaria participated in the invasion and occupation of Greece and Yugoslavia, while Romania, Hungary, and Finland joined the Germans in the assault on the USSR. With the exception of Finland, all Hitler's allies found themselves in a relationship with Nazi Germany that became increasingly unequal over time. Their domestic policies were brought into line with those of Germany, in particular in terms of the implementation of the Holocaust. The degree to which the governments of these countries collaborated with or resisted the Nazis is still the subject of controversy.[4]

If the territorial organisation of the Nazi empire was complicated, the structures that the Germans set up for administering it were more so. Despite the fact that they had long dreamed of a German empire in Europe, the Nazis had made few concrete plans for how they were going to run it. They made up the rules as they went along. No single body was responsible for managing the empire. Instead, a range of organisations and individuals with overlapping jurisdictions competed for domination. Access to Hitler was a key factor that determined which of his Nazi barons, generals, foreign vassals and allies were able to get what they wanted.[5] These complex administrative arrangements were important because they led to substantial differences in how Nazi rule was experienced by Hitler's subjects. Three examples will suffice to give a sense of the diversity of Nazi power structures.

Greater Germany

The arrangements made by the Nazis for the governance of Greater Germany were elaborate. Superimposed on to the pre-existing regions of Germany – such as Prussia, Saxony, and Bavaria – were a series of new

---

[4] See Roni Stauber (ed.), *Collaboration with the Nazis: Public Discourse after the Holocaust* (London: Routledge, 2011), Chapters 10–14.

[5] Alex J. Kay, *Exploitation, Resettlement, Mass Murder: Political and Economic Planning for German Occupation Policy in the Soviet Union, 1940–1941* (New York: Berghahn, 2006), especially Chapters 1 and 2; Thomas J. Laub, *After the Fall: German Policy in Occupied France, 1940–1944* (Oxford: Oxford University Press, 2010), 35–48; Mazower, *Hitler's Empire*, Chapter 8; Jozo Tomasevich, *War and Revolution in Yugoslavia, 1941–1945: Occupation and Collaboration* (Stanford, CA: Stanford University Press, 2001), Chapter 2; Martin Winstone, *The Dark Heart of Hitler's Europe: Nazi Rule in Poland under the General Government* (London: I.B. Tauris, 2015), Chapters 1 and 2.

administrative units called *Gau* (see Map 2). Each *Gau* was governed by a *Gauleiter* who had been appointed by Hitler, and who had significant power in his territory. Alongside the traditional structures of the German state, including the ministries of government and the German armed forces, Hitler created other bodies which exercised state functions. There were two paramilitary formations, the SA (Sturmabteilung) and the SS (Schutzstaffel), both controlled by Heinrich Himmler. There were mass (or 'capillary') organisations, the purpose of which was to mobilise Germans in the service of the state and indoctrinate them according to National Socialist principles. These included the Hitler Youth (Hitler Jugend), the German Labour Front (Deutsche Arbeitsfront), German Women's Welfare (Deutsches Frauenwerk), and the mass leisure organisation Strength through Joy (Kraft durch Freude). There were economic agencies such as the Office of the Four-Year Plan under Hermann Goering (which was supposed to prepare the German economy for war), and the Todt Organisation (which constructed roads, border defences and military installations). Where their roles overlapped, these agencies competed with each other for power. There was no single administrative unit to coordinate policy or make rational decisions about the allocation of resources. It is for this reason that the Third Reich is sometimes referred to as a 'polycratic' state. The key to success, generally, was winning Hitler's favour.[6]

The occupied territories of the Soviet Union

The polycratic style of government that had been introduced in Germany after 1933 was subsequently imposed on other countries. After the German invasion of the USSR in 1941, for instance, the territories that had been conquered by the Wehrmacht were parcelled out to different stakeholders (see Map 3). The Baltic states, large parts of Belorussia and most of Ukraine were placed under *Reichskommissare*. But about half the occupied territory remained under the control of the Wehrmacht. South-western Ukraine was placed under Romanian occupation. The region around Lviv was attached to Frank's Generalgouvernement.

---

[6] Joseph W. Bendersky, *A Concise History of Nazi Germany* (Lanham, MD: Roman & Littlefield, 2007), Chapter 8; Tim Kirk, *Nazi Germany* (Basingstoke: Palgrave Macmillan, 2007), 46–55; D.G. Williamson, *The Third Reich*, 3rd edn (Harlow: Pearson, 2002), Chapter 4.

The governance of the occupied territories in the USSR was further complicated by the large number of overlapping administrative units that were involved in the formulation and implementation of policy. In theory, the occupation of the whole region was coordinated by the East Ministry (Ostministerium) of Alfred Rosenberg. Despite the grandiose title of his ministry, Rosenberg did not enjoy much real power because he was not a member of Hitler's inner circle. The SS, under Himmler, was more important. Not only was the SS responsible for policing behind the lines and implementing racial policies, but it also took control of substantial economic assets. Another leading Nazi who played a major role in the occupation was Fritz Sauckel who, from 1942 onwards, was responsible for rounding up civilians and deporting them as slave labourers to the Reich. Additionally, German business corporations participated in the economic exploitation of the occupied territories. For instance, an organisation made up of representatives of German business interests and the Nazi state, the Berg-und Hüttenwerksgesellschaft (BHO), worked to align the industrial infrastructure of the occupied territories with the needs of the Nazi war economy.[7]

Between these various bodies there was constant rivalry. Some of the Nazi stakeholders – including many of the military commandants and the technocrats of the BHO – were relatively pragmatic in their approach to occupation. Despite his reputation as the Nazis' chief ideologue, Rosenberg was rather flexible on issues such as local self-government. The 'pragmatists' believed that the rational exploitation of the occupied territories in the interests of winning the war should take priority over ideological considerations. They were sometimes in favour of making concessions to win the loyalty of local populations. For example, they initiated efforts to introduce land reform to give the land back to the peasants.[8]

---

[7] Militärgeschichtliches Forschungsamt, *Germany and the Second World War*, Volume V/II: *Organization and Mobilization of the German Sphere of Power: Wartime Administration, Economy, and Manpower Resources 1939–1941* (Oxford: Clarendon Press, 1990), 45–64; Mulligan, *Politics of Illusion*, Chapter 8.

[8] Christian Gerlach, 'Die deutsche Agrarreform und die Bevölkerungspolitik in den besetzten sowjetischen Gebieten', in Christian Gerlach (ed.), *Besatzung und Bundnis. Deutsche Herrschaftsstrategien in Ost- und Südosteuropa* (Göttingen: Verlag der Buchläden, 1995), 9–60.

They allowed Orthodox and Greek-Rite churches to reopen their doors and reinstated religious instruction in schools.[9] They attempted to recruit local troops in order to help alleviate the manpower shortages of the Wehrmacht.[10] They also tried to impede Sauckel's efforts to kidnap workers, not out of humanitarian considerations, but because they regarded it as an inefficient use of labour resources.[11]

The reforming efforts of the 'pragmatists' were resisted by hardliners who dismissed the interests of the local populations as irrelevant. When the Ostministerium sponsored measures to introduce land reform, Koch refused to implement them even though Rosenberg was technically his superior.[12] 'Pragmatists' in the Wehrmacht, particularly in Army Group Centre and in the Supreme Army Command (Oberkommando des Heeres), wanted to raise an army of anti-Stalinist Russians, recruited from Red Army prisoners-of-war (POWs), under the leadership of the turncoat Soviet general, Andrei Vlasov. Blocked at every turn by Nazi officials, and by Hitler himself, the initiative made little progress.[13] In these internecine feuds, the division between 'hardliners' and 'pragmatists' was often blurry. Wehrmacht officers and Nazi officials shifted from one camp to the other depending on the course of the war and their personal interests. For example, Himmler was a 'hardliner' on issues like the economic exploitation of subject populations and the killing of Jewish people.

---

[9] Karel C. Berkhoff, 'Was There a Religious Revival in the Soviet Ukraine under the Nazi Regime?', *Slavonic and East European Review*, 78/3 (2000), 536–567; and *Harvest of Despair: Life and Death in Ukraine under Nazi Rule* (Cambridge, MA: Belknap Press of Harvard University Press, 2004), Chapter 10; Harvey Fireside, *Icon and Swastika: The Russian Orthodox Church under Nazi and Soviet Control* (Cambridge, MA: Harvard University Press, 1971), 83–87 and 117–123; Alexander Voronin, 'The Ukrainian Orthodox Church during WW II', in Taras Hunczak and Dmytro M. Shtohryn (eds), *Ukraine: The Challenges of World War II* (Lanham, MD: University Press of America, 2003), 277–300.

[10] Matthew Cooper, *The Phantom War: The German Struggle against Soviet Partisans 1941–1944* (London: Macdonald and Jane's, 1979), 110–120; Mazower, *Hitler's Empire*, 458–465; Mulligan, *Politics of Illusion*, 148–157.

[11] Mulligan, *Politics of Illusion*, 99–115.

[12] Sean M. McAteer, *500 Days: The War in Eastern Europe, 1944–1945* (Pittsburgh, PA: Red Lead Press, 2008), 45–46; Mulligan, *Politics of Illusion*, 99–100.

[13] Catherine Andreyev, *Vlasov and the Russian Liberation Movement: Soviet Reality and Émigré Theories* (Cambridge: Cambridge University Press, 1987).

But the armed wing of the SS (Waffen-SS) recruited non-Germans and 'non-Aryans', including men whom Hitler would not have regarded as worthy of bearing arms.[14]

Occupied France

The administration of occupied France was equally complex (see Map 4). According to the armistice terms of June 1940, northern France and the Atlantic seaboard were placed under direct military occupation. Southern France was left unoccupied. The French government relocated to the spa town of Vichy in the unoccupied zone, under the leadership of the World War I hero Marshal Pétain. (In November 1942, the Germans occupied the south as well, though the Vichy regime continued to exist.) For military reasons, the two north-eastern departments of the Nord and Pas-de-Calais were placed under the authority of the Wehrmacht authorities in Brussels. Alsace-Lorraine – long a bone of contention between Germany and France – was incorporated into the Greater Reich and Germanised. Some 100,000 of the inhabitants of Alsace-Lorraine, deemed 'unassimilable', were expelled. The Germans also granted a small zone of occupation in south-eastern France to the Italians to placate Mussolini.[15] The degree to which the population of France was subjected to direct German control thus varied greatly from one part of the country to another. In most places, however, day-to-day administration was left largely in the hands of the Vichy regime. French civil servants, mayors and policemen continued to exercise their functions, answering as before to the French government.

The headquarters of the German military occupation, which for much of the war was run by Carl-Heinrich von Stülpnagel, was located in Paris. Stülpnagel was ruthless but pragmatic. In September 1940, he famously noted: 'If one wants the cow to give milk, it must be fed.' Stülpnagel's job, however, was made more complicated by the interference of numerous German agencies. For example, the department in charge of propaganda, while technically part of the military occupation, answered to the German

---

[14] Christopher Hale, *Hitler's Foreign Executioners: Europe's Dirty Secret* (Stroud: History Press, 2011).

[15] Julian Jackson, *France: The Dark Years 1940–1944* (Oxford: Oxford University Press, 2001), 169–174; Raphael Lemkin, *Axis Rule in Occupied Europe* (Washington, DC: Carnegie Endowment for International Peace, 1944), Chapter 18.

propaganda ministry in Berlin under Joseph Goebbels. Policing occupied France increasingly fell to Himmler's SS. Another German voice of influence was that of the ambassador, Otto Abetz, who was stationed in Paris and reported to the foreign ministry of Joachim von Ribbentrop. Married to a French woman, Abetz was a Francophile who favoured a more conciliatory line toward the French – providing that they knew their place.[16] As in other parts of Hitler's empire, the German Ministry of Munitions under Albert Speer, and the Plenipotentiary for Labour, Sauckel, pursued conflicting goals. Speer wanted to shift the production of consumer goods from Germany to France, thereby permitting German firms to focus more on arms production. Sauckel's objective, by contrast, was to harvest as many workers as possible and ship them to Germany to service the war industries of the Reich.[17] The forced requisition of labour, the *Service du Travail Obligatoire* (STO), introduced in 1943 after attempts at encouraging workers to volunteer to leave for Germany had failed, had a profound and negative impact on French public opinion.[18]

Everyday life in Hitler's empire

The choices that people made about how to respond to Nazi rule – in particular whether to resist or to collaborate – were normally shaped by their experiences in everyday life. Conditions differed from one part of Europe to another, and from one section of the population to another. Often these variations were the result of the administrative complexity that we have just described. Another important factor that led to variations in the daily-life experiences of Europeans was Nazi ideology.

According to the Nazis, all the peoples of Europe could be placed in a racial hierarchy. At the top of the pyramid were those Germans whom the Nazis deemed to be 'racially desirable'. Next in line were the 'Nordic'

---

[16] Philippe Burrin, *Living with Defeat: France under the German Occupation, 1940–1944* (London: Arnold, 1996), 84–97.

[17] Mark Spoerer, 'Forced Labour in Nazi-Occupied Europe, 1939–1945', in Marcel Boldorf and Tetsuji Okazaki (eds), *Economies under Occupation: The Hegemony of Nazi Germany and Imperial Japan in World War II* (London: Routledge, 2015), 73–85, 79.

[18] Ian Ousby, *Occupation: The Ordeal of France 1940–1944* (London: Pimlico, 1997), 247–254; Richard Vinen, *The Unfree French: Life under Occupation* (London: Allen Lane, 2006), Chapter 8.

and 'Germanic' peoples of Norway, Denmark and the Netherlands, whom the Nazis regarded as racially akin to the Germans and almost as valuable. Much further down the racial pyramid were the Slavs of Eastern and Central Europe, though some Slavs (for example the Croats and the Czechs) were regarded as more advanced than others (the Poles and the Russians). At the bottom of the hierarchy were Jewish people and Roma, whom the Nazis did not regard as fully human. The political orientation of subject populations also influenced Nazi behaviour. Non-German anti-Semites and anti-Communists were seen as potential allies, while Communists (whom the Nazis conflated with Jews) were seen as arch-enemies and persecuted accordingly.

The consequence of these racial and political considerations was that, generally, Nazi rule was far more brutal in Eastern Europe than in the West. During the first years of the occupation, for example, the German authorities in France behaved fairly correctly towards the bulk of the population (though not towards French Communists, Jewish people or resisters). In the occupied territories of the Soviet Union, by contrast, the Germans were harsh from the outset and became increasingly murderous over time. However, they calibrated their ruthlessness according to politics and ethnicity. Soviet citizens of German origin were favoured, and certain other ethnic groups, such as Estonians and Tatars, were generally treated with less severity.

It is difficult to exaggerate the extent to which the shortage of essential commodities, especially food, influenced people's behaviour. The war led to a massive diversion of resources for military use. To make matters worse, the Allied blockade prevented the importation of foodstuffs and other goods from abroad. Transport and trade were disrupted by war. Above all, the rapacious economic imperialism of the Nazi state led to general impoverishment.[19] The material hardships imposed by the war, however, were not experienced equally. Most severely affected by food shortages were the inmates of concentration and POW camps and of the various Jewish ghettoes that were established by the Nazis in Eastern Europe. For example, the average food ration for Jews in the Warsaw Ghetto in 1941 provided just 184 calories per day. Even when supplemented by food

---

[19] Polymeris Voglis, 'Surviving Hunger: Life in the Cities and the Countryside during the Occupation', in Robert Gildea, Olivier Wieviorka and Anette Warring (eds), *Surviving Hitler and Mussolini: Daily Life in Occupied Europe* (Oxford: Berg, 2006), 16–41.

acquired on the black market, this was far less than the 2,000–3,000 calories that are needed to sustain life.[20] In occupied Greece, food shortages were endemic throughout most of the occupation and, at various times, parts of the country experienced famine.[21] The Red Cross estimated that about 250,000 Greeks perished directly or indirectly as a result of hunger between 1941 and 1943.[22] In the terrible final winter of the war, 4.5 million people in the occupied Netherlands were afflicted by food shortages so acute that an estimated 16,000 died of hunger.[23] In Germany itself, where the shortages were not felt so keenly, the average civilian consumed 2,445 calories per day in 1940 but only 2,078 calories per day in 1943.[24]

Partly as a result of shortages of commodities, but also as a result of the gradual breakdown of civil administration, various forms of crime proliferated. The black market played a central role in daily life almost everywhere. In France, peasants took roughly 21 percent of meat production for private consumption or for sale on the black market.[25] Very often, Nazi officials and officials of client governments colluded in the diversion of commodities on to the black market, or turned a blind eye to racketeering in return for kick-backs.[26] As during the Prohibition era in the United States, but on a vastly greater scale, official restrictions on the operation of the market led to an increase in crime. Some criminal gangs, such as the Bonny-Lafont gang in Paris, forged close links with the occupation

---

[20] Charles G. Roland, *Courage under Siege: Disease, Starvation and Death in the Warsaw Ghetto* (New York: Oxford University Press, 1992), 99–104.

[21] Violetta Hionidou, *Famine and Death in Occupied Greece, 1941–1944* (Cambridge: Cambridge University Press, 2006).

[22] Mark Mazower, *Inside Hitler's Greece: The Experience of Occupation, 1941–44* (New Haven, CT: Yale University Press, 2001), Chapter 3.

[23] William I. Hitchcock, *The Bitter Road to Freedom: A New History of the Liberation of Europe* (New York: Free Press, 2008), Chapter 3, 99.

[24] Tony Judt, *Postwar: A History of Europe since 1945* (London: Pimlico, 2007), 21–22.

[25] Olivier Wieviorka and Jacek Tebinka, 'Resisters: From Everyday Life to Counter-State', in Gildea et al., *Surviving Hitler*, 153–176, 156.

[26] Frank Bajohr, 'The Holocaust and Corruption', in Gerald D. Feldman and Wolfgang Seibel (eds), *Networks of Nazi Persecution: Bureaucracy, Business, and the Organization of the Holocaust* (New York: Berghahn, 2005), 118–140; Richard Grunberger, *A Social History of the Third Reich* (London: Weidenfeld and Nicolson, 1971), Chapter 6; Hein A.M. Klemann and Sergei Kudryashov, *Occupied Economies: An Economic History of Nazi-Occupied Europe, 1939–1945* (London: Bloomsbury, 2013), Chapter 17.

authorities and amassed fortunes through black-marketeering and protection rackets.²⁷ But most criminal activity was small in scale and took the form of pilfering, theft, and the evasion of official restrictions. A particular problem in urban areas was juvenile crime, which resulted from the disruption to schooling and family life, the brutalisation of war, and the pervasiveness of the black market.²⁸ In 1942 the leadership of the Hitler Youth in Germany warned that 'a serious risk of the political, moral and criminal breakdown of youth must be said to exist'.²⁹

Another common experience in Hitler's empire was persecution. The German authorities, as well as their client and allied governments, were repressive. The first victims of Nazi terror after 1933 were the organs of the German labour movement – the Communist Party, the Social Democratic Party, and the trade unions – all of which were crushed within months of the Nazi seizure of power. Jews, Roma, homosexuals, and people with mental and physical disabilities also soon came under attack. By the middle of the 1930s, the Nazis were targeting those elements within the Catholic and Lutheran churches whom they regarded as ideologically hostile, as well as smaller religious groups such as the Jehovah's Witnesses.³⁰ Between 1933 and 1945, 3 million Germans spent time in concentration camps and prisons for political reasons.³¹

As the Nazi empire spread, so was terror visited on ever-widening circles of the European population. The Nazis and their auxiliaries murdered up to 6 million Jewish people and several hundred thousand Roma. During the war, they established perhaps 42,500 places of incarceration throughout occupied Europe, not including those constructed by client governments.³² This was in addition to the thousands of regular prisons,

---

²⁷ Jackson, *France*, 191.

²⁸ Sarah Fishman, *The Battle for Children: World War II, Youth Crime, and Juvenile Justice in Twentieth-Century France* (Cambridge, MA: Harvard University Press, 2002).

²⁹ Quoted in Detlev J.K. Peukert, *Inside Nazi Germany: Conformity, Opposition and Racism in Everyday Life* (London: Penguin, 1987), 153.

³⁰ Wolfgang Benz and Thomas Dunlap, *A Concise History of the Third Reich* (Berkeley, CA: University of California Press, 2006), Chapter 7.

³¹ Peter Hoffmann, 'The Second World War, German Society, and Internal Resistance to Hitler', in David Clay Large (ed.), *Contending with Hitler: Varieties of German Resistance in the Third Reich* (Washington, DC: German Historical Institute and Cambridge University Press, 1991), 119–128, 122.

³² Robert Jan Van Pelt, 'Nazi Ghettos and Concentration Camps: The Benefits and Pitfalls of an Encyclopedic Approach', *German Studies Review*, 37/1 (2014), 149–159.

which were hugely overcrowded. Also incarcerated were millions of Allied soldiers who were taken prisoner, and who were treated according to the racial and political categories of Nazi ideology. Of 232,000 British and American soldiers in Nazi hands, 8,300 died before 1945 – a death rate of 3.6 percent.[33] By contrast, 3.3 million of the 5.7 million Red Army troops taken prisoner by the Germans, or 58 percent, died in captivity.[34] While it is impossible to give precise figures about how many Europeans suffered some form of incarceration or state-sanctioned punishment in Hitler's empire, the number ran into the tens of millions.

The response of the Nazi authorities to any sign of disobedience or resistance was often merciless. This was especially true in Southern and Eastern Europe. During anti-partisan sweeps in the Balkans and the occupied territories of the Soviet Union, it was normal by 1942 for the Germans to kill civilians indiscriminately and to destroy villages that allegedly supported the partisans. When German military personnel were killed by the resistance, the usual German response was to execute hostages, sometimes at the ratio of 10 to one dead German, or 50 to one, or even hundreds to one.[35] Though the behaviour of the Nazis in Western Europe was more restrained, there were atrocities here too, particularly in the last year of the war. The massacre of 335 men, women and children at the Ardeatine caves outside Rome in March 1944 and the murder of 642 inhabitants of Oradour-sur-Glane in Normandy in June 1944 are only two of the most famous examples of such atrocities.[36] Even those civilians who did not suffer direct persecution experienced restrictions on their freedom of movement and of expression. Fear and insecurity were basic facts of life for the majority of Hitler's subjects.

Economic exploitation was also a salient feature of German occupation. Millions of non-Germans were brought to the Reich to work in factories, on farms, or as servants to middle-class German families. By the end of the war, there were approximately 12 million foreigners on German soil, most of whom had been brought there against their will.[37] The Germans

---

[33] Jane Caplan (ed.), *Nazi Germany* (Oxford: Oxford University Press, 2008), 230.

[34] Dieter Fleck and Michael Bothe, *The Handbook of Humanitarian Law in Armed Conflicts* (New York: Oxford University Press, 1995), 324.

[35] Geraldien von Frijtag Drabbe Künzel, 'Resistance, Reprisals, Reactions', in Gildea et al., *Surviving Hitler*, 177–205.

[36] István Deák, *Europe on Trial: The Story of Collaboration, Resistance, and Retribution during World War II* (Boulder, CO: Westview Press, 2015), Chapter 8.

[37] Wieviorka and Tebinka, 'Resisters', 159.

ruthlessly squeezed the economies of all those countries that fell under their rule. In France, 34 percent of industrial production in the first half of 1942 was sent to Germany. By the spring of 1944 this had increased to between 45 or 50 percent.[38] The economic exploitation of the eastern part of Hitler's empire was even more extreme.[39] Most of this plundering of Europe was carried out officially by organs of the German state, and the proceeds were used to shore up Germany's war effort and to maintain living standards on the German home front.[40] But there was also a great deal of private looting. Goering amassed a personal collection of 3,325 *objets d'art*, including 1,160 paintings.[41] Lesser German officials and soldiers likewise plundered their way across Europe.[42]

Popular responses to Nazi rule

How did the populations which fell directly or indirectly under Nazi rule respond to the situation in which they found themselves? In addressing this question, scholars rely above all on two concepts: 'resistance' and 'collaboration'. Historians have defined both terms in different ways, and, as we shall see in Chapter 2, there is still debate about how they should be conceptualised and measured. Because the two terms are so frequently used by historians, it is important to note the kinds of activities that they usually describe.

Collaboration, collaborationism, cooperation and complicity

The word 'collaboration' is an umbrella term describing a wide range of behaviours, from voluntarily taking up arms to fight for the Nazis to fraternising with German troops. Historians often use other terms to identify specific categories of collaboration.

---

[38] Wieviorka and Tebinka, 'Resisters', 155–159.
[39] Klemann and Kudryashov, *Occupied Economies*, Chapter 9.
[40] Götz Aly, *Hitler's Beneficiaries: Plunder, Racial War, and the Nazi Welfare State* (New York: Metropolitan, 2007).
[41] Kenneth D. Alford, *Hermann Göring and the Nazi Art Collection: The Looting of Europe's Art Treasures and Their Dispersal after World War II* (Jefferson, NC: McFarland, 2002), 1.
[42] Gerard Aalders, *Nazi Looting. The Plunder of Dutch Jewry during the Second World War* (Oxford: Berg, 2004); Omer Bartov, *The Eastern Front, 1941–45: German Troops and the Barbarisation of Warfare* (Basingstoke: Macmillan, 1985), 129–141; Grunberger, *Social History*, 146–148.

One such term is 'collaborationist'. This word is generally applied to those who, out of political conviction, actively sought the patronage of the Nazis. If they obtained it, collaborationists worked alongside the Nazis in pursuit of Nazi objectives. Examples of collaborationism include the various fascist parties throughout Europe. For instance, the National Gathering in Norway, which was led by Vidkun Quisling, was closely modelled on the Nazi Party. Quisling was eventually appointed by the Germans as head of a pro-German Norwegian government. So disreputable was Quisling internationally that his surname became a widely used synonym for 'traitor'. Other prominent examples of collaborationists are Anton Mussert (leader of the National Socialist Movement in the Netherlands), Jacques Doriot (head of the French Popular Party – PPF) and Ferenc Szálasi (leader of the fascist Arrow Cross Party in Hungary). Especially in Western Europe, such movements attracted minority support and were rather isolated. Even in those Eastern European and Balkan countries where they enjoyed more popular support, they were nowhere able to take power unless the Nazis willed it.[43]

More numerous by far than political collaborators were those who took up arms in the service of the Reich. Armed collaboration began in some countries immediately after the German invasion, and by the later stages of the war it had become a mass phenomenon. Hundreds of thousands of non-Germans fought as regular troops in the Wehrmacht or the Waffen-SS, or served in non-combatant roles as auxiliary 'volunteers' (*Hilfswillige*). The Germans also established numerous auxiliary police battalions (Schutzmannschaften) which were used to fight the partisans and to round up and kill Jews. There were also a large number of non-German militia organisations which the Germans did not create but which fought alongside the occupying forces. Such paramilitary formations were usually led by men of extreme right-wing views, though the motives of the rank-and-file tended to be more varied. Examples of such militias include the Black Brigades in Italy, the Milice in France, the Omakaitse in Estonia, the Security Battalions in Greece and the Ustaše in Croatia. Finally, in some parts of Europe the Germans encouraged the formation of self-defence

---

[43] John A. Armstrong, 'Collaborationism in World War II: The Integral Nationalist Variant in Eastern Europe', *Journal of Modern History*, 40/3 (1968), 396–410; Nicholas Atkin, *The French at War, 1934–1944* (Harlow: Pearson, 2001), Chapter 5; Hans Fredrik Dahl, *Quisling: A Study in Treachery* (Cambridge: Cambridge University Press, 1999); Jackson, *France*, Chapter 9; Mazower, *Hitler's Empire*, Chapter 13.

'home guard' units in places where local populations were threatened by the activities of bandits and partisans. The militia units established by Muslim Tatars on the Crimean peninsula are an example of this phenomenon. All these varieties of armed collaboration will be discussed in more depth in Chapter 3.

One step down from collaborationism and armed collaboration was active cooperation. We have discussed state collaboration at the level of high politics, but state collaboration also had an impact on the work of people in many different contexts. Participation in the administrative apparatus of the Nazi empire is an example of this cooperation (or 'accommodation', as it is sometimes called).[44] People served the Axis powers as mayors, civil servants, village headmen, policemen and so forth. In some places, as in occupied France, most government officials remained at their posts after the Germans had invaded and were still there after the Germans departed.[45] Elsewhere, as in the occupied territories of the USSR, the state apparatus collapsed almost entirely with the arrival of the Wehrmacht. To fill the administrative vacuum at a local level, the Germans appointed an assortment of tsarist-era officials, ideological collaborators, technocrats, opportunists and criminals.[46] These local officials had significant autonomy. Russian officials who won the confidence of the occupation authorities ruled as 'little tsars'.[47] Even in some of the Jewish ghettoes, powerful individuals emerged – such as Chaim Rumkowski, head of the 'Jewish Council' (Judenrat) in the Lodz Ghetto – who were able to exercise authority over those beneath them, before they, too, were consumed by the Holocaust.[48]

It is important to note that neither the Germans nor the other Axis powers had the human resources to administer by themselves the territories that they had conquered. They required assistance from local populations. For instance, the whole of Denmark in 1942 was occupied by two

---

[44] Laub, *After the Fall*, 21–22.

[45] Mazower, *Hitler's Empire*, 416–417.

[46] Alexander Hill, *The War behind the Eastern Front: The Soviet Partisan Movement in North-West Russia 1941–1944* (London: Frank Cass, 2005), 47–51.

[47] Oleg Anisimov, *The German Occupation in Northern Russia during World War II: Political and Administrative Perspectives* (New York: Research Program on the USSR, 1954), 3–18; Hill, *The War*, 103–106.

[48] Isaiah Trunk and Robert Moses Shapiro, *Łódź Ghetto: A History* (Bloomington, IN: Indiana University Press, 2006), Chapter 2.

under-strength and poor-quality divisions and 215 German officials.[49] The vast lands of Southern Europe, Poland and the occupied territories of the USSR were still more thinly occupied. In October 1943, only 100,000 of 2.6 million German soldiers in the Soviet Union were patrolling the occupied territories. German officials constituted a tiny elite, many of whom possessed neither relevant administrative expertise nor knowledge of local languages.[50] In the Mykolaiv region in Ukraine, 500 German administrative staff ruled a population of 1,920,000 in an area of 17,000 square miles.[51] Where Axis troops were present in large numbers, they could impose the wishes of their political masters. But in most places, most of the time, the day-to-day governance of Hitler's empire was left in the hands of local proxies.

Cooperation between the Germans and subject populations was frequently motivated by economic considerations. For many people, the arrival of the Nazis was a business opportunity. The German war economy created a pan-European market for military equipment, raw materials, consumer goods and foodstuffs. Local producers who were willing to do business with the Germans could make handsome profits.[52] Louis Renault, the famous French manufacturer of automobiles, built military vehicles for the Germans and added thereby to his already considerable fortune. When he was brought to trial after the liberation as a collaborator, Renault claimed that by providing work for thousands of French people he had saved them from being forced to work in the Reich.[53]

---

[49] Bjørn Schreiber Pedersen and Adam Holm, 'Restraining Excesses: Resistance and Counter-Resistance in Nazi-Occupied Denmark 1940–1945', *Terrorism and Political Violence*, 10/1 (1998), 60–89, 62.

[50] Mazower, *Hitler's Empire*, 143–144.

[51] John A. Armstrong, *Ukrainian Nationalism*, 3rd edn (Englewood, CO: Ukrainian Academic Press, 1990), 211–217.

[52] Burrin, *Living with Defeat*, Chapters 15 and 16; Talbot Imlay and Martin Horn, *The Politics of Industrial Collaboration during World War II: Ford France, Vichy and Nazi Germany* (Cambridge: Cambridge University Press, 2014); Fabian Lemmes, 'Collaboration in Wartime France, 1940–1944', *European Review of History*, 15/2 (2008), 157–177; Arne Radtke-Delacor, 'Produire pour le Reich. Les commandes allemandes à l'industrie française (1940–1944)', *Vingtième siècle*, 70 (2001), 99–115.

[53] Anthony Rhodes, *Louis Renault: A Biography* (London: Cassell, 1969), Chapters 5–8; Charles Sowerwine, *France since 1870: Culture, Society and the Making of the Republic* (Basingstoke: Palgrave, 2001), 229–230.

What Renault did on a massive scale was replicated on a smaller scale by innumerable manufacturers, artisans and farmers from one end of occupied Europe to the other.[54] Even in places where the Nazis were most brutal, such as the occupied territories of the Soviet Union, economic collaboration was commonplace.[55] Millions of workers, in one way or another, serviced the Nazi war economy with their labour in return for remuneration. In France alone, 845,000 people were working directly for the Germans by the spring of 1942.[56] Many had little choice, as the alternative was hunger. But there were also many ordinary workers who took advantage of opportunities to improve their material circumstances. In the Netherlands, for instance, unskilled construction workers could earn up to 25 percent more working for the Wehrmacht or the Todt Organisation than outside the war economy.[57]

In 1972, Robert Paxton observed that most people in France had collaborated 'in a functional sense'. By this he meant that people who had not actively resisted had collaborated by default. The term 'functional collaboration' took root and superseded another, 'passive collaboration', which means more or less the same thing.[58] Paxton's concept of functional collaboration underpins most assessments of most people's behaviour in Hitler's empire. Millions of Europeans responded to occupation by attempting to cling on to as much normality as possible in their everyday lives. In those parts of Europe where Axis troops maintained a permanent presence – for example in the cities and major towns – the locals adjusted to the fact that foreign occupation was part of daily life. Axis troops and the civilians of occupied countries often mixed with each other freely, even in those parts of Europe where Nazi rule was most severe. Because local populations did not actively resist, they are accused of functional collaboration.

A final important term that is closely linked to the concept of collaboration is 'complicity'. Given the enormity of the crimes that were perpetrated by the Nazis, the question of guilt casts a shadow over the relationship

---

[54] Burrin, *Living with Defeat*, Chapter 18.

[55] Oleg Zarubinsky, 'Collaboration of the Population in Occupied Ukrainian Territory: Some Aspects of the Overall Picture', *Journal of Slavic Military Studies*, 10/2 (1997), 138–152.

[56] Walter Lipgens (ed.), *Documents on the History of European Integration: Continental Plans for European Union, 1939–1945* (Berlin: Walter de Gruyter, 1985), 266–267.

[57] Robert Gildea, Dirk Luyten and Juliane Fürst, 'To Work or Not to Work?', in Gildea et al., *Surviving Hitler*, 49–87, 45.

[58] See Robert O. Paxton, *Vichy France: Old Guard and New Order, 1940–1944* (New York: Columbia University Press, 1972).

between state and society in Hitler's empire. While the Nazis were the prime architects of the crimes that were committed, a major concern of historians has been to establish the degree to which other groups in society helped them along the way. The behaviour of individuals and groups deemed complicit is placed somewhere on a scale between perpetrators at one pole and bystanders at the other. We explore the important question of complicity and guilt in detail in Chapters 4 and 5.

Resistance, opposition and dissent

Resistance has proved no less difficult to define than collaboration. Most historians still use the term even though they rarely agree about what it means. One distinction they frequently make is between 'active' and 'passive' resistance. The term 'passive resistance' is applied to various kinds of non-conformist behaviour which were relatively free of risk. For example, in the late 1930s, when the Nazis began to harass the Catholic Church, many German Catholics made a point of participating in public religious festivals to demonstrate their confessional loyalty. They were not acting illegally or directly challenging the authority of the Nazis. Nonetheless, given the regime's aspirations for ideological conformity, and the persecution of priests and religious orders, practising Catholics knew that they were engaging in behaviour of which the regime disapproved. Indeed, that was the point.[59] In occupied Denmark in the second half of 1940, thousands of people gathered in the open air every Sunday to sing Danish folk songs. They were not thereby breaking any German rule. However, their public assertion of Danish national identity was a symbol of their refusal to accept the legitimacy of Hitler's new order.[60]

Though it is difficult to draw a clear border between active and passive resistance, the former implies that the behaviour was transgressive and intended to impede the progress of the regime as a whole. The most iconic examples of active resisters are the anti-fascist partisans. The majority of books and articles on resistance in occupied Europe focus on their activities. This preoccupation with the 'pointy end' of resistance is not

---

[59] Martyn Housden, *Resistance and Conformity in Nazi Germany* (London: Routledge, 1997), Chapter 3.
[60] Michael R. Marrus, 'Jewish Resistance to the Holocaust', *Journal of Contemporary History*, 30/1 (1995), 83–110, 94.

surprising, for large numbers of Europeans did indeed take up arms to fight the Nazis. During the final years of the war, partisan movements such as the Home Army (AK) in Poland, the Greek People's Liberation Army (ELAS) and the People's Liberation Army (NOV) in Yugoslavia comprised hundreds of thousands of men and women. Their combat activities were sustained by support networks that embraced millions of people. In Germany itself there were those who sought to use violence to bring an end to Nazi tyranny, most famously the German officers who, led by Count Claus von Stauffenberg, attempted to assassinate Hitler on 20 July 1944.

Political resistance was another widespread form of active resistance. In most occupied territories, an underground press challenged the propaganda of the Nazis and their collaborators. Even the most persecuted group in Hitler's empire – the Jews – maintained a lively political culture that manifested itself in the printed word. Yisrael Gutman has counted 47 underground Jewish periodicals in Warsaw alone. Twenty-six were produced by Zionists and others by members of the Bund, a Jewish socialist party.[61] During the later stages of the war, underground Communist parties flourished in Greece, Yugoslavia, Italy and France. Even in less politically flammable countries such as Belgium, the Netherlands and Denmark, Communists played a central role in the resistance movement and emerged from the war with a much greater base of support and legitimacy.[62] In Germany itself, large-scale underground political organisations had been smashed by 1935. However, especially in working-class and Catholic milieux, the Nazis were never able to eliminate small groups of like-minded friends who kept alive their political traditions. Towards the end of the war, these 'circles of friends' (*Freundschaftskreisen*) began to crystallise into more organised structures called 'anti-fascist committees' (antifas). In some larger cities, the antifas became mass movements which took over the functions of local government during the transition to post-Nazi rule.[63]

Alongside political resistance, and closely linked to it, was economic resistance. Underground trade unions were established in parts of Western Europe. In specific places, it was possible for large numbers of workers to

---

[61] Marrus, 'Jewish Resistance', 96–97.

[62] Archie Brown, *The Rise and Fall of Communism* (London: Bodley Head, 2009), Chapter 8; Donald Sassoon, 'The Rise and Fall of West European Communism: 1939–48', *Contemporary European History*, 1/2 (1992), 139–169.

[63] Gareth Pritchard, *Niemandsland: A History of Unoccupied Germany, 1944–1945* (Cambridge: Cambridge University Press, 2012), Chapter 1.

participate in strikes. In the autumn of 1940 there were strikes throughout North-Western Europe, mainly triggered by anger over shortages of food, soap, clothing, and accommodation. In February 1941, a general strike broke out in Amsterdam in protest at the persecution of Dutch Jews. Three months later, there were major strikes in the mining towns of Belgium and north-eastern France. In April 1942, workers in Athens went on strike to demand higher rations. In October 1942, there were strikes in Lyon and Nantes against the deportation of French workers to Germany. Strikes became more common and larger as the war progressed. In August 1943, a strike of 390,000 workers in Denmark forced the collaborationist government to resign. A strike wave paralysed much of northern Italy in March 1944. Shortly before liberation in August 1944, police officers went on strike in Paris. Sometimes the Germans and collaborationist authorities responded to industrial action by making concessions. More frequently, especially when dealing with workers deemed of lesser racial value, the Germans crushed any sign of industrial unrest. For instance, when workers in the main Warsaw tram garage downed tools in December 1940, the Germans threatened to shoot any strikers who did not go back to work immediately. Faced with such an ultimatum, the strikers returned to their benches.[64]

Armed resistance, participation in underground political movements, and strikes are just a few of the kinds of behaviours that are described as active resistance. Others include gathering intelligence for the Allies, cultural resistance (for example by writers who created literary works that subverted the ruling ideology),[65] religious resistance (for example by Jehovah's Witnesses who categorically refused to stop professing their faith despite relentless persecution by the Nazis)[66] and humanitarian resistance (for example by gentiles who participated in the rescue of Jews).[67] What all these kinds of behaviours had in common was that they involved

---

[64] Tom Behan, *The Long Awaited Moment: The Working Class and the Italian Communist Party in Milan, 1943–1948* (New York: Peter Lang, 1997), Chapter 4; Jørgen Hæstrup, *European Resistance Movements, 1939–1945: A Complete History* (Westport, CT: Meckler, 1981), 92–132; Mazower, *Hitler's Empire*, 479–480; Wieviorka and Tebinka, 'Resisters', 157–158.

[65] Margaret Atack, *Literature and the French Resistance: Cultural Politics and Narrative Forms, 1940–1950* (Manchester: Manchester University Press, 1989); Jackson, *France*, 498–502.

[66] Gabriele Yonan, 'Spiritual Resistance of Christian Conviction in Nazi Germany: The Case of the Jehovah's Witnesses', *Journal of Church and State*, 41/2 (1999), 307–322.

[67] Eva Fogelman, *Conscience & Courage: Rescuers of Jews During the Holocaust* (London: Cassell, 1995); Samuel P. Oliner and Pearl M. Oliner, *The Altruistic Personality: Rescuers of Jews in Nazi Europe* (New York: Free Press, 1988).

taking significant risks. In Western Europe, the Germans occasionally responded to dissenting behaviour with a degree of restraint. But, typically, and especially in the East, they responded to opposition with ruthless severity.

Conclusion

The social history of Hitler's empire is the history of the decisions made by ordinary people under difficult circumstances. When exploring the motives behind and impact of this behaviour, historians use a range of terms such as victim, perpetrator, bystander, collaborator and resister. None of these labels is value-free. All carry moral overtones and all are designed to elicit a specific emotional response.

In the following chapter we shall consider why the historiography has been so influenced by these value-laden terms. For now, it is sufficient to emphasise one central point, namely, that there has been a tendency for historians to locate responses to Nazi rule on a continuum between outright collaboration (collaborationism) at one extreme and armed resistance at the other. We are going to argue that this inflexible and (as we shall see) gendered resistance/collaboration paradigm dominates the historiography of Hitler's empire to such a degree that it can be an obstacle to understanding.

2 The Evolution of the Historiography

Resistance and collaboration in Hitler's empire are of enduring interest to historians.[1] Most general histories of the war rely on the concepts of resistance and collaboration as analytical tools or descriptive terms, and there are thousands of articles and monographs that focus specifically on resistance and collaboration. The resistance/collaboration paradigm dominates the historiographical landscape to the extent that one could easily get the impression that almost everyone in Europe was either a resister or a collaborator. According to Robert Gildea, Olivier Wieviorka and Anette Warring: 'The only escape from the labelling of resister or collaborator has been to be recognised as a victim.'[2]

Making sense of the historiography is not easy. It has changed significantly over time, and there are also substantial variations between national historiographical traditions. Nonetheless, there are general patterns, and it is the purpose of this chapter to identify and to explain them. Firstly, we discuss the historical context in which the concepts of resistance and collaboration emerged. Secondly, we give an overview of the evolution of the historiography in Western and Communist Europe respectively. Finally, we explore some of the definitional and methodological problems in the historiography, all of which are a legacy of the way it has developed since World War II.

---

[1] This chapter draws on our article 'Beyond Resistance and Collaboration: Towards a Social History of Politics in Hitler's Empire', *Journal of Social History*, 48/4 (2015), 865–891.

[2] Robert Gildea et al., 'Introduction', in Robert Gildea, Olivier Wieviorka and Anette Warring (eds), *Surviving Hitler and Mussolini: Daily Life in Occupied Europe* (Oxford: Berg, 2006), 1–15, 5.

The emergence of the terminology of resistance and collaboration

The term 'resistance' was widely employed during the war itself, but from the beginning its usage was polemical. The Nazis preferred to use words such as 'bandits' and 'terrorists' to describe those who opposed them, thereby denying the legitimacy of resistance.[3] Moreover, resisters were not always recognised as such by their compatriots. For example, the inhabitants of villages in the occupied territories of the USSR frequently regarded pro-Soviet partisans in the surrounding forests as bandits. Not only did the partisans take the peasants' food, but their unwelcome presence in the vicinity also brought the danger of German reprisals. It was not uncommon for peasant communities to ask the Germans for permission to form armed self-defence militia units so that they could protect themselves. In parts of Greece, northern Italy and elsewhere, partisan bands were likewise regarded with hostility by local populations.[4]

From 1942 onwards the resistance began to enjoy a greater degree of popular support, though this was not universal. In France, Italy, Poland and Yugoslavia, the anti-Nazi resistance became a genuine mass movement. This growth was due to the increasing brutality of the Nazis and their collaborators, and to the changing fortunes of war. It should be noted, however, that in areas of Eastern Europe – especially the Baltic states and western Ukraine – large sections of the population regarded the USSR, not Nazi Germany, as the primary enemy. In such places, the prospect of 'liberation' at the hands of the Soviets did not fill people with hope and, consequently, they were mistrustful of the anti-German resistance. In Germany itself, many regarded Count Claus von Stauffenberg and his co-conspirators as traitors, rather than as heroes of the resistance.[5]

After the war, the term 'resistance' had positive connotations. Those who were officially acknowledged as resisters were given pensions and medals, and their contribution was celebrated in public ceremonies and monuments. But post-war states used differing criteria to decide whom

---

[3] Charles D. Melson, 'German Counter-Insurgency Revisited', *Journal of Slavic Military Studies*, 24/1 (2011), 115–146.

[4] Alexander Hill, *The War behind the Eastern Front: The Soviet Partisan Movement* (London: Frank Cass, 2005), 62–63, 85–87 and 91–96; Stathis N. Kalyvas, 'Armed Collaboration in Greece', *European Review of History*, 15/2 (2008), 129–142.

[5] Martin Kitchen, *Nazi Germany at War* (London: Longman, 1995), 258.

to commemorate and whom to forget. Choices about commemorative practice were informed by political considerations.[6] Importantly, the process of identifying resisters in the immediate post-war period was also gendered. Membership of formal resistance organisations and the bearing of arms were the main criteria that were used to decide if somebody had belonged to the resistance. Therefore, large numbers of people who had contributed in less obvious ways – women in particular – were excluded. In Yugoslavia, for instance, of the 1,241 individuals who were recognised as 'National Heroes', only 93 (7 percent) were female, even though women had made up at least 13 percent of partisan fighters in the war and had contributed to resistance in myriad ways.[7] In post-war Italy, 200,000 people were formally recognised as members of the partisan movement. But only 35,000 (17.5 percent) of these were women, even though women had been heavily involved in the resistance as well as in the support networks without which armed revolt would have been impossible.[8] Interestingly, where women had been numerically significant in the armed resistance (for example, Yugoslavia and the Soviet Union) there was to be less historical interest in the broader aspects of women's opposition than in places where they rarely engaged in combat (for example, France).[9]

The term 'collaboration' was also in common currency during the war but its meaning shifted over time. At first it was not always used pejoratively. The head of the Vichy regime, Marshal Pétain, said that France had chosen the path of collaboration as a means of rebuilding the country after the defeat of 1940.[10] During the early phases of the occupation, most French people regarded Pétain's government as legitimately constituted, and they supported the Pétainist policy of guarded accommodation with the Germans. That the Vichy regime was also recognised as legitimate by non-belligerent countries, including the United States, added to its authority.[11] However,

---

[6] Pieter Lagrou, 'The Politics of Memory. Resistance as a Collective Myth in Post-War France, Belgium and the Netherlands, 1945–1965', *European Review*, 11/4 (2003), 527–549.

[7] Ivana Pantelić, 'Yugoslav Female Partisans in World War II', *Cahiers balkaniques*, 41 (2013), 2–10, 3.

[8] Jane Slaughter, *Women and the Italian Resistance, 1943–1945* (Denver, CO: Arden Press, 1997), 33.

[9] Vesna Drapac, 'Women, Resistance and the Politics of Everyday Life in Hitler's Europe: The Case of Yugoslavia in a Comparative Perspective', *Aspasia*, 3 (2009), 55–78.

[10] Nicholas Atkin, *Pétain* (London: Routledge, 1998), Chapter 6.

[11] Nicholas Atkin, *The French at War, 1934–1944* (Harlow: Pearson, 2001), 40–43.

more and more French people came to see Vichy officials (though not necessarily Pétain himself) as servants of the enemy. Behaviour which had not been seen as collaborationist in 1940 had thus, by 1944, come to be seen as treacherous.[12] There was a similar trend in the other parts of Hitler's shrinking empire during the later stages of the war. In many contexts, the word 'collaborator' became synonymous with the word 'traitor'.

The degree to which the term 'collaborator' was politically constructed becomes clear if we look at what happened in Europe immediately after liberation. In those parts of Europe that fell to Communism, guilt was assessed in collective terms. Entire ethnic groups, such as the Crimean Tatars, the Chechens and the Sudeten Germans, were punished on account of their alleged collaboration with the Nazis. Thus, millions of people were driven from their homes in orchestrated episodes of ethnic cleansing. Economic elites were likewise targeted by the Communists on the grounds that Nazism and fascism had represented the class interests of the rich. Many of those who were punished behind the Iron Curtain were war criminals, but millions of innocent people also suffered. As the Communists consolidated their power in East Germany, Poland, Hungary, Czechoslovakia, Romania, Bulgaria, Yugoslavia and Albania, they used the accusation of collaboration first as a means of denigrating their political rivals, and then as a justification for liquidating them.[13]

In Western Europe the process of punishing collaborators took a different course. Whereas the Communist approach was based on the assumption of collective guilt, governments in France, the Low Countries, Scandinavia and Italy established judicial procedures to establish the guilt of individuals. The process was more thorough in some countries than in others. In Denmark, where there had been relatively few collaborationists, 374 out of every 100,000 citizens were sentenced to prison in post-war trials. In France, by contrast, where collaboration had been more common, the

---

[12] Philippe Burrin, *Living with Defeat: France under German Occupation, 1940–1944* (London: Arnold, 1996), Chapter 12; Julian Jackson, *France: The Dark Years 1940–1944* (Oxford: Oxford University Press, 2001), 272–283.

[13] Keith Lowe, *Savage Continent: Europe in the Aftermath of World War II* (London: Penguin, 2012), Chapters 12–15; Giles MacDonogh, *After the Reich: The Brutal History of the Allied Occupation* (New York: Basic Books, 2009), Chapter 4; Norman M. Naimark, *Fires of Hatred: Ethnic Cleansing in Twentieth-Century Europe* (Cambridge, MA: Harvard University Press, 2001), 89–107; J. Otto Pohl, *Ethnic Cleansing in the USSR, 1937–1949* (Westport, CT: Greenwood Press, 1999), Chapters 6 and 10.

corresponding figure was 94 in every 100,000, and most of those who had been incarcerated were released under an amnesty in 1947.[14] However, 49,723 French collaborators were subjected to 'National Degradation', which meant that they were not allowed to stand for election, to vote, to teach, to practise law, to serve in the armed forces or to work in the communications industries.[15] In Italy, by contrast, where the Fascists had been in power since the 1920s, the circle of complicity encompassed a wider section of the population. Elites in business and the civil service were particularly compromised. Since a thorough purge would have destabilised the fragile post-war political order, the new authorities in Italy preferred to draw a line under the past. By February 1946, a mere 1,580 government employees had been dismissed and the first amnesties were announced the following June.[16]

In the three western zones of occupied Germany, the British, French and Americans introduced a system of tribunals and questionnaires, the purpose of which was to evaluate the degree to which millions of individual Germans had been complicit in the crimes of the Third Reich. However, in the western zones, this process of punishing Nazis soon became mired in bureaucratic, political, and legal difficulties. It was impossible to implement thorough denazification, partly because of the conditions of the time, and partly because the Western Allies lacked the resources to undertake a more comprehensive purge. The deteriorating relationship with the Soviets also made it politically unwise to alienate too wide a section of the West German population. By the end of the 1940s, denazification in the western zones had largely been abandoned.[17]

From the beginning, the concepts of 'resistance', 'collaboration' and 'complicity' were thus politically constructed. They emerged and were first applied in the concrete historical circumstances of wartime Europe and the opening phases of the Cold War. Because the two halves of

---

[14] Tony Judt, *Postwar: A History of Europe since 1945* (London: Pimlico, 2007), 44–46.

[15] Milton Dank, *The French against the French: Collaboration and Resistance* (London: Cassell, 1974), 320.

[16] Judt, *Postwar*, 47–48.

[17] Tom Bower, *The Pledge Betrayed: America and Britain and the Denazification of Post War Germany* (New York: Doubleday, 1981); Toby Thacker, *The End of the Third Reich: Defeat, Denazification & Nuremberg, January 1944–November 1946* (Stroud: Tempus, 2006), Chapters 6 and 8.

Europe developed in radically different ways, it is necessary to deal separately with the evolution of the historiography in Western Europe, and the Communist and post-Communist states of Eastern Europe and the Balkans.

Western Europe

In post-war Western Europe, historians played an important role in establishing the narratives about wartime resistance and collaboration that were central to the self-understanding of political elites. In France, for instance, historians celebrated the record of the resistance movement and of its most prominent leader, Charles de Gaulle. They thereby legitimised the new order and restored national honour after the humiliation of the German occupation. In the interests of stability, difficult questions about the behaviour of the population during the occupation were avoided. The French were portrayed as a 'nation of resisters'. French historians from this period blamed the excesses of Vichy on a small number of traitors such as Pierre Laval, who had served as Pétain's prime minister from April 1942 to August 1944. Other important figures in the Vichy regime (many of whom still held positions of power and responsibility in post-war France) wrote self-serving memoirs, the general line of which was that they were patriots who had tried to protect France by putting themselves between the Germans and the French population. This interpretation was supported by historian Robert Aron in 1954 in a landmark book which argued that, when the Vichy regime did collaborate, it was playing a double game, keeping bridges open to the British while shielding the French from the Germans.[18]

In West Germany in the 1950s and early 1960s, the prevailing climate of the historiography was likewise conservative and patriotic. Nazism was portrayed as a phenomenon that had no deep roots in German society or history. It was argued that a tragic combination of circumstances had made

---

[18] Robert Aron, *The Vichy Regime, 1940–44* (London: Macmillan, 1958); Julian Jackson, 'Occupied France: The Vichy Regime, Collaboration, and Resistance', in Thomas W. Zeiler and Daniel M. DuBois (eds), *A Companion to World War II* (Hoboken, NJ: Wiley-Blackwell, 2012), 825–840.

it possible for a band of Nazi adventurers to seize control of the German state and to use that power for criminal purposes. Almost nothing was written during this period about the complicity of ordinary people.[19] As Richard Evans points out: 'Very little was said about Nazism. Next to nothing was taught about it in schools. ... Critical enquiry into the German past was discouraged.'[20] There were, however, certain aspects of the history of the Third Reich about which West German historians were eager to write. The victimhood of the churches at the hands of the Nazis was emphasised, along with the heroism of figures such as Bishop Clemens August von Galen who had spoken publicly against the so-called euthanasia campaign.[21] The officers who had participated in the July 1944 assassination attempt on Hitler – above all Stauffenberg – were celebrated. Such work helped to consolidate the Federal Republic by embedding it in a narrative that was anti-Nazi but patriotic, anti-Communist and democratic.[22]

The 1960s and 1970s marked a turning point in the historiography. In the more critical intellectual and political climate of that era, a younger generation of historians emerged, most of whom had no adult memories of World War II. Key figures among this second generation of historians included Martin Broszat (born 1926), Pierre Laborie (1936), Jean-Pierre Azéma (1937), Detlev Peukert (1950), and Henry Rousso (1954). An important contribution was also made by British and American historians such as Robert Paxton (born 1932), Tim Mason (1940), and Ian Kershaw (1943). Second-generation historians tended to be much more interested in social history and the history of everyday life. They sought out novel sources and questioned established methodologies. Unlike their predecessors, they did not focus solely on male elites. They studied groups

---

[19] Nicholas Berg, *The Holocaust and the West German Historians: Historical Interpretation and Autobiographical Memory* (Madison, WI: University of Wisconsin Press, 2003), Chapter 2.

[20] Richard J. Evans, *In Hitler's Shadow: West German Historians and the Attempt to Escape from the Nazi Past* (London: I.B. Tauris, 1989), 11–12.

[21] John S. Conway, 'Coming to Terms with the Past: Interpreting Church Struggles 1933–1990', *German History*, 16/3 (1998), 377–396.

[22] Ian Kershaw, *The Nazi Dictatorship: Problems and Perspectives of Interpretation*, 4th edn (London: Arnold, 2000), 186–187; Frank McDonough, 'Resistance inside Nazi Germany', in Zeiler and DuBois, *Companion to World War II*, 813–824, 814–815.

previously ignored, in particular, workers, young people and, eventually, women.[23]

Another preoccupation of these second-generation historians was critiquing the dominant conservative narratives. The new historiography of the 1960s and 1970s emphasised the degree to which European elites had collaborated with the Nazis. Even those well-known figures who had resisted them – such as the Wehrmacht officers who tried to kill Hitler, or the German clerics who had criticised the Nazis – were subjected to closer scrutiny and found to be wanting. The opposition of elites to the Nazis, it was now claimed, had been motivated by self-interest or an objection to specific Nazi policies rather than a root-and-branch rejection of Nazi ideology. Most importantly, second-generation historians broke the wall of silence that had surrounded the issue of popular collaboration. Paxton, as we have seen, argued that most French people during the occupation had either passively accepted the Vichy regime or actively collaborated with it. So great was Paxton's influence that historians refer to the 'Paxtonian revolution' of the 1970s. The historiography of the Third Reich was similarly transformed by a steady flow of books and articles that explored the degree to which millions of Germans had willingly participated in the 'popular dictatorship' of the Nazis.[24] We shall explore this theme in more detail in Chapters 4 and 5.

A related development in the historiography dating from the 1960s and 1970s was the emergence of the Holocaust as a major field of enquiry. An event which sparked greater interest in the Holocaust was the 1961 trial, in Jerusalem, of Adolf Eichmann, who had been one of the principal architects of the Holocaust. In the same year, Raul Hilberg published his

---

[23] In the case of Germany, for example: Daniel Horn, 'Youth Resistance in the Third Reich', *Journal of Social History*, 7/1 (1973), 26–50; T.W. [Tim] Mason, 'Labour in the Third Reich', *Past and Present*, 33 (1966), 112–141; and 'National Socialism and the Working Class, 1925–May, 1933', *New German Critique*, 11 (1977), 49–93; Allan Merson, *Communist Resistance in Nazi Germany* (London: Lawrence & Wishart, 1986); Lutz Niethammer, Ulrich Borsdorf and Peter Brandt (eds), *Arbeiterinitiative 1945* (Wuppertal: Hammer, 1976).

[24] Sarah Fishman et al. (eds), *France at War: Vichy and the Historians* (Oxford: Berg, 2000); Kershaw, *Nazi Dictatorship*, 186–190; Francis R. Nicosia and Jonathan Huener (eds), *Business and Industry in Nazi Germany* (Oxford: Berghahn, 2004); Robert O. Paxton, *Vichy France: Old Guard and New Order, 1940–1944* (New York: Columbia University Press, 1972); Michael Schmidtke, 'The German New Left and National Socialism', in Philip Gassert and Alan E. Steinweis (eds), *Coping with the Nazi Past: West German Debates on Nazism and Generational Conflict, 1955–1975* (New York: Berghahn, 2006), 176–193.

monumental *Destruction of the European Jews*.[25] Historians began to investigate the Holocaust in more depth, and their findings influenced profoundly the evolution of the wider historiography. By the 1970s, consciousness of the Holocaust had spilled beyond the academy into mainstream Western society. Indeed, it would be difficult to exaggerate the impact of the Holocaust on the way that the history of Hitler's empire is conceptualised. For professional historians and members of the public alike, the Holocaust became a 'negative icon' in West European consciousness.[26]

Since the late 1960s, questions about the response of Europeans to the Holocaust have been at the forefront of scholarly and public debate about World War II. The Nazis were primarily responsible for the Holocaust, but what role was played by others? Which individuals and groups helped the Nazis to kill Jewish people? Which individuals and groups tried to obstruct the Nazis and to save Jews? How many people simply looked the other way and pretended not to notice? How did Jewish people themselves respond to the existential predicament in which they found themselves? Could the Allies have done more to save the Jews by bombing the railway lines that took them to the death camps? Controversies about these questions rarely stay confined to academia. A well-known instance was the furore that was sparked by the publication in 1996 of *Hitler's Willing Executioners* by Daniel Goldhagen. According to Goldhagen, the Holocaust was the result of a unique form of 'eliminationist' anti-Semitism that was embedded in German culture. His sensationalist thesis provoked public argument and academic derision.[27] In the late 1990s and early 2000s, a touring exhibition on the war crimes of the Wehrmacht likewise led to a public debate about the degree to which ordinary German soldiers had participated in the implementation of Hitler's racial policies.[28]

Starting in the 1980s, a third generation of historians came to maturity. They inhabited an academic environment that was less politically charged than that of the 1960s and 1970s. We are now seeing the emergence of a

---

[25] David Cesarani (ed.), *After Eichmann: Collective Memory and Holocaust since 1961* (Abingdon: Routledge, 2005).

[26] Ljiljana Radonic, *Krieg um die Erinnerung: Kroatische Vergangenheitspolitik zwischen Revisionismus und europäischen Standards* (Frankfurt: Campus Verlag, 2009), 53–60.

[27] Geoff Eley (ed.), *The 'Goldhagen Effect': History, Memory, Nazism – Facing the German Past* (Ann Arbor, MI: University of Michigan Press, 2000).

[28] Gabriel Fawcett, 'The Wehrmacht Exhibition', *History Today*, 52/4 (2002), 2–3.

fourth generation of scholars who have no adult memories even of the Cold War, and who therefore look at the history of World War II with different ideological preconceptions. These third- and fourth-generation historians possess a number of traits in common: their work is less obviously politicised; they build on the methodological advances of previous decades; and they are eclectic in their interests. Traditional topics, such as the military activities or the high politics of resistance and collaboration, are still widely researched. But there are now more studies of diverse aspects of social life in Hitler's empire, including music, humour, leisure, fashion, sexuality, disability, sport, and family life.

Since the collapse of Communism, third- and fourth-generation scholars from Western Europe have also found their way into the archives of Eastern and Southern Europe. As a result, more attention has been paid to Eastern Europe than was the case before 1989. Though we still know much more about daily life in Western Europe during the war, ground-breaking studies are being published on resistance, collaboration and everyday life in Eastern Europe, the Balkans, and the occupied territories of the USSR. Above all, the historiography of the Holocaust is rich and methodologically innovative and, as we will see in Chapter 5, it influences wider perceptions of resistance and collaboration.[29]

Communist and post-Communist states

Wartime resistance and collaboration also interested historians in Communist states. However, to an even greater extent than in the West, the history of Hitler's empire was instrumentalised in the service of politics. In Communist historiography, Nazism represented capitalism and German imperialism. From this perspective, resistance and collaboration

---

[29] A few examples of third- and fourth-generation scholars who have made important contributions would include: Karel C. Berkhoff (Russian and Eastern European history); Bernhard Chiari (Belarusian history); Martin Conway (Belgian history); Jan T. Gross (Polish history); Alexander Hill (Soviet history); Stathis N. Kalyvas (Greek history); Pieter Lagrou (Memory studies); Wendy Lower (Holocaust studies, German and Ukrainian history); Mark Mazower (Greek and Balkan history); Per Anders Rudling (Ukrainian history); Kevin Spicer (German and church history); Dan Stone (Holocaust studies); Nikica Barić (Croatia); Jovan Byford (Serbia); Cathie Carmichael (former Yugoslavia); Tomislav Dulić (former Yugoslavia); Emily Greble (Bosnia); Marko Attila Hoare (former Yugoslavia); and Sabine Rutar (Slovenia and Serbia).

were driven by class interests. The Communists accused European elites of having collaborated with the Nazis in the pursuit of imperialist and reactionary objectives. On the other hand, claimed the Communists, Nazis and collaborationists were resisted by a popular front of workers, peasants, and progressive sections of the middle classes.

According to the official narrative, a cross-class anti-fascist movement had emerged right across Europe, at the forefront of which were the Communists. In Germany, it was claimed, the Communists spearheaded the resistance to Hitler. The state that the Communists constructed in East Germany – the German Democratic Republic (GDR) – was referred to as an 'anti-fascist state' and anti-fascism was central to its self-legitimisation.[30] Throughout Eastern Europe, the achievements of Communist resisters were celebrated in innumerable books, scholarly articles and memoirs, as well as public monuments, museums, and films.[31] One such monument, constructed by the GDR authorities at the concentration camp at Buchenwald, is portrayed on the front cover of this book.

During the 45 years of Communist rule in East-Central Europe, the broad outlines of the narrative of wartime resistance and collaboration remained relatively stable. Minor corrections were made in order to take account of shifts in Communist Party policy. Individuals who had fallen from grace were discreetly removed from history books. The wartime resistance of individuals who had risen up the party hierarchy was celebrated, and on occasion fabricated.[32] During the later years of

---

[30] Eve Rosenhaft, 'The Uses of Remembrance: The Legacy of Communist Resistance in the GDR', in Francis R. Nicosia and Lawrence D. Stokes (eds), *Germans Against Nazism: Nonconformity, Opposition, and Resistance in the Third Reich* (New York: Berg, 1990), 369–388.

[31] Hill, *The War*, 2–11; James Gow, 'The People's Prince – Tito and Tito's Yugoslavia: Legitimation, Legend, and Linchpin', in Melissa K. Bokovoy et al. (eds), *State-Society Relations in Yugoslavia, 1945–1992* (New York: St. Martin's Press, 1997), 35–60; David Marples, *Stalinism in the Ukraine in the 1940s* (New York: St. Martin's Press, 1992), 54–57; Catherine Plum, *Antifascism after Hitler: East German Youth and Socialist Memory, 1949–1989* (London: Routledge, 2015), especially Chapter 2. See also the bibliography in Marko Attila Hoare, *Genocide and Resistance in Hitler's Bosnia: The Partisans and Chetniks 1941–1942* (Oxford: Oxford University Press, 2006) which contains over four pages (355–360) of references to autobiographies, diaries, eyewitness accounts and literature.

[32] Catherine Epstein, *The Last Revolutionaries: German Communists and Their Century* (Cambridge, MA: Harvard University Press, 2003), Chapter 7.

Communism, the tone of the historiography became more patriotic and less internationalist. In Yugoslavia in the 1980s, Serb and Croat historians gave the Communist narrative of World War II a nationalist twist.[33] But, in most respects, Communist historiography – like Communist technology and Communist fashion – remained stuck in the 1950s until the very end.

It was a different story in the East European diaspora. Communist states imposed orthodoxy on historians behind the Iron Curtain but they had no control over Europeans who had fled to the West. Among the diasporic communities of Poles, Hungarians, Balts, Ukrainians, Serbs, Croats and others, there emerged alternative narratives of World War II which were the polar opposite of the official Communist versions. For example, émigré Lithuanian or Ukrainian writers did not depict Communist partisans as heroes, but as traitors and collaborators who had served the interests of the Soviets. Lithuanian and Ukrainian nationalist writers in the West celebrated the memory of their compatriots who had fought alongside the Germans and against the Soviets. Whereas Communist historiography vilified the Baltic partisans known as the Forest Brothers and the Ukrainian Insurgent Army (UPA) as collaborators and terrorists, émigré writers commemorated them as patriots and freedom fighters.[34] In the case of Serbia, this alternative history had its roots in the war itself and the writings of émigrés as well as British operatives who had been part of the mission to Serb irregulars known as Chetniks. There was a deep anti-Partisan sentiment in this literature based on Serbian ultra-nationalism and nostalgia for the Chetniks.[35]

---

[33] Radonic, *Krieg um die Erinnerung*, 118–122.

[34] Examples of this genre of writing include: Juozas Audenas (ed.), *Twenty Years' Struggle for the Freedom of Lithuania* (New York: Supreme Committee for Liberation of Lithuania, 1963); A.M. Budreckis, *The Lithuanian National Revolt of 1941* (Boston, MA: Lithuanian Encyclopedia Press, 1968); Yuriy Tys-Krokhmaliuk, *UPA Warfare in Ukraine: Strategical, Tactical, and Organizational Problems of Ukrainian Resistance in World War II* (New York: Society of Veterans of Ukrainian Insurgent Army, 1972).

[35] See David Martin, *Ally Betrayed: The Uncensored Story of Tito and Mihailovich*, foreword by Rebecca West (New York: Prentice-Hall, 1946); Michael Lees, *The Rape of Serbia: The British Role in Tito's Grab for Power 1943–1944* (San Diego, CA: Harcourt Brace Jovanovich, 1990). For a discussion of this phenomenon, see Vladislav Marjanović, 'L'historiographie contemporaine serbe des années 80: de la démystification idéologique à la mystification nationaliste' and 'L'histoire politisée. L'historiographie serbe depuis 1989', in Antoine Marès (ed.), *Histoire et pouvoir en Europe médiane* (Paris: L'Harmattan, 1996), 139–170 and 283–308.

The existence in the diaspora of an alternative memory of World War II is important because it underpinned the nationalist interpretations of resistance and collaboration which emerged after the fall of Communism. The official rehabilitation in Serbia in 2015 of the leader of the Chetniks, Dragoljub (Draža) Mihailović, who collaborated with the Axis powers, is an example of the effect of this phenomenon. In Ukraine, the memory of Stepan Bandera, Roman Shukhevych and other Ukrainian nationalists who also collaborated with the Germans and fought against Soviet partisans was transformed into an official cult.[36]

Another crucial difference between the historiography in Western Europe and the post-Communist states of East-Central Europe pertains to the complicity of local populations in the Holocaust. As we shall explore further in Chapter 7, the Holocaust is now widely regarded in Western Europe as the central tragedy of the twentieth century.[37] By contrast, in former Communist states, it is common in public and academic debate for the crimes of the Nazis to be linked to those of the Communists. The subject peoples of the Communist empire, it is claimed, suffered a 'double genocide' at the hands of Nazi and Soviet totalitarianism.[38] The role of local populations in the Holocaust is downplayed, as is the collaboration of local leaders such as Miklós Horthy, Jozef Tiso, Bandera and Shukhevych. Instead, historians focus their attention on the 'resistance' of local actors to the Communists as well as to the Nazis. This relates to the way in which the war was fought in the East and, often, to the brutal experience of 'liberation' by the Red Army. It is also a result of the simplified official Communist master-narratives of resistance and collaboration. What the Communists preached in their propagandistic tracts is no longer the dominant discourse. The resulting vacuum has been filled by

---

[36] Per Anders Rudling, 'Historical Representation of the Wartime Accounts of the Activities of OUN-UPA', *East European Jewish Affairs*, 36/2 (2006), 163–189; David R. Marples, 'Stepan Bandera: The Resurrection of a Ukrainian National Hero', *Europe-Asia Studies*, 58 (2006), 555–566.

[37] Radonic, *Krieg um die Erinnerung*, 53–67.

[38] Yitzhak Arad, 'Popular Collaboration in the Baltic States: Between Evasion and Facing a Burdensome Past', in Roni Stauber (ed.), *Collaboration with the Nazis: Public Discourse after the Holocaust* (London: Routledge, 2011), 53–67; David Bankier, *Expulsion and Extermination: Holocaust Testimonials from Provincial Lithuania* (Jerusalem: Yad Vashem, 2011); Georges Mink and Laure Neumayer (eds), *History, Memory and Politics in Central and Eastern Europe: Memory Games* (Basingstoke: Palgrave Macmillan, 2013).

a national counter-narrative of World War II with a new set of heroes and villains.[39]

In post-Communist Russia, the historiography has developed in a different direction but is no less subservient to the requirements of nationalism and state-building. Those who collaborated with the Nazis are still, as in Soviet times, described as traitors. The partisan resistance is portrayed, as it always was, as an authentic uprising of the mass of the people against foreign invaders. The major difference between the post-Communist Russian and Soviet versions is that the role of the Communist Party is now downplayed, whereas the mobilising influence of Russian nationalism is emphasised. Under the increasingly authoritarian and nationalistic regime of Vladimir Putin, there was a deliberate attempt by the Russian state, and by those historians who are patronised by the Kremlin, to appropriate the history of World War II for political purposes.[40]

There is thus a three-way division between the work on World War II published by contemporary Western, Eastern European, and Russian academics. Much of the scholarship on resistance and collaboration published in former Communist states is still politicised and polemical. In some respects this work is similar to that which was written in the West during the first two decades after World War II. In Western Europe in the later 1940s and the 1950s, as in post-Communist Europe since the 1990s, the priority was the smooth transition to a new political order. This resulted in the construction of national myths which were used to legitimise those who had taken power, while delegitimising those who had lost it. In Western Europe, these myths were deconstructed by decades of critical enquiry, though, in some cases, old myths were replaced by

---

[39] Delphine Bechtel, 'The 1941 Pogroms as Represented in Western Ukraine Historiography and Memorial Culture', in *The Holocaust in Ukraine: New Sources and Perspectives* (Washington, DC: Centre for Advanced Holocaust Studies United States Holocaust Memorial Museum, 2013), 1–16; John-Paul Himka, 'Obstacles to the Integration of the Holocaust into Post-Communist East European Historical Narratives', *Canadian Slavonic Papers*, 50/3 (2008), 359–372; Dovid Katz, 'On Three Definitions: Genocide; Holocaust Denial; Holocaust Obfuscation', in Leonidas Donskis (ed.), *A Litmus Test Case of Modernity: Examining Modern Sensibilities and the Public Domain in the Baltic States at the Turn of the Century* (Bern: Peter Lang, 2009), 259–277; Raphael Vago, 'Hungary: Continuing Trials of War and Memory', in Roni Stauber (ed.), *Collaboration with the Nazis: Public Discourse after the Holocaust* (New York: Routledge, 2010), 229–244.

[40] Hill, *The War*, 10–13.

new ones. In the case of France, the Paxtonian revolution turned what had been a 'nation of resisters' into a 'nation of collaborators'. But in post-Communist Europe, the need to create nationalist narratives of victimhood and resistance is still in evidence. This has led to a degree of friction when Western historians have criticised the failure of their Eastern colleagues to engage openly with the past.[41] The historiographical lag has also led to polarisation within historical communities whereby the 'new nationalists' are pitted against the 'old guard', as in Croatia.[42] The name-calling and finger-pointing in these debates has yet to subside.

Problems of definition

As we have seen, regimes in both halves of Europe in the immediate aftermath of World War II set about trying to determine who should be rewarded for resistance or punished for collaboration. This was the context in which the first histories of resistance and collaboration were written. Questions of definition were a central concern, and have remained so. The historiography of World War II has never escaped from this need to identify resisters to celebrate and collaborators to castigate. In many instances, the differences between resisters and collaborators were indeed clear-cut. Few would dispute that Quisling, the servile leader of the Norwegian version of the Nazi Party, was a collaborator. Nor would many historians dispute the heroism of Jean Moulin, the French resistance leader who was tortured and killed by the Gestapo in 1943. But between Quisling and Moulin lie a host of different motives and behaviours, the categorisation of which has provoked ongoing debate.

The word 'collaborator', for instance, is morally and politically loaded and difficult to use dispassionately. The correlation between the concepts of 'collaboration' and 'treachery' is particularly problematic. Olga Kucherenko, in her study of the wartime experience of the Ukrainian city of Odessa, defines collaboration as 'co-operation with the enemy

---

[41] Aleida Assmann, 'Europe's Divided Memory', in Uilleam Blacker, Alexander Etkind and Julie Fedor (eds), *Memory and Theory in Eastern Europe* (Basingstoke: Palgrave Macmillan, 2013), 25–41.

[42] Srdjan Cvijic, 'Swinging the Pendulum: World War II History, Politics, National Identity and Difficulties of Reconciliation in Croatia and Serbia', *Nationalities Papers*, 36/4 (2008), 713–740.

against the interests of one's country'.[43] Most historians, either explicitly or implicitly, adopt a similar approach. But on what basis can historians objectively decide what constituted 'the interests' of particular countries? Moreover, the very concept of 'one's country' was problematic in East-Central Europe and the Balkans. The majority of the state borders in the region had been recently established and were themselves the products of a previous war. The new 'nation-states' that had won the right to self-determination included multiple and substantial ethnic minorities.

The province of Galicia illustrates well the problems involved in applying Kucherenko's definition. Before World War I, Galicia had been the easternmost province of the Habsburg Empire. Its population was ethnically and linguistically diverse. In the countryside, most peasants spoke dialects of Ukrainian. The towns were mainly inhabited by people who spoke Polish, German or Yiddish. In 1919, Galicia was incorporated into the newly-created state of Poland. Ukrainian speakers were discriminated against in a state that was increasingly dominated by strident Polish nationalists. In September 1939, following the Molotov-Ribbentrop Pact, the territory was annexed by the USSR. The Soviets imposed a Communist – and Russified – dictatorship and tens of thousands of people were arrested, deported or killed.[44] In relation to the interests of which state, then, should the behaviour of Galicians be measured? Did they owe their loyalty to the USSR, or to Poland, or to an (imagined) independent Ukrainian state? Any attempt to apply Kucherenko's definition of collaboration to Galicia becomes mired in contradictions.

Questions about how to define resistance are also problematic. In attempting to define and measure resistance, should we look at motives, at the behaviour itself, or at outcomes? Were people who rejected Nazi rule in its entirety, but who engaged in only small-scale acts of opposition, more or less worthy of the label 'resisters' than people who accepted or even agreed with aspects of Nazi rule, but who risked their lives to resist a specific Nazi policy? How far should we take into account the opportunities that were available to resist in measuring people's behaviour? Was an elderly woman who made the most of limited opportunities to resist more of a resister than a high-ranking Wehrmacht officer who made less use

---

[43] Olga Kucherenko, 'Reluctant Traitors: The Politics of Survival in Romanian-Occupied Odessa', *European Review of History*, 15/2 (2008), 143–155.
[44] Marples, *Stalinism*, 64–66.

of much greater opportunities, but whose limited opposition had more impact? These questions lie at the heart of ongoing debates about the nature and extent of resistance.

When attempting to define and measure resistance, some historians focus on the risks involved. But high-risk activities that were punished as oppositionist were not necessarily politically motivated. This was the case for much juvenile delinquency in wartime Germany. Nonetheless, delinquent youths posed a threat to the authority of the regime. They were sent to prisons and concentration camps, or executed.[45] The problem was exacerbated when, in October 1939, the Nazis ruled that 16-year-olds were to be punished as adults.[46] Can we compare the 'resistance' of these young people to that of, say, a Protestant pastor who made critical comments about the regime in sermons but who ran only a small risk of punishment by doing so?

Some scholars privilege motive and state of mind in their definitions of resistance. According to Roger Gottlieb, resistance involved 'acts motivated by the intention to thwart, limit, or end the exercise of power of the oppressor group over the oppressed'. From Gottlieb's perspective, 'an act is more fully an act of resistance the more fully the agent understands it as such'.[47] Olivier Wieviorka and Jacek Tebinka agree that the key to defining resistance lies not in the action but in the intention that drove the action. They argue that a man who helped Jews to escape for money cannot be considered a resister because his action was motivated not by ethical or political considerations but by self-interest. 'Resistance', argue Wieviorka and Tebinka, 'is a commitment – a desire to participate in a concrete and collective action against the occupier or its ally'.[48]

There are problems with any definition of resistance that gives primacy to motives and intentions. Those who became involved in resistance often had a range of motives, some of which may have had little to do with political commitment, and resisters may not themselves have

---

[45] Catherine A. Epstein, *Nazi Germany: Confronting the Myths* (Chichester: Wiley Blackwell, 2015), 193.

[46] Kitchen, *Nazi Germany at War*, 179.

[47] Quoted in Michael R. Marrus, 'Jewish Resistance to the Holocaust', *Journal of Contemporary History*, 30/1 (1995), 83–110, 90.

[48] Olivier Wieviorka and Jacek Tebinka, 'Resisters: From Everyday Life to Counter-State', in Gildea et al., *Surviving Hitler*, 153–176, 153–155.

known which of their motives were more important. It is often impossible for the historian to know why people made the decision to resist. Most of those involved in resistance left no record of their motives, and those who later spoke or wrote about their motivations did not necessarily give an accurate account of what they were thinking in the 1940s. A motive-orientated definition of resistance is difficult to sustain methodologically and empirically.

Other historians have emphasised what people actually did and the consequences of their actions. Walter Hofer argues that the most important thing in measuring resistance is the impact on the ability of Hitler's regime to achieve its objectives.[49] Broszat claims that defining resistance in terms of actions and impact is more objectively verifiable than speculating about purposes and intentions. According to Broszat, 'what counts politically and historically is above all what was *done* and *accomplished* (*bewirkt*), not just desired or intended'.[50] But focusing on outcomes rather than on motives does not resolve the conceptual problems involved in defining and measuring resistance. If the most important criterion in measuring resistance is impact, it follows that a black marketeer who successfully assisted Jews for profit can be regarded as more of a resister than someone who tried to help Jews out of humanitarian principle but failed.

Linked to the issue of whether we should prioritise motive or impact is the question of whether we should take a broad or narrow approach to defining resistance. Those, like Broszat, who focus on what was accomplished tend to adopt a broader definition of resistance. They are often more interested in the cumulative impact of millions of small acts of opposition which sometimes blocked important aspects of Nazi policy. For example, raising the birth rate among 'racially desirable' Germans was a central goal of the regime. Yet, for all the Nazis' blandishments and inducements, millions of German women made decisions about their fertility based on their own situation and needs rather than the wishes of the state.[51] (The same was true in Italy and Vichy France.) If we look at resistance primarily in terms of impact, here we have an example of

---

[49] In McDonough, 'Resistance', 817.
[50] Quoted in Kershaw, *Nazi Dictatorship*, 194. Emphases in the original.
[51] Fridolf Kudlien, 'The German Response to the Birth-Rate Problem during the Third Reich', *Continuity and Change*, 5/2 (1990), 225–247.

an important Nazi policy that was obstructed by popular non-conformity. In the same way, millions of Germans refused to abandon their Christian affiliations despite the neo-pagan ideology of the regime and the partial persecution of the German churches. By the end of the Nazi period, Germans were flocking to their churches in unprecedented numbers.[52] For Broszat, such low-level types of subversion were 'more capable of undermining the totalitarian dictatorship than efforts at fundamental opposition, which had little chance of success under the watchful and pervasive system of Nazi control'.[53]

Some historians have rejected outright this attempt to broaden or 'democratise' the definition of resistance. By placing too much emphasis on day-to-day opposition, they argue, we risk trivialising the heroism and self-sacrifice of those who took a more uncompromising stance. According to Kershaw, there was 'a broad gulf separating ... "opposition" from the inner core of "resistance" proper' and crossing that gulf 'amounted to a "quantum leap" in attitude and behaviour', making it inappropriate to confuse the two categories.[54]

One way of attempting to resolve these definitional problems is to apply elaborate typologies of resistance that differentiate between degrees of motive and/or impact. Broszat argues that there were two main kinds of oppositional behaviour: *Widerstand* and *Resistenz*. Both these German words translate into English as 'resistance', but they have different connotations. *Widerstand*, for Broszat, was the open and intentional opposition either to the Nazi regime as a whole or to certain Nazi policies; it signifies active resistance. *Resistenz* is a term more suggestive of an organism being 'resistant' to microbes, or of a material object being 'resistant' to conducting electricity.[55] From this perspective, the German Communists or military men who practised *Widerstand* achieved little, but the German women's *Resistenz* to Nazi pro-natal policies accomplished a great deal.

---

[52] Martyn Housden, *Resistance and Conformity in the Third Reich* (New York: Routledge, 1996), Chapter 3.

[53] Martin Broszat, 'A Social and Historical Typology of the German Opposition to Hitler', in David Clay Large (ed.), *Contending with Hitler* (Washington, DC: German Historical Institute and Cambridge University Press, 1991), 25–33, 29–30.

[54] Kershaw, *Nazi Dictatorship*, 207.

[55] Martin Broszat, '*Resistenz* and Resistance', in Neil Gregor (ed.), *Nazism* (Oxford: Oxford University Press, 2000), 241–244.

Kershaw articulates a slightly more complex model by identifying three levels of oppositional behaviour: resistance, opposition and dissent. For Kershaw, 'resistance' was the smallest category, as it included only those acts that were inspired by a total rejection of the Nazi regime and its ideology. Kershaw defines 'opposition' as behaviour in the public sphere that was motivated by a rejection, not of Nazism as a whole, but of a single issue or specific Nazi policy such as the killing of disabled people. 'Dissent', for Kershaw, was by far the largest category, for it embraced the millions of small acts of refusal, usually in the private sphere, which Broszat describes as *Resistenz*.[56]

Where Broszat identifies two categories of oppositional behaviour and Kershaw argues that there were three, Werner Rings, in his analysis of Jewish responses to the Holocaust, identifies five different types of resistant behaviour. These are: (1) symbolic resistance – small but significant acts by Jewish people to assert their cultural and religious identity; (2) polemic resistance – telling the truth about the Holocaust and maintaining a distinct Jewish culture through the written or spoken word; (3) defensive resistance – the self-help of Jewish communities and the mutual solidarity of Jewish individuals to help and protect each other in the face of Nazi persecution; (4) offensive resistance – the use of violence by Jewish people against their tormentors; and (5) resistance unchained – the struggles of Jewish freedom fighters in the camps or ghettoes. What matters most to Rings is not the level of violence, or the outcome, but the motivations and objectives of resisters.[57]

Some typologies of resistance are even more elaborate. According to Peukert, oppositional acts can be located at some point in a graph in which the X-axis represents the sphere within which dissident behaviour took place, ranging from the private to the public. The Y-axis in Peukert's graph represents the scope of the criticism of the system, ranging from partial (the rejection of a specific Nazi policy) to general (the total rejection of Nazism). Within the graph, Peukert saw an escalating series of steps from the bottom-left-hand corner (partial rejection in the private sphere) to the top-right-hand corner (general rejection in the public

---

[56] Ian Kershaw, *Popular Opinion and Political Dissent in the Third Reich: Bavaria 1933–1945* (Oxford: Clarendon Press, 1983), 2–4.
[57] In Marrus, 'Jewish Resistance', 90–104.

The Evolution of the Historiography

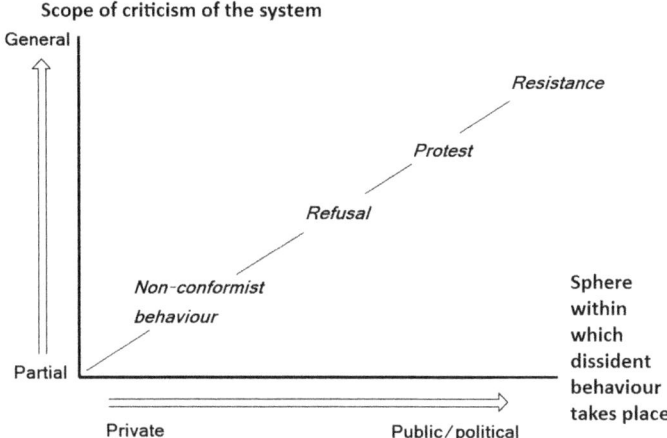

Figure 2.1 Peukert's model of non-conformism, refusal, protest and resistance (1987).[58]

sphere). He called these four steps: 'non-conformist behaviour', 'refusal', 'protest' and 'resistance' (see Figure 2.1).[59]

One of the most convoluted typologies has been proposed by Martyn Housden. His model allows us to build up a personal profile of each resister according to four categories: political aims, means used, personal motives and social context (see Figure 2.2). In theory, each individual can be given a unique profile according to the scores achieved against specified criteria. The resulting grid resembles the kind of grading rubrics that are used in schools and universities to mark the work of students, and the similarity is not accidental. Housden notes that, as far as he is concerned, the higher the value that the individual or act scores in the four categories, the greater the worth of the resistance.[60] Whether it is appropriate or even possible for the historian to attempt to grade people's responses to Nazi rule like high-school essays is the question to which we now turn.

---

[58] Detlev J.K. Peukert, *Inside Nazi Germany: Conformity, Opposition and Racism in Everyday Life* (New Haven, CN: Yale University Press, 1987), 83–84.
[59] Peukert, *Inside Nazi Germany*, 83–84.
[60] Housden, *Resistance and Conformity*, 166–168.

Political aims	Personal motives
Actions which:	Actions which were:
1 Lacked all but a notional political agenda. 2 Were based on piecemeal political views at odds with only elements of the Nazi system. 3 Foresaw the creation of a totalitarian, Communist state. 4 Envisaged the creation of an authoritarian, Bismarckian state. 5 Aimed at the creation of an essentially free, democratic state.	1 To do with protecting oneself from National Socialism. 2 To protect family and friends. 3 For the good of anyone suffering.

Means used	Social context
Actions which involved: 1 Personal mental protection. 2 The deliberate carrying on of traditional community life in the face of Nazi preferences to the contrary. 3 Anti-Nazi discussions with close circles of friends. 4 Open dissent. 5 Public protest. 6 Concerted conspiracy using 'low key' means (for example, the secret distribution of leaflets) to subvert Nazi policies. 7 Open rebellion against elements of the Hitler state. 8 Revolution against the whole Hitler state.	1 Individuals who (a) made use of opportunities for opposition activity only rarely and/or (b) exploited available opportunities only slightly. 2 Individuals who (a) made use of some opportunities for opposition and/or (b) stopped short of exploiting those which were available fully. 3 Individuals who (a) made use of all opportunities and/or (b) exploited their opportunities to the full. 4 Individuals who roughly manufactured opportunities for opposition deliberately. 5 Individuals who planned opposition activity in detail.

Figure 2.2 Martyn Housden's typology of resistance (1990).[61]

---

[61] Housden, *Resistance and Conformity*, 166–168.

The Evolution of the Historiography

Conceptual and methodological problems

Underlying these differences of definition are a number of problems, all of which have their roots in the way that the historiography evolved after 1945. Here, we would like to highlight two of the most important: (1) the teleological character of the resistance/collaboration paradigm that has been imposed by historians; and (2) the uneven and inadequate incorporation of gender into the dominant resistance/collaboration paradigm.

Problem 1: The dominance of the resistance/collaboration paradigm

The resistance/collaboration paradigm provides the interpretative framework for most social histories of Hitler's empire. Behaviours which cannot easily be located within this paradigm – for instance, family relationships, sexual practices, the daily observance of cultural and religious traditions, and work practices – are ignored or relegated to books of popular, depoliticised social history. Large areas of private and public life are thus treated superficially or not at all.

The dominance of the resistance/collaboration paradigm also leads historians to analyse specific behaviours in isolation from their wider social context. Christians, for example, are discussed in historical accounts when they take measures actively to resist, or express support for, a Nazi or collaborationist regime, or when they help, or fail to help, or denounce Jews. But, as we shall demonstrate in Chapter 6, the critical element that binds all these behaviours together – faith and membership of faith communities – remains unexplored. For the vast majority of Europeans, resistance and collaboration were part of a wider nexus of social relationships and can only be understood in that context.

For all their sophistication, the taxonomies that distinguish between various forms of resistance are, in fact, one-dimensional. As we have intimated already, they seek to analyse complex behaviours by locating them at some point on a scale between pure, heroic resistance and ideologically driven collaboration. They are also teleological because they privilege outcomes over process. In other words, decisions about what behaviours to explore in a study of resistance or collaboration are made on the basis of their actual or (allegedly) intended political or military impact. Therefore, all social conduct is assessed from the perspective of the military and political goals of the main belligerent powers. Behaviours are labelled as resistance because they seemingly led to, or were intended to lead to, the victory of the Allies, the defeat of the Nazis, or the obstruction of particular Nazi polices. Other behaviours are labelled collaborationist because they seemingly led to, or were intended to lead to, the opposite. This is regardless of the fact that, in many cases, particularly with regard to collaboration, no causal link can be established between the behaviour in question and its (supposed) outcome.[60]

Problem 2: The uneven application of gender as a category of analysis

A second problem with the resistance/collaboration paradigm is that when it is expanded to involve wider sections of society it begins to break down. The very questions that historians have posed about women as a group, whether they were victims or perpetrators, or whether they were complicit or defiant, presuppose and further entrench stereotypes. Moreover, the paradigm has led to double standards relating to the definition of what counts as resistance and collaboration. Salient examples of this phenomenon are armed resistance and collaboration (see Chapter 3), daily-life resistance and collaboration (Chapter 4) and the churches (Chapter 6). Our view is that these double standards have grown out of the inconsistent application of gender as a category of analysis.

One of the most important claims that we want to make in this book is that gender has been incorporated into definitions of resistance and collaboration in a lopsided way. The result is that women have been marginalised in the resistance narrative but are fully embedded in the counter-myth of broad-based collaboration and complicity. Since the 1970s, many works on women's experiences under Nazi rule – particularly in Germany and France – have used resistance and collaboration as the primary categories of analysis. But whereas the concept of collaboration has been broadened and 'feminised', the concept of resistance has not. This is in spite of the fact that historians of women in the resistance have addressed this definitional problem. Generally speaking, studies of active resistance still privilege the spectacular, individualised, heroic ideal. As we shall see in the next chapter, little has been written about non-combatant roles performed by women in armed resistance. Yet all acts of resistance, whether

---

[60] For a more detailed critique of the paradigm, see Drapac and Pritchard, 'Beyond Resistance and Collaboration'.

spectacular or prosaic, emerged from distinctive social milieux and were grounded in social networks in which women played a critical role.

There is a direct link between the way that women are discussed in the historiography and the definitions of resistance and collaboration. The whole point of the typologies is to draw distinctions between various types of behaviour along the resistance–collaboration scale, rather than to explore the connections between them. This can obscure the interconnectedness of different forms of opposition and collaboration. The 'pointy ends' (people with guns) should not be separated from the social and political networks that sustained them.

Whereas hierarchies of resistance place private acts of refusal very low on the spectrum of dissident behaviour, current approaches to collaboration often trace a straight line between private acts and the worst crimes of the Nazi and collaborationist regimes. According to Claudia Koonz, Elizabeth Harvey, Robert Gellately and others, women exercised considerable agency in daily life and they must therefore be held accountable for their actions and for the (generally unforeseen) political consequences of those actions. They were not mere 'bystanders' but culpable. Women who denounced other people to the Gestapo, or who provided emotional and domestic support to men who were agents of the ideology, or who simply failed to resist in ways deemed by historians to be sufficiently active, are often portrayed as complicit (collaborators) and even as perpetrators.[62] As far as Koonz is concerned: 'Far from remaining untouched by Nazi evil, women operated at its very centre.'[63]

There is thus a stark definitional difference between women's resistance and women's collaboration. Resistance is defined either in terms of motive (the desire to topple the Nazi regime or at the very least to obstruct certain of its policies) or in terms of impact (the impeding of Nazi policy). But the women who are judged as collaborators were rarely motivated by a desire to support the regime. Even Gellately and Koonz

---

[62] Robert Gellately, *Backing Hitler: Consent and Coercion in Nazi Germany* (Oxford: Oxford University Press, 2001); Elizabeth Harvey, *Women and the Nazi East: Agents and Witnesses of Germanization* (New Haven, CT: Yale University Press, 2003); Claudia Koonz, *Mothers in the Fatherland: Women, the Family, and Nazi Politics* (New York: St. Martin's Press, 1987); Klaus-Michael Mallmann and Gerhard Paul, 'Omniscient, Omnipotent, Omnipresent? Gestapo, Society and Resistance', in David F. Crew (ed.), *Nazism and German Society, 1933–1945* (New York: Routledge, 1994), 166–196.

[63] Koonz, *Mothers in the Fatherland*, 6.

concede that female denouncers were usually driven by private concerns. Nor did such women's actions have much, if any, impact on the government. Furthermore, Nazi women's organisations were peripheral to the running of the state, and their leaders had no role in determining policy.[64] According to the taxonomies, female resistance requires either motive or impact to be considered valid. Yet female collaboration requires neither.

The resistance/collaboration paradigm is thus a blunt instrument for analysing the complexity of women's lives under Nazi rule. A clear example is to be found in the historiography on the role of women in the French resistance, often referred to as the 'shadow army'. When women's memoirs began to be published and the social history of the war was amplified to incorporate women's experiences, it became evident that accepted definitions of resistance were inadequate. These definitions did not take into consideration the factors that influenced the way that women behaved. Firstly, historians of resistance have often emphasised the importance of choice over circumstance: the true resister resisted no matter what. Yet the opportunity to resist (or collaborate) differed significantly across time and place. As François Marcot notes, the structure of a resistance network was determined by its main functions. For instance, those in flight would be more likely to need the help of transport workers and hoteliers. But in order to assist escapees, one had to live in proximity to an escape route.[65] Secondly, any act of resistance necessitated the cooperation of many people. Those who did not have the requisite skills or personality traits to carry out specific tasks (for example, assassinating a German soldier) were nonetheless necessary to nurture and sustain resistance. Thirdly, the paradigm makes it more difficult to take account of the 'total' nature of modern warfare by which the home front also becomes a battle front. As Claire Andrieu pointed out in 1997, it has proved difficult to write a resistance narrative that includes those in the shadow of the shadow army. When, she asked, would historians seek out the 'other resistance', resistance 'in the home'?[66] In the following decades this challenge was not taken up.

---

[64] Gisela Bock, 'Nazi Gender Policies and Women's History', in Françoise Thébaud (ed.), *A History of Women in the West*, Vol. 5 (Cambridge, MA: Belknap Press of Harvard University Press, 1994), 149–176.

[65] François Marcot, 'Pour une sociologie de la Résistance: intentionnalité et fonctionnalité', *Le Mouvement social*, 180 (1997), 21–41.

[66] Claire Andrieu, 'Les résistantes, perspectives de recherche', *Le Mouvement social*, 180 (1997), 69–94.

Conclusion

Three key points emerge from this overview of the historiography of resistance and collaboration. Firstly, historians are always influenced by the political environment in which they think and write about the past. This is particularly true of historians of resistance and collaboration, and their books and articles must be read with this in mind.

Secondly, the historiography of resistance and collaboration has evolved through several phases. In Western Europe, the emphasis of most historians in the 1950s and 1960s was on high politics and the construction of national narratives. This strand in the historiography did not disappear. But in the late 1960s it was joined by another type of historical writing that was more focused on the everyday lives of ordinary people, and on the deconstruction of established narratives. From the 1980s and 1990s, there has emerged a new type of scholarship that is less obviously politicised, highly empirical and methodologically sophisticated, of which recent work on the Holocaust is the most obvious example. Behind the Iron Curtain, the historiography developed along different lines. For more than four decades, the history of World War II was subordinated to the ideological demands of Communist states. The collapse of the Soviet Bloc shattered the old narratives, but they were replaced by a new set of myths based on ideas of national victimhood and national resistance.

Thirdly, there are conceptual problems embedded in all the major strands of the historiography. These problems are a legacy of the way that the historiography evolved. The concepts of 'resistance' and 'collaboration' still dominate to a degree that impedes the study of the social history of Hitler's empire – including resistance and collaboration themselves. As a result, gender has never been adequately integrated as a category of analysis.

3 Armed Resistance and Collaboration

During World War II, hundreds of thousands of Europeans joined paramilitary armed bands in order to fight the Nazis and their proxies. But many hundreds of thousands of non-German Europeans also served in the Wehrmacht and the Waffen-SS or fought in militia and police units that were sponsored by the German authorities. Both armed resistance and armed collaboration were mass phenomena. They constitute the extreme poles of the resistance/collaboration paradigm as it is usually applied by historians.

In this chapter we provide an overview of the historiography of this much-discussed topic. Building on the critique of the historiography that we outlined in the previous chapter, we argue that, if we set aside the resistance/collaboration paradigm, a new picture begins to emerge of a pan-European 'war of the armed bands'. Though intimately related to the big war fought between the Allied and the Axis powers, this war of the armed bands had a distinct character and chronology. It was driven by a cycle of paramilitary violence which began in the 1930s and which lasted until the later 1940s.

The development of armed resistance

Armed resistance to Nazi rule began at different times in different parts of Europe. In Poland, partisan bands began to form in the forests soon after the German invasion of September 1939. In Italy, by contrast, armed resistance commenced only after the Germans occupied northern and central Italy in the autumn of 1943. Everywhere, however, the partisans were at first few in number, poorly organised and badly equipped. In many places they did not initially enjoy popular support. The first partisan bands were often regarded as extremists, whose violent actions could provoke German reprisals against the civilian population.

In the early days of the armed resistance, the ability of the higher echelons of resistance movements to coordinate the activities of combat units on the ground was limited. The Soviet partisan movement, for instance, was one of the best organised in Europe. It was backed by the resources of the Soviet state and, in theory, it was subject to the discipline of the Red Army and the Communist Party. Yet in 1942 the majority of partisan units in the occupied territories of the USSR did not possess a radio and acted more or less autonomously.[1]

Many of those who took up arms during the early days did so out of political conviction. Some of the first partisan movements to emerge were led by Communists, such as the Greek People's Liberation Army (ELAS), the National Liberation Movement (NLM) in Albania, and the People's Liberation Army (NOV) in Yugoslavia. Others, such as the Home Army (AK) in Poland, were led by conservative nationalists. A few partisan movements espoused extreme ethnic nationalism, for example the Serbian Chetniks, the National Military Organisation (NOW) in Poland, and the Ukrainian Insurgent Army (UPA). The leaders of armed resistance movements were usually either army officers, who fought out of a sense of patriotic duty, or radical political activists. In Ukraine, officers of the UPA were often members of a terrorist party, the Organisation of Ukrainian Nationalists (OUN), which had been established in 1929.[2] A key role in the nascent partisan movement in Italy was played by veteran anti-fascists of the Spanish Civil War, who had strong political convictions and relevant combat experience.[3] Table 2 provides a list of some of the main armed resistance movements that emerged between 1939 and 1943. It should be noted that this list is far from exhaustive.

---

[1] Bernd Bonwetsch, 'Sowjetische Partisanen 1941–1944', in Gerhard Schulz (ed.) *Partisanen und Volkskrieg* (Göttingen: Vandenhoeck and Ruprecht, 1985), 92–124.

[2] Per Anders Rudling, 'Historical Representation of the Wartime Accounts of the Activities of OUN-UPA', *East European Jewish Affairs*, 36/2 (2006), 163–89, 170.

[3] Jane Slaughter, *Women and the Italian Resistance, 1943–1945* (Denver, CO: Arden Press, 1997), 37–38.

Table 2 The formation of partisan movements, 1939–43.

Year	Country	Movement	Political orientation
1939	Poland	National Military Organisation (NOW)	Right-wing nationalist
1940	Belgium	Mouvement National Royaliste	Ultra-conservative
		Partisans Armés	Communist-led
		Légion Belge	Right-wing nationalist
	France	Combat	Gaullist
	Poland	Peasant Battalions (Bataliony Chłopskie)	Nationalist
1941	France	FTP (Francs-tireurs et partisans)	Communist-led
		Libération	Socialist
	Greece	National Republican Greek League (EDES)	Left-wing nationalist
	Norway	Milorg	Anti-fascist democratic
	USSR	Soviet partisan movement	Communist
	Yugoslavia	Chetniks	Ultra-nationalist, Serb royalist
		People's Liberation Army (NOV)	Communist-led
1942	Albania	National Liberation Movement (NLM)	Communist-led
	Greece	Greek People's Liberation Army (ELAS)	Communist-led
		National and Social Liberation (EKKA)	Nationalist republican
	Poland	Home Army (AK)	Nationalist
		National Armed Forces (NSZ)	Right-wing nationalist
		People's Guard (GL)	Communist-led
	Ukraine	Ukrainian Insurgent Army (UPA)	Ultra-nationalist

1943	Greece	Slav-Macedonian National Liberation Front (SNOF)	Left-wing nationalist
	Italy	Garibaldi Brigades	Communist-led
		Justice and Freedom (Giustizia e Libertà)	Progressive democratic
		Matteotti Brigades	Socialist

Another motive for joining the partisan resistance was desperation. In eastern Poland and western Belorussia, for instance, some of the Jews who had fled to the forests gradually coalesced into bands. Eventually they were able to procure weapons and become partisans. The best-known Jewish band was led by Tuvia Bielski, whose wartime activities were celebrated in the 2008 feature film *Defiance*, but there were many others.[4] In the occupied territories of the Soviet Union, the core of the partisan movement was at first made up of Red Army soldiers who had been caught behind German lines. Because they knew how badly the Germans treated Red Army personnel who surrendered, many such troops escaped to the forests and survived as partisans.[5]

With the turn of the war in the period 1942–43, partisan activity against German rule became more widespread. By 1944 ELAS comprised up to 150,000 armed fighters and controlled three-fifths of the territory of Greece.[6] Approximately 250,000 men and women joined the partisan movement in the occupied territories of the USSR.[7] The largest partisan movement of all, the NOV in Yugoslavia, consisted at its height of

---

[4] Nechema Tec, *Defiance: The Bielski Partisans* (Oxford: Oxford University Press, 1993), Chapters 1–6. See also Frank Blaichman, *Rather Die Fighting: A Memoir of World War II* (New York: Arcade Publishing, 2009), Chapters 1–3.

[5] Alexander Hill, *The War behind the Eastern Front: The Soviet Partisan Movement in North-West Russia 1941–1944* (London: Frank Cass, 2005), 76–79.

[6] Jonathan M. House and Spencer C. Tucker, 'Ellinikós Laïkós Apeleftherotikós Stratós', in Spencer C. Tucker (ed.), *Encyclopedia of Insurgency and Counterinsurgency: A New Era of Modern Warfare* (Santa Barbara, CA: ABC-CLIO, 2013), 154–155.

[7] Matthew Cooper, *The Phantom War: The German Struggle against Soviet Partisans 1941–1944* (London: Macdonald and Jane's, 1979), viii.

up to 800,000 male and female fighters.[8] Many movements became well-organised, well-equipped guerrilla armies which were capable of major operations against Axis forces. In mountainous or forested terrain, the partisans became a serious threat to the ability of the German authorities to assert their control. Writing in 1944, a British intelligence officer in Italy noted that 'the great horse shoe of the Apennines and the Alps is infested with Partisans. If the enemy wishes to move to any particular place, even in the mountains, sufficiently strongly, he will always get there. But he cannot be everywhere at once, and immediately he moves away again the Partisans return to their old haunts.'[9] At this stage of the war, German control over much of Greece, Yugoslavia and southern Poland was equally tenuous. Because the forests and mountains were full of partisans, the Germans rarely strayed far from the beaten track, except in large numbers.

There were several reasons for the changing character and extent of armed resistance. The increasing professionalism of the partisans was in part a result of the logistical and intelligence support that they received from bodies such as the British Special Operations Executive (SOE), the American Office of Strategic Services (OSS), and the Soviet Central Headquarters of the Partisan Movement. The increasing scale of armed resistance was in part a consequence of the German defeats in Stalingrad and North Africa in the early months of 1943, after which an Allied victory seemed more likely and armed resistance began to appear less hopeless. The cruelty of Nazi occupation policy, along with the worsening material situation, created incentives to join the armed resistance. This in turn had a dramatic impact on the composition of the partisan movement. Whereas the first partisans came from sections of the population that were marginal in some way (for example Communists, Jews and fugitive soldiers), the second wave of recruits represented a much broader cross-section of society. They were women and men who were typical of the societies from which they came, and whose lives had been disrupted by war.

Motives for joining the armed resistance after 1942 varied considerably. For some people, material factors were paramount. In the towns and cities of the occupied territories of the Soviet Union, where food was particularly

---

[8] Philip Green, 'Tito', in David T. Zabecki (ed.), *World War II in Europe: An Encyclopedia* (London: Routledge, 2015), 521–524.

[9] The National Archives (TNA), War Office (WO), 204/7283, 2–3, Nov–Dec 1944.

scarce, joining the partisans was the only way that some people could survive.[10] Another factor that led ordinary people to join the armed resistance was the desire to evade conscription or compulsory labour service. Many people fled to remote areas where they gravitated to the partisans. In France, young men seeking to evade the *Service du Travail Obligatoire* (STO) ran off to the rough countryside of southern France and the Massif Central where some of them joined the bands of 'Maquis' (so-called after the French word for 'thicket' or 'the bush').[11] Other people were influenced to join the partisans by the need to prove their political credentials in anticipation of the Allied victory. Those who had got a bit too close to the Germans now attempted to expiate their former collaboration by demonstrating their loyalty to the resistance.[12] Additional motives for joining the armed resistance included revenge and self-enrichment. According to the same British intelligence officer quoted above, the partisan bands by the later stages of the war comprised all sorts of people: 'Their motives vary from democratic idealism to personal ambition. They vary just as much in the lengths to which they are prepared to go to assist in the accomplishment of their aim – from desperate solitary enterprises to sitting by a railway counting trains. They are indeed an astonishing mixture.'[13]

By the end of the war, partisan movements were made up of patriots and political fanatics, freedom fighters and criminals, as well as people who were trying to survive. They included individuals whose lives had hitherto been unremarkable, but who had taken up arms after the war had transformed their circumstances. The anti-Nazi partisan bands had become microcosms of wider society.

Armed collaboration

If armed resistance became a mass phenomenon, so did armed collaboration. At least to begin with, especially on the Eastern Front, but also in other theatres, it is likely that more people took up arms to fight for the Germans than to fight against them.

---

[10] Hill, *The War*, 159.
[11] Jørgen Hæstrup, *European Resistance Movements, 1939–1945: A Complete History* (Westport, CT: Meckler, 1981), 121–122.
[12] Hill, *The War*, 154–156.
[13] TNA, WO 204/7283, 1, Nov–Dec 1944.

The Germans became reliant on armed collaboration because they did not have enough resources to police the vast lands that they had won through military conquest. Nor did they have the manpower to implement their murderous occupation policies. Consequently, they outsourced much of the violence to local volunteers. There was no shortage of men who were willing to do their bidding. For example, soon after the German invasion of Yugoslavia in April 1941, paramilitary units of radical Croatian nationalists (Ustaše), at the behest of the Germans, attacked the local Jewish population. Acting on their own initiative, these militiamen also launched a wave of terror against the Serb minority in Croatia.[14] A similar situation emerged in the Baltic states during the first weeks after the German invasion of the USSR. In Lithuania, members of militia units called the 'white-arm-banders' rounded up and killed Jews, Communists and other alleged 'national traitors'. In Latvia, a militia unit led by Viktors Arājs murdered at least 26,000 Jews between July 1941 and the summer of 1942.[15] In Belorussia and Ukraine, the auxiliary police battalions (Schutzmannschaften) assisted in anti-partisan operations and participated in the implementation of the Holocaust. Without the assistance of such local paramilitary forces, the Germans could not have organised the murder of so many Jewish people across such an enormous region in so short a period of time.[16]

From 1942 onwards, these militia and auxiliary police units were joined by other kinds of armed bands that were motivated by the need of communities to defend themselves. The partisan units in the forests and mountains of Europe normally survived by seizing food from the local population. Armed groups of escaped POWs, displaced persons and

---

[14] Sabrina Petra Ramet, *The Three Yugoslavias: State Building and Legitimation, 1918–2005* (Washington, DC: Woodrow Wilson Centre Press and Indiana University Press, 2006), 119–120.

[15] Christopher Hale, *Hitler's Foreign Executioners: Europe's Dirty Secret* (Stroud: History Press, 2011), 180–184 and 190–192.

[16] Martin Dean, 'Local Collaboration in the Holocaust in Eastern Europe', in Dan Stone (Ed.), *The Historiography of the Holocaust* (Basingstoke: Palgrave Macmillan, 2004), 120–140; Hale, *Hitler's Foreign Executioners*, 172–173; John-Paul Himka, 'The Ukrainian Insurgent Army and the Holocaust' (paper prepared for the 41st national convention of the American Association for the Advancement of Slavic Studies, Boston, 12–15 November 2009), available at <www.academia.edu/1071581/The_Ukrainian_Insurgent_Army_UPA_and_the_Holocaust> (accessed 24 March 2017).

bandits did the same. Unsurprisingly, the villagers from whom food was being taken did not appreciate the practice. In some parts of Europe, the Axis powers provided local communities with weapons and training so that they could defend themselves. One Soviet partisan fighting in Belorussia noted in his memoir that 'any former partisan leader who mentions the problems of feeding his men must admit that most of the food, clothes, horses and tools had to be looted from the peasants. ... Most villages had strong police or home-guard garrisons, which greeted us with machine-gun and rifle fire.'[17] Such self-defence militia units were also common in parts of the Balkans, the Baltic states and regions of southern Russia that were inhabited by non-Russian minorities.

In many parts of Europe, the rising power of the Communists from 1943 led to an anti-Communist backlash and a new wave of recruits to collaborationist units. In France, 50,000 men joined the Milice, the pro-German auxiliary police force. In Greece, nationalists and conservatives feared that the Communist-led ELAS partisan movement was about to seize power. In response, thousands of Greeks entered the collaborationist Security Battalions or joined one of the many self-defence militia units that were established by the Germans and the Bulgarians. In Italy, after Mussolini was installed by the Germans as the head of the 'Salò Republic' in 1943, the struggle against the Communist Party (PCI) was carried on by armed bands such as the Black Brigades and the Republican National Guard. Wherever they existed, paramilitary formations played a key role in the armed struggle against the partisans.

In addition to those who bore arms in locally raised militia and police units, hundreds of thousands of Europeans fought for Hitler's empire in Wehrmacht uniforms. By the end of 1941, 24,000 Frenchmen, Croats, Spaniards and Walloons were serving in the German army on the Eastern front in what was portrayed as a crusade to save Europe from Bolshevism. The Wehrmacht also recruited Soviet citizens to serve as 'volunteers' (*Hilfswillige*) in German units. By June 1943, there were at least 320,000 such volunteers. Most worked as cooks, chauffeurs, translators and so forth, but between 20 and 30 percent were involved in combat operations. In some German units, these *Hiwis* (as they were nicknamed) comprised

---

[17] Quoted in Olga Baranova, 'Nationalism, Anti-Bolshevism or the Will to Survive? Collaboration in Belarus under the Nazi Occupation of 1941–1944', *European Review of History*, 15/2 (2008), 113–128.

up to 20 percent of personnel.[18] The Wehrmacht also raised regular military units from disaffected national minorities of southern Russia and the Caucasus, including Cossacks, Chechens, Dagestanis, Kazakhs, Kyrgyz, and Uzbeks. In the spring of 1943, 21 battalions of 'Eastern Troops' (*Osttruppen*) were fighting for the Wehrmacht against the Red Army in the Caucasus alone.[19] The Germans also recruited Russian POWs to help them fight their war against Stalin. Some 310,000 Red Army POWs volunteered to join the so-called Russian Army of Liberation (ROA), though, due to opposition from high-ranking Nazis, the number who were put into ROA uniforms and given weapons was much smaller.[20] By 1945, at least one in eight men in German uniform had been a citizen of the USSR in 1941.[21]

The Waffen-SS was even keener to enlist non-Germans than the Wehrmacht. Himmler's recruiting agents began looking for volunteers in Scandinavia in 1941, and thereafter in the Low Countries and France. In total, some 125,000 men from Western Europe served in the Waffen-SS, including 50,000 Dutchmen, 40,000 Belgians, and 20,000 Frenchmen. There was even a handful of British recruits from the POW camps. But far more important as a source of new soldiers were the ethnic German communities of Eastern and Southern Europe. By the end of the war, 500,000 men had been recruited to the Waffen-SS on the grounds that they were of German descent and bore 'valuable German blood', though many of them could barely speak German. Also recruited in large numbers to the Waffen-SS were Estonians, Latvians, Ukrainians, and Bosnian Muslims. By 1945, 19 of the 38 divisions of the Waffen-SS – and over half its total manpower – were made up of foreigners.[22] Some of the last troops defending Berlin in the final days of the war were Frenchmen of the Charlemagne Division, along with Danes and Norwegians of the Nordland Division.[23]

---

[18] Cooper, *Phantom War*, 113.

[19] Cooper, *Phantom War*, 116–117; Hale, *Hitler's Foreign Executioners*, 329–331.

[20] Joachim Hoffmann, *Die Geschichte der Wlassow-Armee* (Freiburg: Verlag Rombach, 1984). See especially Chapters 3 and 5.

[21] Jeffrey Burds, 'The Soviet War against "Fifth Columnists": The Case of Chechnya, 1942–4', *Journal of Contemporary History*, 42/2 (2007), 267–314.

[22] Mark Mazower, *Hitler's Empire: Nazi Rule in Occupied Europe* (London: Allen Lane, 2008), 454–457.

[23] Julian Jackson, *France: The Dark Years 1940–1944* (Oxford: Oxford University Press, 2001), 568–569; Peter Scharff Smith, Niels Bo Poulsen and Claus Bundgård Christensen, 'The Danish Volunteers in the Waffen SS and German Warfare at the Eastern Front', *Contemporary European History*, 8/1 (1999), 73–96.

The officers of these pro-German military and paramilitary formations were usually extreme nationalists or anti-Communists with a history of political violence. The French Milice, for instance, was founded and led by Joseph Darnand, who in the 1930s had been a prominent member of a right-wing terrorist group, La Cagoule.[24] Another collaborationist unit in France, the Legion of French Volunteers Against Bolshevism, was established by, among others, a former Communist, Jacques Doriot. Having renounced Communism in the mid-1930s, Doriot founded the ultra-nationalist French Popular Party (PPF). During the German occupation, the PPF was the most dynamic and best organised of all the collaborationist parties in France. Doriot himself served as a volunteer on the Eastern Front and was decorated with an Iron Cross.[25] For men such as Darnand and Doriot, armed collaboration with the Germans was a means to move to the forefront of the political stage, even though their radical right-wing political views were shared only by a minority of their compatriots.

It was the same story in Eastern Europe. Roman Shukhevych, for instance, was an ethnic Ukrainian from Galicia, which, as we saw in Chapter 2, was part of Poland during the inter-war period. In the 1930s, Shukhevych became a leading member of the OUN. Having been involved in the assassination of opponents (including other ethnic Ukrainians), he was accustomed to the use of violence for political purposes. After the German invasion of Poland in 1939, the OUN sought the patronage of the Nazis against their common enemies: the Poles, the Jews and the Russians. Serving as the commander of a battalion of Ukrainian nationalists in German uniform, Shukhevych entered Soviet Ukraine in 1941 in the wake of the German invasion. His unit, Nachtigall (Nightingale), participated in the pogrom that broke out in Lviv at the end of June. He subsequently went on to serve as an officer in one of the many Schutzmannschaften that played an important role in German anti-partisan operations and in the implementation of the Holocaust.[26]

---

[24] Nicholas Atkin, *The French at War, 1934–1944* (Harlow: Pearson, 2001), 74–75.

[25] Philippe Burrin, *Living with Defeat: France under German Occupation* (London: Hodder Arnold, 1996), 417–426.

[26] Per Anders Rudling, 'Dispersing the Fog: The OUN and Anti-Jewish Violence in 1941', *Yad Vashem Studies*, 44/2 (2016), 227–245 and 'Schooling in Murder: *Schutzmannschaft* Battalion 201 and *Hauptmann* Roman Shukhevych in Belarus 1942', available at <www.academia.edu/536217/Schooling_in_Murder_Schutzmannschaft_Battalion_201_and_Hauptmann_Roman_Shukhevych_in_Belarus_1942> (accessed 24 March 2017).

Almost everywhere in Hitler's empire, armed collaborators became locked in cycles of violence with armed resisters. Each violent act by either side provoked reprisals. In Belgium, the resistance announced in April 1942 that all collaborators would 'perish as dogs'. True to their word, the partisans assassinated 60 prominent collaborators in the second half of 1942. Attacks by resisters on those who collaborated with the Germans were more common than on the Germans themselves. By the time that Belgium was liberated, the partisans claimed to have killed 1,100 traitors. During the final phase of the German occupation, members of collaborationist militia in Belgium no longer felt protected by the Germans and engaged in retaliatory killings. Several hundred people were killed by Belgian fascists.[27] Even in Denmark, one of the countries in occupied Europe least scarred by political violence, the resistance assassinated 300 informers. Danish collaborators, with German support, murdered 125 people, planted bombs and set fire to buildings.[28]

In Southern and Eastern Europe, the escalating wars of revenge were much more intense. In Greece, the propensity of communities to provide volunteers to the collaborationist Security Battalions was directly related to the amount of ELAS violence that had been experienced in the neighbourhood. Both ELAS and the Security Battalions targeted civilians and perpetrated massacres.[29] In occupied Crimea, there was a bitter armed conflict between German-sponsored Tatar militia units and the Soviet partisans. Before the German invasion, the Tatar ethnic community had not been particularly anti-Soviet. During the occupation, however, the partisan movement in Crimea largely consisted of urban, ethnic Slavs who had fled to the hills, where the Tatars lived. Since the partisans had not prepared for the underground struggle, they were desperately short of supplies and took what they needed from the Tatars. In response, some of the Tatars sought – and received – weapons and logistical support from the Germans. Thus an urban–rural division became

---

[27] Pieter Lagrou, 'Belgium', in Bob Moore (ed.), *Resistance in Western Europe* (Oxford: Berg, 2000), 27–63.

[28] Bjørn Schreiber Pedersen and Adam Holm, 'Restraining Excesses: Resistance and Counter Resistance in Nazi-Occupied Denmark 1940–1945', *Terrorism and Political Violence*, 10/1 (1998), 60–89.

[29] Stathis N. Kalyvas, 'Armed Collaboration in Greece', *European Review of History*, 15/2 (2008), 129–142.

ethnicised by the geographical accident that the towns were mainly Slav, whereas the hilly Crimean hinterland was inhabited by Muslim Tatars. Both sides committed atrocities. Tatar militiamen killed any partisan they encountered, and Tatar farmers carried guns when they worked in the fields to protect themselves from their partisan enemies.[30] In Greece and Crimea, as well as in other parts of Europe, the struggle between armed resisters and armed collaborators began to take on features of a civil war.

Paramilitarisation as social process

Hitherto, the history of paramilitary violence in Hitler's empire has been viewed almost exclusively through the prism of resistance and collaboration. In the rest of this chapter, we discuss three important benefits of looking at paramilitary violence in the 1940s from a different perspective. We are not arguing that the terms 'resistance' and 'collaboration' should be abandoned. We merely wish to demonstrate that there are other ways of organising knowledge about irregular warfare during the 1940s.

We believe that the concept of 'paramilitarisation' can provide us with new insights into the nature of armed resistance and collaboration. By 'paramilitarisation' we mean the gradual loss by the state of its monopoly over the use of armed force, and the increasing use of political and criminal violence by citizens against the state, and by citizens against other citizens. The process of paramilitarisation had begun in some countries before the outbreak of war,[31] but it was massively aggravated by the devastating impact of a total war waged by a totalising dictatorship. There are many ways in which the concept of paramilitarisation can help us to understand the nature of civic violence in the 1940s. Here, we confine ourselves to three examples.

---

[30] Alexander Statiev, 'The Nature of Anti-Soviet Armed Resistance, 1942–44: The North Caucasus, the Kalmyk Autonomous Republic and Crimea', *Kritika*, 6/2 (2005), 285–318.

[31] Robert Gerwarth and John Horne, 'Vectors of Violence: Paramilitarism in Europe after the Great War, 1917–1923', *Journal of Modern History*, 83/3 (2011), 489–512; and (eds), *War in Peace: Paramilitary Violence in Europe after the Great War* (Oxford: Oxford University Press, 2012).

Armed resistance and armed collaboration were not separate categories

Most historians have treated armed resistance and collaboration as discrete categories. This was true of the first wave of academic studies published in the aftermath of the war and it is still true today. There are innumerable works on armed resistance in particular countries or across Europe as a whole. There are also books that deal with specific aspects of armed collaboration in individual countries. But few authors discuss armed collaboration and armed resistance together as part of the same interpretative framework.[32] Even in general histories of the Nazi occupation of specific countries, which deal with both resistance and collaboration, the two are usually discussed in separate chapters. The conceptual paradigm underlying the approach of historians is that armed resistance and collaboration stood like bookends at either extreme of popular responses to Nazi rule.

In fact, it is not always easy to draw a clear line between armed resistance and armed collaboration. It was not uncommon for individuals or groups to change sides, and many partisans at different times fought both for and against the Axis powers. In 1943, for example, Shukhevych defected from his auxiliary police unit in order to join the UPA, which fought against both the Germans and the Soviets. In Yugoslavia, the Chetniks carried out military operations not only against the Germans, the Italians and the Ustaše, but against Tito's Partisans as well. Moreover, once the Chetniks had identified the Communists as their primary enemy in the region, they cooperated with the Axis powers against the common foe. Not only did the Chetniks accept arms deliveries from the Germans (while simultaneously taking arms from the British), but they also participated with Axis forces in military operations against the Partisans.[33]

In Greece, meanwhile, members of nationalist partisan groups such as EDES, which had originally taken the field against the German and Italian occupiers, had also begun by 1943 to regard the Communists as their most dangerous enemy. As a result, many of these partisans gravitated

---

[32] An exception is Stathis N. Kalyvas, *The Logic of Violence in Civil War* (Cambridge: Cambridge University Press, 2006).

[33] Mario Jareb, 'Allies or Foes? Mihailović's Chetniks during the Second World War', in Sabrina P. Ramet and Ola Listhaug (eds), *Serbia and the Serbs in World War Two* (Basingstoke. Palgrave Macmillan, 2011), 155–174; Enver Redžić, *Bosnia and Herzogovina in the Second World War* (London: Frank Cass, 2005), Chapter 3.

towards the German-equipped Security Battalions in order to fight the Communist-led ELAS guerrillas. This did not mean that they were any more sympathetic to the Germans. Most of them were actually pro-British. But they realised that German rule would shortly come to an end, and in the meantime they needed German weapons and logistical support to prevent the Communists from taking over. From their perspective, collaborating with the Germans was a short-term expedient that was in Greece's long-term interests. As soon as the British arrived at the end of 1944, many nationalists switched their loyalty to the new occupying power and continued – now with British support – to wage war on their local Communist enemies.[34] As in Ukraine and Yugoslavia, local actors in Greece were thus engaged in a complex, many-cornered struggle in which loyalties were contingent and shifting. In such circumstances, mutually exclusive labels such as resistance and collaboration are not always helpful.

Both armed resistance and armed collaboration were manifestations of the process by which societies became increasingly paramilitarised. As we have seen, many who joined the armed resistance did so for a variety of reasons, not all of which were 'political' in the narrow, party sense of the word. The same could be said of those who became involved in armed collaboration. Indeed, the motives behind armed collaboration were often not so different from those behind armed resistance. For some, it was a means of avoiding labour service or captivity. For others, the decision to join a collaborationist military or paramilitary unit was driven by hunger. Others again got involved in armed collaboration in pursuit of self-enrichment or revenge. In 1944, a British military intelligence officer in Greece wrote a report in which he identified six main types of volunteer in the Security Battalions:[35]

1. People from very poor backgrounds who joined in order to survive.
2. Criminal types for whom service in the Security Battalions provided an opportunity for plunder and violence.
3. Volunteers inspired by hatred of ELAS, including those whose relatives had been killed by the Communists.
4. Political opportunists for whom service in the Security Battalions was a calculated career move.

---

[34] Kalyvas, 'Armed Collaboration'.
[35] TNA, WO 208/713, 'PIC Paper No.55. Greek Security Battalions', 18 July 1944.

5. Former army officers who saw fighting the Communists as a patriotic duty.
6. Members of other non-Communist resistance movements who had joined the Security Battalions after their original organisations had been destroyed by ELAS.

With just a few changes to the vocabulary, this list would look similar to reports written by other observers on the varied backgrounds and motives of armed resisters.

In other words, if we look at armed resistance and collaboration as pan-European social processes, they no longer seem like polar opposites. Instead, they can both be regarded as products of the collapse of state authority, an increase in the scale of civic violence, and the paramilitarisation of whole societies. Unleashed by the collapse of civil society and regular administration, the war of the armed bands did not come to a tidy conclusion with the end of World War II in Europe in May 1945. Political violence, along with violent crime and banditry, persisted in many European countries for months or even years after the official cessation of hostilities. In some countries, such as Greece, Ukraine and the Baltic states, it was not until the end of the 1940s that the state finally reimposed its monopoly over the use of armed force.[36]

Paramilitarisation was a pan-European and transnational phenomenon

The armed bands were a transnational phenomenon. Overwhelmingly, however, they have been studied within national categories. This is evident from the works cited in books that explore Hitler's empire in a comparative and transnational context. Such studies rely on a historiography that is essentially national in its orientation.[37] It is not unusual, of course, for works of historical synthesis to draw on local (or national) studies for source material. But there is no reason why local studies have to take the nation as the primary (or only) frame of reference. For example, studies of German anti-partisan warfare will often discuss the operations of

---

[36] For an overview of political and criminal violence in post-war Europe, see Keith Lowe, *Savage Continent: Europe in the Aftermath of World War II* (London: Penguin, 2012).

[37] See, for example, works cited by Mazower in his chapter on opposition in *Hitler's Empire*, 638–641.

particular military units which appear on the scene, fight the partisans and then disappear again. Yet the Wehrmacht and the Waffen-SS were inherently transnational organisations. Their component units often saw service in a wide range of countries. As we have seen, both the Wehrmacht and the Waffen-SS were made up of troops of many nationalities and ethnicities. All these factors influenced the way that German units behaved towards civilian populations.[38] Even if our focus is only on anti-partisan warfare in a specific geographical area, we must not lose sight of these wider connections.

The dominance of the national paradigm, and the dearth of comparative and transnational approaches, is equally obvious if we look at the edited volumes that discuss armed resistance and collaboration in occupied Europe. Such volumes are normally divided into separate chapters that examine the topic in individual countries, with little or no attempt at systematic comparison. A typical example of the genre is *Resistance in Europe: 1939–1945* (1975), edited by Stephen Hawes and Ralph White, which mostly consists of individual chapters on aspects of the resistance in France, Germany and Poland.[39] A more recent example is *Resistance in Western Europe* (2000), edited by Bob Moore. The book comprises chapters on six European countries as well as the Channel Islands. The individual contributors rarely refer to events in countries other than the ones on which they are writing.[40] In 2013, Phillip Cooke and Ben Shepherd published an edited volume entitled *European Resistance in the Second World War*, which follows exactly the same pattern, albeit with an even wider geographical scope.[41]

It is not inappropriate to explore the role of the armed bands in the history of specific countries. Indeed, given the centrality of armed resistance and collaboration in the national narratives that were constructed by postwar states, relating the bands to their role in national history is essential.

---

[38] Peter Lieb, 'Repercussions of Eastern Front Experiences on Anti-Partisan Warfare in France 1943–1944', *Journal of Strategic Studies*, 31/5 (2008), 797–823; Ben Shepherd, *Terror in the Balkans: German Armies and Partisan Warfare* (Cambridge, MA: Harvard University Press, 2012), 216–232.

[39] Stephen Hawes and Ralph White (eds), *Resistance in Europe: 1939–1945* (London: Allen Lane, 1975).

[40] Moore, *Resistance*.

[41] Phillip Cooke and Ben Shepherd (eds), *European Resistance in the Second World War* (Barnsley: Praetorian Press, 2013).

However, the dominance of national categories has impeded the application of comparative approaches to the study of the armed bands. Any historian who writes about paramilitary violence will make claims about the origins, character and function of the armed band in question. But in the absence of comparative references it is impossible to distinguish which features were local and which were manifestations of deeper regional or pan-European trends. Studying the armed bands within national categories alone will reveal their outer form, but comparative history can lay bare the dynamics of the processes that drove them.

Along with comparative approaches, a transnational framework of analysis can also be instructive, in part because the armed bands were often made up of people of many nationalities and ethnicities. A British military report of July 1944, for instance, estimated that around 50,000 Communist partisans were fighting in the Paris area, of whom no fewer than 20,000 were Italians, Poles, Spaniards, Hungarians, and Jews of all nationalities.[42] In May 1943, the head of the Greek-Rite Orthodox Church in western Ukraine, Metropolitan Andrei Sheptyts'kyi, reported to the Pope, Pius XII: 'All of Volhynia and part of Galicia are full of bands which have a certain political character. Some are made up of Poles, others of Ukrainians, and others of Communists; others are truly bandits, people of all nationalities, Germans, Jews, and Ukrainians.'[43] The point here is that World War II uprooted and intermingled populations on an unprecedented scale. Many of those whose lives were turned upside-down by war found their way into armed bands of one kind or another, where they fought alongside people of different languages, religions and nationalities.

Not all the armed bands were multinational. The AK, for instance, was made up largely of ethnic Poles. The Chetniks were overwhelmingly Serbs. Yet even those bands which were ethnically homogenous are better understood in a transational context. It was common for the operations of the armed bands to cross national and ethnic borders. Thus the AK operated in Poland, western Ukraine, Belorussia and Lithuania, while the Chetniks fought in Bosnia, Croatia, Macedonia, Montenegro, Serbia and Slovenia. Above all, almost all the armed bands were enmeshed in a complicated transnational matrix of patron–client relationships that connected them to one or more of the belligerent powers. Armed bands on the ground in

---

[42] TNA, WO 202/12725, 'Military Attache Report', 3 July 1944.
[43] Quoted in Alfred J. Rieber, 'Civil Wars in the Soviet Union', *Kritika*, 4/1 (2003), 129–162, 153.

Europe searched for patronage as a means of gaining an advantage over local rivals, and the belligerent powers were happy to supply it.

A good example of the transnational nature of irregular warfare is furnished by northern Italy in 1944 and 1945. The partisan units fighting in the foothills of the Alps were made up, not just of Italians, but of people from across the world: Russians, Poles, Czechs, Alsatian deserters from the Wehrmacht, as well as American, British, Indian, Canadian, New Zealand and French servicemen who had escaped from the Italian POW camps after the collapse of the Mussolini regime in 1943. Some of the partisans were pro-British or pro-American, while others were Italian Communists whose primary allegiance was to Moscow. Others again were Slovene guerrillas who were closely connected to Tito's Partisan movement in Yugoslavia. The political and military behaviour of all these units was influenced by their patrons, who in turn were influenced by developments elsewhere in Europe. The Anglo-Americans, for instance, were acutely aware of the similarities between Italy and Greece, and were determined to prevent Italy from following the path of Greece towards Communist insurrection.[44]

The situation in Italy was further complicated by the intrusion of partisan units from outside the country. At the end of the war, large numbers of French Gaullist partisans moved into some of the valleys of north-western Italy where they began assimilating these territories into France. So enraged were the Italian partisans by the unwelcome arrival of their French counterparts that, for several weeks in May and June 1945, the Allies were worried that fighting might break out between the two groups.[45] In north-eastern Italy, meanwhile, the struggle of the partisans against the Germans became entangled with Tito's claims on the territories to the east of the River Isonzo. British military observers noted that, in the region of Friuli, there was not only a significant degree of conflict between the pro-Communist Garibaldi partisans and the anti-Communist Osoppo partisans, but the Communists were themselves divided between the 'Italian Communists', who opposed Tito's territorial claims, and the 'pro-Slav Communists', who supported them.[46]

---

[44] TNA, WO 204/10066, Report of Lt Raoul De Lauzieres; WO 204/1866, 'JANL Activity in N.E. Italy', 13 January 1945.

[45] TNA, WO 204/1869, Memo 15, Army Group to Field Marshall Alexander, 11 May 1945.

[46] TNA, WO 204/10066, Report of Lt Raoul De Lauzieres; WO 204/1866, 'JANL Activity in N.E. Italy', 13 January 1945.

Any analysis of insurgency and counter-insurgency in northern Italy which confines itself to the actions of paramilitary forces within a single national context will be unable to incorporate the complex interplay of these transnational influences. A similar point could be made about the study of armed resistance and armed collaboration in almost every other part of Hitler's transnational empire.

The armed bands had many functions of which combat was only one

A third striking feature of the historiography of armed resistance and collaboration is that much of the literature is preoccupied with military issues in isolation from the social context. Therefore, it is also highly gendered. The resistance/collaboration paradigm necessarily focuses the attention of historians on military activities undertaken by the armed bands either for or against the Axis powers. For this reason, the study of armed resistance and armed collaboration has largely been conducted by military historians.

Traditional military history is primarily concerned with command decisions, strategy and tactics, and military outcomes. Consequently, much of the military historiography on armed resistance and collaboration is written from a top-down perspective. The question at the core of this literature is the impact of the armed bands on the military outcome of the war. All Soviet historians, for example, emphasised the importance of the partisans to the victory of the Red Army. Post-Soviet Russian historians also generally depict the partisan movement as a mass, popular phenomenon that made a major contribution to the defeat of the Germans. Some Western authors, such as Leonid Grenkovich and J.F.C. Fuller, have come to similar conclusions. Most Western military historians, however, such as Basil Liddell Hart, John Armstrong and Alexander Hill, tend to downplay both the popular nature of the Soviet partisan movement and its military significance.[47] There have been similar debates about the military contribution of the partisan resistance elsewhere. There seems to be general agreement that resistance was important for morale but was militarily critical in only a few places, such as Yugoslavia.[48]

---

[47] Hill, *The War*, 2–20.

[48] For the classic exposition of this thesis see M.R.D. Foot, *Resistance: An Analysis of European Resistance to Nazism* (St Albans: Granada Publishing and Paladin, 1979), 61.

The focus on operational matters was in part a result of the fact that many of the authors who worked in this field had military backgrounds. Some of the most important historians writing about this topic had themselves been involved in some way with armed resistance during World War II. For example, one of the best-known historians of this topic in Britain was M.R.D. Foot. During the war, he served in the French resistance and was subsequently awarded the Croix de Guerre by a grateful French government. The pioneering Anglophone historian of the resistance movement in Greece was Christopher (Monty) Woodhouse. In September 1942, Woodhouse had been parachuted into Greece as an SOE operative. Alexander Dallin, a prominent American historian of armed resistance and collaboration on the Eastern Front, served in the Military Intelligence Corps of the US army from 1943 to 1946. The influential historian of the Italian resistance, Roberto Battaglia, was himself a former partisan leader, as was Henri Michel, the first significant historian of the French resistance. One of the standard Soviet texts on the subject was written by P.K. Ponomarenko. During the war, Ponomarenko had been head of the Central Headquarters of the Partisan Movement at the Stavka (high command) of the Red Army. Today, the armed forces and intelligence services of the Russian Federation, Ukraine, the Baltic states, the United States, and other countries continue to sponsor academic research on armed resistance and collaboration in the 1940s.

The emphasis on military operations reinforces the hierarchical concept of resistance and collaboration that we discussed in Chapter 2. It also creates an artificial division between military resistance and other kinds of resistance, including political resistance and resistance in everyday life. Olivier Wieviorka and Jacek Tebinka, for example, estimate that between 1 and 3 percent of French people, 2.4 percent of Belgians, and 1–2.5 percent of Danes were involved in resistance during World War II.[49] In arriving at these statistics, Wieviorka and Tebinka are counting those individuals who were active members of formal resistance organisations. Yet, as Jørgen Hæstrup has pointed out, to make

---

[49] Olivier Wieviorka and Jacek Tebinka, 'Resisters: From Everyday Life to Counter-State', in Robert Gildea, Olivier Wieviorka and Anette Warring (eds), *Surviving Hitler and Mussolini: Daily Life in Occupied Europe* (Oxford: Berg, 2006), 153–176, 153.

such a clear-cut distinction between 'active' and 'passive' resistance is misleading. According to Hæstrup:

The organised Resistance infiltrated the apparently normally functioning community, and exploited it. ... Production, transport, communications and the administration were tools of the Occupying Power, but these and other functions of society also became tools of the organised Resistance, which succeeded, with great skill, in using the possibilities of legal society. ... As this infiltration increased, any dividing line between passive and active resistance disappeared.[50]

Moving beyond the resistance/collaboration paradigm requires us to acknowledge that combat was only one of many activities in which paramilitary groups engaged. Frequently, it was not even the most important. For many partisan groups, physical survival was the primary concern and consequently they spent much of their time avoiding combat by retreating deep into the forests or the mountains. Both the Soviet high command and British military intelligence complained that many partisan units spent too much time hiding and not enough time fighting.[51] One of the major preoccupations of the armed bands was finding food. It was not uncommon for plunder to become an objective in itself. Many of the armed bands, while aligning themselves with one or other of the belligerent powers, engaged in indiscriminate banditry. Violent criminal gangs and bands multiplied. All these forms of civil violence were a consequence of the loss by the state of its monopoly over the use of armed force, the terrible economic circumstances, the ready availability of weapons, and the brutalising dynamic of a totalising war.[52]

One of the benefits of moving beyond the resistance/collaboration paradigm, and studying paramilitarisation as a social process, is that it allows us to explore more fully the role that was played by women in the armed bands. In most histories of armed resistance and collaboration, women are only discussed when they took part in combat. The numerous other functions of women in the armed bands are rarely studied. The extensive

---

[50] Hæstrup, *European Resistance Movements*, 140–141.

[51] Cooper, *Phantom War*, 61–63.

[52] Gareth Pritchard, 'Power Relations during the Transition from Nazi to Post-Nazi Rule', in Nicholas Doumanis (ed.), *The Oxford Handbook of European History, 1914–1945* (Oxford: Oxford University Press, 2016), 593–612.

literature on the Soviet partisan movement, for example, tells us very little about the relationship between the partisans and the peasant villages – largely made up of women – which supported them. Nor are we told very much about the women who lived in the partisan camps and who provided essential services to the fighters. The same is true of the historiography of armed groups that fought against the Soviets, such as the UPA in Ukraine and the Forest Brothers in the Baltic states. Yet large sections of the population, including women, and not only those who actually bore arms, were involved in some way in armed collaboration or (more especially) armed resistance. Here we have another example of the double standard to which we referred in Chapter 2. Partisans who carried guns (usually male) are discussed by historians; partisans who performed other tasks (usually women) are sidelined.

It would be wrong to say that the role of women has been ignored. Authors such as Jomarie Alano, Jelena Batinić, Hanna Diamond, Juliane Furst, Paula Schwartz, Jane Slaughter and others have stressed the degree to which women were essential to the effectiveness of resistance organisations, and the wide-ranging and often dangerous tasks that women undertook within these movements.[53] There is no doubt that the work of women's historians has made a major contribution to our understanding of paramilitary movements. Yet general histories of armed resistance do not take sufficient account of this work. Thus the conceptual paradigm within which armed resistance is situated has not been adapted to incorporate the findings of gender historians.

Behind every armed action there was a long chain of people. In any regular army, only a small proportion of personnel are combat troops. Without logistical officers, intelligence officers, doctors, dentists, nurses, stenographers, clerks, cooks, and so forth, it would be impossible for

---

[53] Jomarie Alano, 'Armed with a Yellow Mimosa: Women's Defence and Assistance Groups in Italy, 1943–45', *Journal of Contemporary History*, 38/4 (2003), 615–631; Jelena Batinić, *Gender, Revolution, and War: The Mobilization of Women in the Yugoslav Partisan Resistance during World War II* (Stanford, CA: Stanford University Press, 2015); Hanna Diamond, *Women and the Second World War in France, 1939–48: Choices and Constraints* (Harlow: Longman, 1999); Juliane Furst, 'Heroes, Lovers, Victims – Partisan Girls during the Great Fatherland War', *Minerva*, 18/3–4 (2000), 38–75; Paula Schwartz, '*Partisanes* and Gender Politics in Vichy France', *French Historical Studies* 16/1 (1989), 126–151; and 'Redefining Resistance: Women's Activism in Wartime France', in Margaret Randolph Higgonnet et al. (eds), *Behind the Lines: Gender and the Two World Wars* (New Haven, CT: Yale University Press, 1987), 141–153.

an army to sustain combat operations. Large-scale armed resistance was dependent on 'civilians' who performed analogous tasks. (This was also true but to a much lesser extent for most forms of armed collaboration. Generally speaking, armed collaborators were men who were equipped and trained by the Germans or their client regimes, and therefore less dependent on 'bottom-up' support.) As we have seen, a number of scholars have devised influential typologies of resistance which clearly distinguish between 'active' resistance and mere 'opposition', thereby drawing a sharp line between the 'pointy end' and the social networks which sustained it. This represents a failure to recognise the interconnectedness of different forms of opposition and collaboration. Since women played a central role in the networks that sustained paramilitary violence, they need to be brought into the historian's field of vision.

We can push this point even further. In the case of many armed bands, even to portray women as performing an essential 'service' role is misleading. The primary function of many of the bands, as we have seen, was survival rather than combat. From this perspective, their priority was not military activity, but rather the task of providing for the material needs of the group. In the difficult work of finding food and fuel, and making the most of limited resources, the leading role was often played by women. Only when we look at the bands from outside the resistance/collaboration paradigm can we see that many of them are best defined as semi-autonomous, armed communities of men and women whose primary motives might have had little or nothing to do with the goals of the belligerent powers.

Conclusion

The military conflict between the Axis and the Allied powers, coupled with the willingness of both to outsource violence to local clients, led to a pan-European process of paramilitarisation. Especially in Southern and Eastern Europe, paramilitarisation was linked to the weakness of civil society before the war, the collapse of the regular structures of the state, the breakdown of social order, the radicalisation of populations, and the brutal – and brutalising – character of Nazi rule. Under these circumstances, armed bands proliferated across much of the European continent.

Many were disciplined military units. Many engaged in ethnic cleansing or indiscriminate banditry. All were engaged in local conflicts that were produced by, but often distinct from, the military struggle between the Great Powers. In the words of John-Paul Himka:

> The Second World War, with its tremendous violence and massive scale, unleashed a large number of smaller conflicts fought alongside it and within it, in Eastern Europe and elsewhere. Political movements that represented none of the principal protagonists of the war made use of the militarization and disruption of society and the diffusion of weapons to pursue their own agendas of political, territorial, and ethnic transformation.[54]

Only by moving beyond the resistance/collaboration paradigm can we begin to analyse the paramilitarisation of European society in the 1940s as a social process. A number of historians have indeed begun to investigate the social roots of the phenomena referred to as 'armed resistance' and 'armed collaboration'. For example, both Mark Mazower and Stathis Kalyvas have already deconstructed the paradigm with their insightful studies of partisan warfare in Greece.[55] Their work teaches us that armed resistance and armed collaboration were about much more than attitudes to the Nazis. Resistance and collaboration were part of a social process that was normally (but not always) rooted in pre-war tensions. Where they existed, these tensions were massively exacerbated (often in unpredictable ways) by the impact of total war and totalising dictatorship. In other cases, it was the war itself which created divisions where before there had been none. Yet even the most innovative scholars tend to use the terms 'resistance' and 'collaboration' as a frame of reference. The paradigm has been challenged, but remains dominant.

---

[54] John-Paul Himka, 'Former Ukrainian Policemen in the Ukrainian National Insurgency: Continuing the Holocaust outside German Service', in Wendy Lower and Lauren Faulkner Rossi (eds), *Lessons and Legacies XII: New Directions in Holocaust Research and Education* (Evanston, IL: Northwestern University Press, 2017), 139–163.

[55] Kalyvas, *The Logic of Violence*; Mark Mazower, *Inside Hitler's Greece: The Experience of Occupation, 1941–1944* (New Haven, CT: Yale University Press, 1993).

4 Resistance and Collaboration in Everyday Life

Historians began to write about armed resistance and armed collaboration even before the war was over. But the first generation of historians showed much less interest in resistance and collaboration in everyday life. Only in the 1960s did the social history of Hitler's empire become a subject of serious scholarly enquiry. In the following decades, a large number of thematic and regional studies reconstructed the social history of Nazi Germany, Fascist Italy and Vichy France. Since the collapse of Communism, the methodology of social history has increasingly been applied to Eastern Europe and the Balkans. However, there are still large gaps in our knowledge, and the question of daily-life resistance and collaboration remains controversial.

This chapter will discuss the evolution of the study of non-combatant resistance and collaboration. It examines different approaches to interpreting the relationship between state and society in Hitler's Europe and how these have influenced the conceptualisation of resistance and collaboration in daily life. In particular, it explores the connection between totalitarian theory and the resistance/collaboration dichotomy. But first it is necessary to look at typical examples of everyday resistance and collaboration in order to provide context for the discussion that follows.

Conceptualising daily-life resistance and collaboration

While there are a number of historians who reject the rigidly dichotomous approach to the study of daily life at this time of crisis,[1] the organising principle, explicit or implicit, for understanding social life in Hitler's Europe

---

[1] See, for example, Robert Gildea, *Marianne in Chains: In Search of the German Occupation, 1940–1945* (London: Macmillan, 2002) in which the author eschews the embedded binaries in a richly

has always been the resistance/collaboration paradigm. Resistance and collaboration could be spectacular with high (visible) impact, but they could also be more prosaic and difficult to discern.

The concept of daily-life resistance refers to a range of activities that did not involve formal membership of a network or movement. Activities that preserved the vestiges of civil society and traditional norms of behaviour have been described as constituting resistance in daily life or, in the words of Jacques Semelin, 'unarmed' or 'civil' resistance.[2] Much active resistance, such as producing underground papers and pamphlets or gathering intelligence, was also unarmed but would not normally be categorised as daily-life resistance. The idea of resistance in daily life suggests defending or conserving, in routine ways, traditions or values or institutions that were under threat. It denotes a refusal to succumb to the will of the enemy or of collaborators. In rural settings, daily-life resistance included hiding produce from the occupying forces for local consumption or for barter with people who came from the city looking for extra supplies. Resistance in daily life for a teacher involved maintaining the old school curriculum and not including new materials that were racist or collaborationist. A doctor resisted in daily life by providing treatment to social and racial outcasts. For some, resistance in daily life meant turning a blind eye to subversive activities. For others, it meant refusing to take up a lucrative job that was ethically or politically compromising. The idea of 'hibernation' was also put forward to describe a way of maintaining personal integrity by keeping one's head down until the moment to act presented itself.[3]

French historians of occupation note that living with the enemy challenged different people in different ways, and they identify nuances in daily-life resistance or 'resistances'.[4] In occupied France (as elsewhere in Hitler's empire), people spoke in a code of sorts. They talked of holding on (*tenir*) and referred to the occupation as the ordeal (*l'épreuve*).

---

detailed study of life in the Loire Valley during the occupation. Gildea introduces the subtle concept of 'cohabitation'. See also Robert Gildea, Olivier Wieviorka and Anette Warring (eds), *Surviving Hitler and Mussolini: Daily Life in Occupied Europe* (Oxford: Berg, 2006).

[2] Jacques Semelin, *Unarmed against Hitler: Civilian Resistance in Europe, 1939–1943* (Westport, CT: Praeger, 1993).

[3] Michael Balfour, *Withstanding Hitler in Germany 1933–1945* (London: Routledge, 1988), 62–63.

[4] See Hanna Diamond, *Women and the Second World War in France, 1939–48: Choices and Constraints* (Harlow: Longman, 1999), Chapter 5.

Navigating one's way through the ordeal involved multiple negotiations or accommodations. People embarked on a kind of double life. Outward conformity, or 'silence', masked people's true feelings and beliefs, as well as their hostility towards the occupiers and towards collaborationism.[5] The fact that one was not in a resistance network did not necessarily signify acceptance of the legitimacy of the new status quo. For the powerless, opposition involved a resolute focus on the regular features of daily life. The point was to maintain routines that defined one's private and public mores in opposition to the new order. It was thus imperative for life to 'go on'. Behaving 'normally' was an aspiration and one of a number of the 'weapons of the weak'.[6] It demonstrated a wilful disregard for Nazis and collaborationists. It also posed a barrier to the penetration of their ideology, and denoted a refusal to make unacceptable compromises. Building immunity or *Resistenz* involved the maintenance of established, everyday relationships in the face of efforts by the Germans and their local auxiliaries to undermine or sever them.

An example of the significance of the continuity of 'normal' activities is the response of ethnic Poles to occupation and oppression. The German attack on Polish identity was extreme. There were 3,000 Polish deaths for every day of German occupation.[7] The struggle to survive was itself an expression of resistance in daily life. Poles were fighting on every front: military, social, intellectual, religious, and cultural. The basic aspects of Poles' everyday life 'as Poles' were pursued privately and collectively, and sometimes almost entirely, underground. The Polish Underground State comprised various administrative units including a Department of Education and Culture. Speaking, writing and worshipping in Polish and organising clandestine schools and university classes in Polish were forms of resistance in daily life. Polish theatre, music and literature were nurtured with purpose and in opposition to the Germans' directives.[8] The Secret

---

[5] Pierre Laborie, '1940–1944: Double-Think in France', in Sarah Fishman et al. (eds), *France at War: Vichy and the Historians* (Oxford: Berg, 2000), 181–190.

[6] For the classic exposition of this concept, see James C. Scott, *Weapons of the Weak: Everyday Forms of Peasant Resistance* (New Haven, CT: Yale University Press, 1985).

[7] R J. Crampton, *Eastern Europe in the Twentieth Century* (London: Routledge, 1994), 197.

[8] Marek Jan Chodakiewicz, *Between Nazis and Soviets: Occupation Politics in Poland, 1939–1947* (Lanham, MD: Lexington Books, 2004); Jan Tomasz Gross, *Polish Society under German Occupation: The Generalgouvernement, 1939–1944* (Princeton, NJ: Princeton University Press, 1979).

Theatrical Council oversaw the activity of over 40 theatre groups, while concerts were held illegally in private homes and other locations.[9] This was the atmosphere in which the young Karol Wojtyła, future Pope John Paul II, was formed.

Collaboration in daily life also entailed a range of behaviours. Moreover, if one were to accept the premise that Europeans who did not engage in active resistance were collaborators, one would have to conclude that almost every adult who lived and worked in Hitler's empire was culpable or complicit in some way. Making money on the black market, profiting from the changed circumstances by taking up a position in the service of the occupiers or collaborators, consorting with occupation troops, and denouncing suspected oppositionists and Jews, are just some examples.[10] Farmers across Europe sold their produce to the Germans. Millions of European workers propped up the German war economy as their employers fulfilled German contracts. Civil servants could also be accused of having legitimised German hegemony by acting as intermediaries between local populations and the occupiers or collaborationists.

With the deconstruction of the 'resistance myth' in the late 1960s and early 1970s, there was more focus on daily-life collaboration than on daily-life resistance. Moreover, what had once been considered a form of non-cooperation was now interpreted as the opposite: the preservation of daily-life norms – and survival itself – could be seen as forms of accommodation, complicity or collaboration. Retreating from the world into the safety of the home could be understood as having been motivated by self-interest rather than the desire to maintain personal integrity. According to this line of thinking, sitting on the fence, choosing to 'wait and see' (*attentisme*, in French historiography)[11] before making up one's

---

[9] Martin Winstone, *The Dark Heart of Hitler's Europe: Nazi Rule in Poland under the General Government* (London: I.B. Tauris, 2015), 194–248. For insights into debates on the demystification of the Polish underground see Klaus-Peter Friedrich, 'Collaboration in a "Land without a Quisling": Patterns of Cooperation with the Nazi German Occupation Regime in Poland during World War II' and John Connelly, 'Why Poles Collaborated So Little – And Why That Is No Reason for Nationalist Hubris', Forum, *Slavic Review*, 64/4 (2005), 711–746, 771–781.

[10] See, for example, Jean-Pierre Azéma and François Bédarida, *Le Régime de Vichy et les Français* (Paris: Fayard, 1992); Gildea, *Marianne in Chains*.

[11] For an explanation of this term, see Julian Jackson, *France: The Dark Years 1940–1944* (Oxford: Oxford University Press, 2003), 239ff.

mind about what to do, implied keeping one's options open rather than seeking refuge in private life as a form of protest. Many historians concluded that the French and other occupied peoples simply did not want to 'put all their eggs in one basket'. Instead, most people had pragmatically refrained from choosing to collaborate or to resist until it was evident which decision would be more personally advantageous.

A number of premises about resistance and collaboration, as well as the double standards to which we have already alluded, make it difficult to apply the terms to everyday life in a meaningful way. Firstly, as noted in Chapter 2, historians assess and judge social life in Hitler's empire from within a framework that privileges a narrow view of resistance and a broad view of collaboration. Having been democratised or coded as feminine, the term collaboration is applied loosely to a wide range of everyday behaviours. At the same time, the definition of resistance remains tightly circumscribed. Moreover, the image of resistance as transgression is hard to reconcile with the idea of daily-life resistance. Secondly, according to the hierarchies, also discussed in Chapter 2, resistance in daily life had an extremely low impact. But collaboration in daily life is considered to have had a high impact to the point that it kept the otherwise 'chaotic' empire of Hitler afloat. German housewives, for instance, have been described as the mainstay of the regime. Thirdly, distortions in interpretations of social behaviour during the war, which derive from this line of thinking, are exacerbated by the association of resistance with an ethical, heroic stance and the association of collaboration with its opposite. Changing views about responsibility for the Holocaust have raised the stakes in interpreting all resistance and collaboration, whether it was active and armed or unspectacular and 'private'. We will discuss this in more detail in Chapter 5.

In the following sections we argue that the way historians interpret daily life in wartime Europe depends on their assessment of the interplay between control, consensus and coercion. Historians make judgements about daily-life behaviours based on their perception of (1) the extent of the power of the Nazis and their collaborators, (2) the freedom that remained to individuals to embrace, to resist or to ignore them, and (3) the impact or otherwise of Nazification and collaborationism on people's social relationships and on their capacity to reject Nazi policies.

Social control, social agency, social revolution

Historians who have studied resistance and collaboration in daily life have been greatly influenced by wider debates about the nature of the relationship between state and society. Within this literature there are three main, overlapping currents of thought which focus on social control, social agency and social revolution. Because these three currents are so important in shaping the perspectives of historians of everyday life in Hitler's empire, it is necessary to consider them in some detail.

Social control

Works that emphasise social control focus on the limited opportunity and capacity of ordinary people to contest twentieth-century dictatorships. These works take as their point of departure the lack of freedom under Fascist and Nazi rule and the arbitrary and violent imposition of police states by powerful leaders. Historians who emphasise social control also note that the collapse of the rule of law, the total control of all governing processes by a one-party dictatorship, and the comprehensive silencing of opposition, meant that there was no public space for the expression of alternative modes of thinking. If pockets of dissent existed, they were soon infiltrated and neutralised.

Historians who write in this tradition have used the word 'totalitarian' because they believe that a fundamental characteristic of these dictatorships was the state's attempt to abolish the division between public and private spheres. A number of (mainly conservative) philosophers and political scientists – above all in the United States and West Germany – began to see fundamental systemic similarities between Nazi Germany, Fascist Italy, and the Soviet Union.[12] They came to the conclusion that the three dictatorships could be described as 'totalitarian' because they all sought to create a new social reality which could only be achieved through total domination. In a more traditional, authoritarian dictatorship, there was still a division between the public and the private spheres. Totalitarian dictatorships, by contrast, aspired to transform all aspects of social life and subordinate them to state control.

---

[12] This thesis was most famously articulated in Carl Friedrich and Zbigniew Brzezinski, *Totalitarian Dictatorship and Autocracy* (Cambridge, MA: Harvard University Press, 1956).

Through the 1950s and 1960s, totalitarian theory had an enormous influence on the work of historians of Nazi Germany. Two of the leading first-generation post-war historians, Karl Dietrich Bracher and Klaus Hildebrand, used the concept of totalitarianism to describe the process by which the Nazis imposed their control, first on the German state, and then on the whole of German society. In the words of Hildebrand: 'The party set about achieving its ends immediately after the change of government in January 1933, and in a relatively short time the Reich was subjected to the will of its new masters.'[13] From this perspective, the story of Hitler's dictatorship and his domination of Europe was about the imposition by the state of a violent new order. Nazism was the active agent, and the role of society was essentially passive. The terror of the police state and its arbitrariness were integral to understanding the nature of totalitarian rule and its impact on social life. Violence permeated state structures and created a climate of fear and intimidation, further bolstering the power of the Nazi regime and its agents.

Eventually the totalitarian paradigm was critiqued and, in the 1990s, it fell out of favour.[14] Its detractors regard totalitarian theory as a Cold War construct, the goal of which was to discredit the Soviet Union while at the same time relativising (or even normalising) the crimes of the National Socialist and Fascist dictatorships.[15] Critics of totalitarian theory argue that the structures of the police state, including the Gestapo and the SS, had become an 'alibi' for people's complicity in daily life.[16] Furthermore, historians who reject the totalitarian paradigm claim that it is a static concept and artificially separates 'state' from 'society'. They remark on the over-simplification of the relationship between the 'dominant' and the 'dominated', noting that power in those states derived from the legitimacy invested in them by people from all walks of life who accommodated

---

[13] Klaus Hildebrand, *The Third Reich* (London: Routledge, 1994), 21.

[14] See Peter Lambert, 'The Third Reich: Police State or Self-Policing Society?', in Alf Lüdtke (ed.), *Everyday Life in Mass Dictatorship: Collusion and Evasion* (Basingstoke: Palgrave Macmillan, 2016), 37–54.

[15] Michael Geyer and Sheila Fitzpatrick, 'Introduction', in Michael Geyer and Sheila Fitzpatrick (eds), *Beyond Totalitarianism: Stalinism and Nazism Compared* (Cambridge: Cambridge University Press, 2008), 1–38.

[16] Jürgen Matthäus, 'Historiography and the Perpetrators of the Holocaust', in Dan Stone (ed.), *The Historiography of the Holocaust* (Basingstoke: Palgrave Macmillan, 2004), 197–215.

or sustained dictatorships for a range of reasons.[17] The term totalitarian is now rarely used to describe the Third Reich or Hitler's Europe. A reaction against the blanket rejection of the idea of totalitarianism emerged in the mid-2000s but has had limited impact to date.[18]

Social agency

The critique of the totalitarian model was also informed by a different approach to history and historical actors. This approach, as we have suggested above, was predicated on the belief that individuals had more freedom and 'soft power' than the totalitarian model allowed. The new social historians argued that totalitarian theory – with its top-down focus on ideology and state structures – placed people who did not have power in the traditional sense outside the historical process. Research into daily life (*Alltagsgeschichte*), on the other hand, presented a different historical narrative. Its bottom-up focus on social life under Nazi rule cast the assumptions and findings of historians who had focused on the totalitarian model and on control and coercion in a new light.

Micro-studies of the daily life of communities under dictatorship, such as those conducted under the auspices of the 'Bavaria Project' directed by Martin Broszat, revealed cracks in the totalitarian façade of Nazi rule.[19] At first this approach had broadened the scope of the understanding of daily-life resistance. It was shown that people exercised a degree of social agency in multiple ways and that, in certain circumstances, they could withstand the intrusions of the state. National Socialism had not won over everyone: far from it. Privately, some were able to subvert the totalitarian impulse of the dictatorship. Humour at the expense of the

---

[17] See various essays in Geyer and Fitzpatrick, *Beyond Totalitarianism*.

[18] For a summary of this discussion, see Lambert, 'Third Reich'. See also Roger Griffin, 'Introduction: God's Counterfeiters? Investigating the Triad of Fascism, Totalitarianism and (Political) Religion', *Totalitarian Movements and Political Religions*, 5/3 (2004), 291–325; Peter Grieder, 'In Defence of Totalitarianism Theory as a Tool of Historical Scholarship', *Totalitarian Movements and Political Religions*, 8/3–4 (2007), 563–589; Yong Woo Kim, 'From "Consensus Studies" to History of Subjectivity: Some Considerations on Recent Historiography on Italian Fascism', *Totalitarian Movements and Political Religions* 10/3–4 (2009), 327–337.

[19] For a discussion of the Bavaria Project, see Ian Kershaw, *The Nazi Dictatorship: Problems and Perspectives of Interpretation*, 4th edn (London: Arnold, 2000), 192–194, 202–205.

regime, grumbling, keeping children out of state-run youth groups, non-participation in compulsory parades and municipal ceremonies; these were just some of the ways in which people maintained a sense of themselves and created a barrier to the penetration of the ruling ideology and the state into their private lives. As previously noted, Broszat and others referred to such non-conformity in daily life and the persistence of some established routines as constituting or building immunity (*Resistenz*). A similar pattern was evident in research into the nature of life in Fascist Italy.[20] However, in due course there was a shift in thinking and perspective about everyday resistance or opposition under dictatorship and then in the Nazi empire as a whole.

If society under the Nazis was active rather than passive – and if citizens could exercise choice, or agency – it followed that ordinary people should be held accountable for their behaviour. According to this line of thinking, the failure to bring down the Fascist and National Socialist regimes indicated varying levels of accommodation and acceptance of those regimes. Social historians began to use the word 'consensus', among other terms, to describe the dominant attitude towards dictatorship in both Italy and Germany. Having moved away from concepts like 'indoctrination' and even 'propaganda' – which denied agency – these historians spoke of the dictators as 'manufacturing consensus'.[21] It was thereby suggested that the regimes enjoyed the 'compliant acceptance' or 'active complicity' of the majority of the population.[22] Total control was neither possible nor necessary and there was 'room for manoeuvre' in various milieux.[23] But how much room for manoeuvre one had depended on a range of factors, including one's age, place of residence and standing in the state's social, racial, gendered and political hierarchies. More recently historians have applied the concept of 'gesture politics' in their study of the small ways in

---

[20] See Paul Corner, 'Collaboration, Complicity, and Evasion under Italian Fascism', in Lüdtke, *Everyday Life in Mass Dictatorship*, 75–93. See also R.J.B. Bosworth, *The Italian Dictatorship: Problems and Perspectives in the Interpretation of Mussolini and Fascism* (London: Arnold, 1998), Chapters 5 and 6; and *Mussolini's Italy: Life under Dictatorship 1915-1945* (London: Penguin Books, 2006), Chapters 8 and 9.

[21] Victoria de Grazia, *The Culture of Consent: Mass Organization of Leisure in Fascist Italy* (Cambridge: Cambridge University Press, 1981).

[22] Alf Lüdtke, 'Ordinary People, Self-Energising, and Room for Manoeuvering: Examples from Twentieth Century Europe', in Lüdtke, *Everyday Life in Mass Dictatorship*, 13–34.

[23] Lüdtke, 'Ordinary People'.

which individuals expressed their identification or otherwise with dictatorial regimes.[24]

A new interpretative model displaced the totalitarian paradigm. Indeed, some of those who conceptualised this new model believed that their work constituted a 'paradigm shift'.[25] Historians such as Robert Gellately, Eric Johnson, and Claudia Koonz argued that the Third Reich rested on a high degree of approval and acceptance, not mere acquiescence.[26] Gellately noted, for example, that the Gestapo were too few in number to police effectively a country as large as Germany, let alone the whole of Hitler's empire. He alleged that the small number of active Gestapo agents relied for much of their information – and hence their power – on the thousands of people who denounced each other. In short, through their unsolicited denunciations, these ostensibly 'ordinary Germans' demonstrated their approval of and willing participation in the regime. This conclusion was put forward even though, as we saw in Chapter 2, denouncers normally acted out of self-interest rather than ideological commitment to Nazism,[27] and regardless of the fact that few denunciations resulted in prosecution.[28] Consensus was also evident in the adoration of Hitler, or people's attachment to what Ian Kershaw referred to as the 'Hitler myth'.[29] Therefore, control was not simply imposed from the top down and the state's authority derived from 'bottom-up' active support. A completely new understanding of the police state and the nature of Nazi terror emerged: the Third Reich was policed 'from below' and its violence also emanated 'from below'.[30] In this model, Nazi Germany was 'self-policing'. People had considerable agency in their daily life and actively negotiated their position in society.

---

[24] See, for example, Mary Fulbrook, 'Embodying the Self: Gestures and Dictatorship in Twentieth-Century Germany', *Past and Present*, 203, Supplement 4 (2009), 257–279.

[25] For a critique, see Lambert, 'Third Reich', 39ff.

[26] Claudia Koonz, *Mothers in the Fatherland: Women, the Family, and Nazi Politics* (New York: St. Martin's Press, 1987); Klaus-Michael Mallmann and Gerhard Paul, 'Omniscient, Omnipotent, Omnipresent? Gestapo, Society and Resistance', in David F. Crew (ed.), *Nazism and German Society, 1933–1945* (London: Routledge, 1994), 166-196; Robert Gellately, *Backing Hitler: Consent and Coercion in Nazi Germany* (Oxford: Oxford University Press, 2001).

[27] Gellately, *Backing Hitler*.

[28] Lambert, 'Third Reich', 43.

[29] Ian Kershaw, *The 'Hitler Myth': Image and Reality in the Third Reich* (Oxford: Oxford University Press, 1989).

[30] Lambert, 'Third Reich', 39.

The evolution of the historiography of other parts of Hitler's empire resembled trends in the scholarship on the Third Reich. In the case of France, the myth of a 'nation of resisters' was in part based on the idea that an alien, totalitarian system had been imposed on the French people by the German occupiers and by a small number of politically driven collaborationists in Paris such as Joseph Darnand and Jacques Doriot. At the time of the publication of Robert Paxton's *Vichy France* in 1972, historians began to write more about the daily collaboration of the French population and, eventually, the complicity of French officials, policemen and politicians in the deportation of Jews to the death camps.[31] The emphasis was placed on the agency that the French people still possessed under occupation. Rather than use that agency to resist the Germans or to protect targeted groups (especially the Jews), the majority of the French chose to look the other way, to carry on with their lives as best they could, and – if the opportunity arose – to feather their own nests. The German occupiers did not figure much at all in these revised accounts of the daily complicity of French people. Instead, there was talk of the descent into what amounted to a civil war, '*la guerre franco-française*', a perspective that reinforced the rigid binaries of resistance and collaboration.

The argument that Hitler's empire was not in essence totalitarian often generalises from the examples of Germany and Western Europe, where the war was not as devastating as it was in Eastern Europe and the Balkans. It proceeds also from what Nikolaus Wachsmann, who has written extensively on Nazi prisons and concentration camps, refers to disparagingly as the 'concept of the happy dictatorship'.[32] This thesis posits that living in Nazi Germany or under occupation was not so bad after all, at least for those who were materially well off, out of the line of direct combat and regarded by the regime as racially desirable. The premise of this thesis is that, by their daily acquiescence and accommodations, people willingly and enthusiastically entered into a 'pact' with the new order.

Critics of the totalitarian approach also stress that Nazi and Fascist rule was far from revolutionary. The now familiar story told by these

---

[31] Michael R. Marrus and Robert O. Paxton, *Vichy France and the Jews* (New York: Basic Books, 1981).

[32] 'Forum: Nazi Terror', in *German History*, 29/1 (2011), 79–98, 97. Questions formulated by Neil Gregor. Respondents: Norbert Frei, Anna Hájková, Armin Nolzen and Nikolaus Wachsmann.

historians is as follows: existing class and social relations were not overturned and the basic unit of society, the family, remained intact.[33] Mothers remained mothers. Workers remained workers. Peasants remained peasants. Musicians cared more about their performances than about politics. Artists who wanted to paint did not worry about anything else so long as they could produce new works. Filmmakers made films regardless of the fact that their Jewish colleagues were now absent. The rich and famous remained rich and famous, oblivious or indifferent to the suffering around them. According to Peter Lambert: 'Scarcely any historian of the Third Reich would now argue that there was anything less than a broad social and political consensus sustaining Nazi rule for the greater part of its duration.'[34]

Such was the shameful account of daily consent and collusion in the Nazi state and, by association, empire. But the critiques of the totalitarian model failed to take account of the self-consciously dynamic impulse of the totalitarian project. Its ideological drive and social imperative were undervalued or ignored in the new orthodoxy about daily life in Hitler's empire.

Social revolution

Between the notions of (near) absolute control and relative freedom is a position which maintains that Fascism and National Socialism aimed to and did affect social relations. This way of interpreting the Fascist and Nazi states and Hitler's empire also emerged in the 1960s. It focuses on the concept of 'social revolution'.

The historian most closely associated with this term is David Schoenbaum. In his monograph, *Hitler's Social Revolution*, first published in 1966,[35] Schoenbaum argued against the common perception that the Nazi regime had been backward-looking and reactionary. On the contrary, in order to mobilise Germany for war, the Nazis had encouraged

---

[33] Kershaw, *Nazi Dictatorship*, Chapter 7. See also Hester Vaizey, 'Husbands and Wives: An Evaluation of the Emotional Impact of World War Two in Germany', *European History Quarterly*, 40/3 (2010), 389–411.

[34] Lambert, 'Third Reich', 38.

[35] David Schoenbaum, *Hitler's Social Revolution: Class and Status in Nazi Germany 1933–1939* (Garden City, NY: Doubleday, 1966).

modernisation and industrialisation as well as Nazification. This, claimed Schoenbaum, had a revolutionary effect on German society and beyond. He maintained that traditional social divisions between men and women, between Catholics and Protestants, between young and old and between the classes had been eroded. In addition, Schoenbaum noted that there were Germans who took advantage of the opportunities for social mobility which had been offered to them and thereby breathed life into the ideology that underpinned the regime.

Schoenbaum's idea of social revolution can be seen as something of a hybrid between the 'top-down' historiography of the first generation of post-war historians, and the 'bottom-up' approaches of the second. His concept had similarities with the totalitarian approach. Like Bracher and Hildebrand, he emphasised the active and transformative nature of Nazi rule. But, like many other social historians of this period, he also stressed the role of those Germans who were either Nazified or pragmatic careerists. Historians like Ralf Dahrendorf and Richard Grunberger contributed to this discussion.[36] In the 1980s, Detlev Peukert and Jeffrey Herf, addressing the problem of balancing the seemingly contradictory characteristics of National Socialism – its reactionary and modernising elements – assessed the nature of the regime slightly differently again. They argued that racial ideology, which propelled the regime, subsumed those apparent contradictions and that social relations were shaped and realigned according to the new racial hierarchies.[37]

Historians, for the most part, remained sceptical about claims that there was any kind of social revolution in Nazi Germany. Kershaw has explicitly rejected the analyses of Schoenbaum and Dahrendorf. According to Kershaw, Hitler wanted to create a new racial identity but was otherwise 'uninterested in tampering with the social order'.[38] The Nazis made no attempt to break down the fundamental structures of the German economy. Nor were family, church associations or class relations transformed. Thus Kershaw and others use the same argument against the concept of

---

[36] Ralf Dahrendorf, *Society and Democracy in Germany* (Garden City, NY: Doubleday, 1967); Richard Grunberger, *A Social History of the Third Reich* (London: Weidenfeld and Nicolson, 1971).

[37] Jeffrey Herf, *Reactionary Modernism: Technology, Culture, and Politics in Weimar and the Third Reich* (Cambridge: Cambridge University Press, 1984); Detlev J.K. Peukert, *Inside Nazi Germany: Conformity, Opposition and Racism in Everyday Life* (New Haven, CT: Yale University Press, 1987).

[38] Kershaw, *Nazi Dictatorship*, 173.

social revolution that they use against totalitarian theory. They emphasise continuity, rather than change. Society adapted to or accommodated Nazi rule relatively easily, and the basic institutions and structures that were there in 1933 were still there in 1945.

However, the creation of a new 'racial identity', not only in the Greater Reich but in Hitler's empire as a whole, did involve 'tampering with the social order'. Thomas Saunders, for instance, wrote that the social force of National Socialism could not be understood if one focused only on what was measurable in the conventional sense, or 'objectively'.[39] Class relations were unlikely to be completely overturned in such a short period even if this had been a goal of the Nazi ideologues, which it clearly was not. One had also to consider qualitative changes, or the 'subjective' social revolution. Saunders maintained that one would not find evidence for the 'subjective' social revolution in relations between workers and bosses. Rather, the real revolution took place in terms of norms of behaviour and professional practice. For example, there were radical changes in the behaviour of medical experts, health workers and employees of various welfare agencies. These changes entailed, in the first instance, forced sterilisation of people of questionable 'racial health', and then their murder in the 'euthanasia' programme. Similarly, encounters between soldiers on the Eastern Front and their racial and political enemies provide us with a sense of the transformative capacity of Nazi ideology and its progressive radicalisation in total war. Historians like Michael Burleigh and Wolfgang Wippermann have analysed these behaviours in terms of a Nazi 'racial revolution' and the goal of racial purity.[40]

Nazi racial ideology, notably its anti-Semitism, was so radical in practice that it permeated all kinds of relationships between states and citizens, between citizens, and between the occupiers and the occupied. In other words, the application of Nazi racial ideology constituted a profound 'tampering' with social norms. This 'tampering' might not have resulted in a revolution that transformed relations between classes or between generations, but it heralded revolutionary changes nonetheless. Nazi racial ideology underpinned rule in the empire, in the centre and

---

[39] Thomas Saunders, 'Nazism and Social Revolution', in Gordon Martel (ed.), *Modern Germany Reconsidered, 1870–1945* (London: Routledge, 1992), 159–177.

[40] Michael Burleigh and Wolfgang Wippermann, *The Racial State: Germany 1933–1945* (Cambridge: Cambridge University Press, 1991).

on the periphery. In the context of total war, racial thinking contributed to the mass murder of civilians on an unprecedented scale and then to genocide. Everyday resistance and collaboration can only be understood with proper regard for the massive social dislocation and disruption occasioned by the war, as well as the interplay between coercion, control and consensus in Hitler's empire.

'Measuring' daily-life resistance and collaboration

In Chapter 2 we noted that the organising principle for the study of social behaviour in Hitler's empire is a continuum with active resistance at one extreme and collaborationism at the other. We suggested that the problem with this paradigm is that it is difficult to apply to a wide range of social behaviours. Regardless of the many declarations that the old binaries (such as coercion versus consent, or control versus collusion) have been superseded,[41] the urge to judge or classify the gamut of everyday behaviours as resistance or collaboration, or as gravitating towards one or the other, persists. This tendency has skewed assessments of resistance and collaboration in daily life, as is revealed if we look briefly at three problems of perception embedded in the historiography. These are (1) the under-emphasis of the social impact and radicalisation in war of the racial imperative of National Socialist ideology, (2) the implication that resistance and collaboration are appropriate moral or ethical markers of all social behaviour, and (3) the linear and teleological approach that assesses behaviour from the perspective of the endpoint – or desired outcome – of an Allied victory.

Agency inflation has resulted in an under-emphasis of the impact of ideology, state power and state violence on daily life

Those who conceived of the totalitarian or total state never meant it to be a simple top-down instrument of control, let alone a static entity. The term 'totalitarian' derives from Mussolini's vision of an all-encompassing or total state which would cater to every human need and within which the

---

[41] See Lüdtke, 'Ordinary People'.

contradiction between the individual and the collective would finally be resolved. This totalising vision was summed up in his famous slogan: 'All within the state, nothing outside the state, nothing against the state.'[42] But, in order to create this utopian state, it would also be necessary to create a new kind of human being (the 'Fascist person') whose identity was inextricably entwined with the collective. This would be achieved through the establishment of a plethora of capillary associations that regulated people's working lives as well as their private time, and through which Fascist values would be inculcated from cradle to grave. It soon became clear that positive reinforcement (propaganda) was insufficient to create a nation of enthusiastic Fascists, and so control, indoctrination, and coercion became integral to the system.

Hitler was impressed by Mussolini's social vision. He subsequently sought to fill German people's lives with a similarly comprehensive range of capillary organisations. These were designed to replace existing patterns of social interaction and engagement with new relationships based on National Socialist values. The leader of the German Labour Front, Robert Ley, wrote that 'the only person who is still a private individual in Germany is somebody who is asleep'.[43] At the same time, Nazi ideologues developed highly sophisticated methods of propaganda and control in a variety of forms: new work practices, school curricula, print, film, radio programming, state-sponsored leisure pursuits, and elaborately choreographed public ceremonies. The goal was not mere distraction through escapist entertainment and consumerism. It was, rather, to instil strong emotional and personal ties to the regime through joyful and pleasurable activities.[44] Unlike the Italian Fascists, the Nazis did not use the term 'totalitarian' to describe their project. But they did talk about 'coordination' (*Gleichschaltung*), by which they meant the total Nazification of the state, society and all those individuals who were deemed to be 'desirable'. Those who were unwanted, by contrast, were to be excluded from the racially determined national community (*Volksgemeinschaft*), forced into

---

[42] Ann T. Allen, *Women in Twentieth-Century Europe* (Basingstoke: Palgrave Macmillan, 2007), 52.

[43] Quoted in Hannah Arendt, *The Origins of Totalitarianism*, 2nd edn (Cleveland, OH: Meridian Books, 1958), 339.

[44] See Pamela E. Swett, Corey Ross and Fabrice d'Almeida (eds), *Pleasure and Power in Nazi Germany* (Basingstoke: Palgrave Macmillan, 2011).

emigration, or liquidated. Opponents of the regime were to be intimidated into conformity, incarcerated or killed.

Hannah Arendt, who fled Nazi Germany in 1933 to escape persecution, famously theorised totalitarianism. According to Arendt, totalitarian dictatorships successfully coerced populations into conformity. But at the same time they created new elites, some of whom were true believers in the official ideology, and some of whom were careerists who implemented without question the policies of the state.[45] To describe the routine and bureaucratic character of mass terror and killing in totalitarian dictatorships, Arendt coined the phrase 'the banality of evil'.[46] According to Arendt, stasis – and hence mere compliance – was anathema to the proponents of the total state because it demonstrated that the revolutionary élan was abating, or was spent. The notion of daily life as stasis, or 'business as usual', was unacceptable because it was a deadening influence and blocked the revolutionary potential of radically transforming regimes. To achieve their goals, totalising states had constantly to be in motion. Arendt's identification of atomisation in totalitarianism went hand-in-hand with her ideas concerning the establishment and control of new associational ties and 'energising the everyday' in the total state. It was in the war that the full potential of the totalitarian or totalising state was realised.

World War II was an ideological war. It constituted a struggle between competing views of the world: liberal, nationalist, fascist, Communist and National Socialist. The nature of the war was unprecedented both in terms of its scale and its disruption to daily life. The war itself was also a radicalising and polarising agent. This was evident at the centre and on the periphery of Hitler's empire. It was evident in a political and in a social sense.

Politically, the war led to the collapse of moderate forces and the rise to power of fringe, often extreme, groups. We noted this in our discussion of the paramilitarisation of society in Chapter 3. Where states had

---

[45] Hannah Arendt, *The Origins of Totalitarianism* (New York: Harcourt, Brace, 1951). See also Hannah Arendt, 'Authority in the Twentieth Century', *Review of Politics*, 18/4 (1956), 403–417; Steven E. Aschheim, 'Nazism, Culture and *The Origins of Totalitarianism*: Hannah Arendt and the Discourse of Evil', *New German Critique*, Special Issue on Germans and Jews, 70 (1997), 117–139.

[46] Hannah Arendt, *Eichmann in Jerusalem. A Report on the Banality of Evil* (New York: Viking Press, 1963).

fallen apart, the new political elites had particular force. Some collaborationist groups had been on the periphery of the body politic before the war, while others came to the fore entirely as a result of the changed circumstances. In the case of Yugoslavia, there were only a few hundred Ustaše in the inter-war period and almost all of them lived in exile. They had no mandate and were beholden to the Germans and Italians who had installed them in power after the invasion of Yugoslavia in 1941.[47] Similarly, Dutch and Norwegian Nazis had little or no traction before the war.[48] Slovak collaborationists, on the other hand, had a higher profile and electoral support in the 1930s, but nonetheless became the direct beneficiaries of the dismemberment of the Czechoslovak state in 1938.[49] War thus led to the breakdown of established power relations within society. External forces invested new elites with an authority that they would not have had otherwise.

Collaborationist regimes emulated their protectors by regulating and controlling the lives of people over whom they exercised authority. As the dominant ideology, National Socialism determined political agendas that impacted on social norms across Hitler's empire. Assuming the methods of the Fascists and the Nazis, collaborationists wanted to create a new social reality and transform people's quotidian routines by 'energising the everyday' and by absorbing into state-run capillary associations those who had been outside the reach of the state, especially women and young people.[50] In France, the Vichy regime launched a 'National Revolution' on the principles of 'Work, Family, Nation'. In Croatia, the Ustaše created a

---

[47] Sabrina P. Ramet, *The Three Yugoslavias: State-Building and Legitimation, 1918–2005* (Washington, DC: Woodrow Wilson Center Press and Indiana University Press, 2006), 114–115.

[48] Dietrich Orlow, *The Lure of Fascism in Western Europe: German Nazis, Dutch and French Fascists, 1933–1939* (Basingstoke: Palgrave Macmillan, 2009); Salvatore Garau, 'Anticipating Norwegian Fascism: The Radicalization of Urban Right-Wing Nationalism in Inter-War Norway', *European History Quarterly*, 43/4 (2013), 681–706.

[49] Nadya Nedelsky, 'The Wartime Slovak State: A Case Study in the Relationship Between Ethnic Nationalism and Authoritarian Patterns of Governance', *Nations and Nationalism*, 7/2 (2001), 215–234. See also James Mace Ward, *Priest, Politician, Collaborator: Jozef Tiso and the Making of Fascist Slovakia* (Ithaca, NY: Cornell University Press, 2013).

[50] Sheila Fitzpatrick and Alf Lüdtke, 'Energizing the Everyday: On the Breaking and Making of Social Bonds in Nazism and Stalinism', in Geyer and Fitzpatrick, *Beyond Totalitarianism*, 266–301.

youth movement, a women's organisation and a university students' association, among other specialised groups.[51] The goal of such structures – wherever they were introduced – was to establish new relationships that would undermine the liberal concept of civil society which embraced everyone equally in the 'universe of obligation'.[52] In the emergent social orders across Hitler's empire, loyalties were determined by ethnicity, race or political affiliation, rather than by universal values.

Historical explanations of daily-life resistance and collaboration must also take into account the intensity of terror, and the extent to which fear seeped into social relations. In pursuit of their political, racial and national agendas, the Nazis and collaborationist regimes did not tolerate opposition. Wachsmann argues that we need to regard the system of concentration camps as an integral feature of the new European order. The mere presence of the camp system had a regulatory effect.[53] Within the territory contained in the current borders of Poland there were 5,800 internment facilities including ghettoes, concentration and labour camps, and prisons, not to mention the death camps.[54] We know that 'at least 18 million Europeans passed through the camp system [and] that at least 11 million died in it' during the war.[55] Moreover, as noted in Chapter 1, approximately 3 million Germans were interned at some point in the history of the Third Reich. Mary Fulbrook reminds us that 'gestures were ... almost entirely ineffectual in face of the machinery of death'.[56]

Opposing the Third Reich or collaborationists did not simply incur personal risk. If one had the opportunity to leave Germany, and then

---

[51] Ramet, *Three Yugoslavias*, 117.

[52] Sociologist Helen Fein coined the term 'universe of obligation'. See Helen Fein, *Genocide: A Sociological Perspective* (London: Sage, 1993). Discussed in Adam Jones, *Genocide: A Comprehensive Introduction*, 2nd edn (London: Routledge, 2011), 4.

[53] See Nikolaus Wachsmann, *KL: A History of the Nazi Concentration Camps* (London: Little, Brown, 2016); 'Forum: Nazi Terror', in *German History*; Christian Goeschel and Nikolaus Wachsmann (eds), *The Nazi Concentration Camps, 1933–1939: A Documentary History* (Lincoln, NE: University of Nebraska Press, 2012). See also Nikolaus Wachsmann, *Hitler's Prisons: Legal Terror in Nazi Germany* (New Haven, CT: Yale University Press, 2004).

[54] Dieter Pohl, 'War, Occupation and the Holocaust in Poland', in Stone, *Historiography of the Holocaust*, 88–119, 96.

[55] Konnilyn Feig, 'Non-Jewish Victims in the Concentration Camps', in Michael Berenbaum (ed.), *A Mosaic of Victims: Non-Jews Persecuted and Murdered by the Nazis* (New York: New York University Press, 1990), 161–178, 162.

[56] Fulbrook, 'Embodying the Self', 269.

criticised it from without, or if one became involved in dissident activities from within, one's entire family and social network were at risk. The German state's recourse to 'family punishment' (*Sippenhaft*), which was technically illegal, was a powerful disincentive to potential critics.[57] State terror, resulting in the harsh punishment of trivial offences, was an important form of social control, as was collective punishment. The arbitrariness of reprisals made them all the more effective as deterrents. Reprisals could be so extreme as to call into question the worth of the initial act of resistance that prompted the reaction. There was a relentless ideological drive in German counter-insurgency measures that resulted in the mass murder of civilians, including women and children.[58] The point was to eradicate actual and potential opposition, whatever the cost in human terms.

Furthermore, all manner of subversive behaviours were held to be serious crimes and could lead to incarceration, torture and death. In 1942, a 73-year-old man who was struggling to support himself and his wife wrote 'Hitler must be killed to end the war' on the wall of a public toilet in Germany. The Nazis caught him and executed him. According to the typologies of resistance, writing graffiti counts as a 'low-level transgression' and an 'unobtrusive or minor obstruction'.[59] Yet, for the victim, neither the act itself nor the consequences were 'minor'. This man's story may have been the exception rather than the rule, but it dramatically illustrates the ramifications of even 'minor' acts of non-conformity in daily life.

The notion of 'self-policing' dictatorships, invested with legitimacy through the 'happy' consensus of ordinary people, especially women, has gone too far. Unsolicited denunciations might have contributed to the feeling of fear, but the broad application of the term collaboration to such behaviours distorts its very nature. The real work of surveillance was not carried out by random 'volunteers', as reprehensible and as distasteful as they were, but by functionaries employed by the state. The actual coercive power of the Gestapo and other policing agencies came from their paid informers, from the many hundreds of thousands of block wardens who

---

[57] Robert Loeffel, 'The Sinews of the Modern Terror State: An Analysis of the Role and Importance of Family Punishment in Nazi Germany', *Australian Journal of Politics and History*, 58/3 (2012), 380–393.

[58] Henning Pieper, 'The German Approach to Counterinsurgency in the Second World War', *International History Review*, 37/3 (2015), 631–642.

[59] Balfour, *Withstanding Hitler*, 63–64.

monitored their neighbours and the ubiquitous factory spies in the pay of the Labour Front, among others. The rejection of totalitarian theory has resulted in an underestimation of the extent of the assault on norms of behaviour and daily life in totalitarian regimes. Lambert argues that one myth, that of the all-seeing Gestapo, has given way to another, that of the 'omnipresent army of snitches', and furthermore that it is misleading to describe denouncers as 'ordinary Germans'.[60] The assortment of terms used to describe the various European regimes at this time, including 'mass', 'participatory', 'consensus', 'self-mobilising' and 'self-energising' dictatorships, is similarly misleading.

What Timothy Snyder has called 'agency inflation' has resulted in an exaggerated sense of the options that were available to people in Hitler's Europe. He has used his term in a specific context where he discusses Polish-Ukrainian literature on the war and Holocaust historiography.[61] We believe that his evocative phrase and the idea behind it have more general applicability and that people's capacity to act independently in Hitler's New European Order has been 'inflated'. The totalitarian paradigm – in which people were 'controlled' – has been replaced by the view that individuals had a number of acceptable options. In this new interpretative framework ordinary people had a plurality of choices, and by choosing not to resist in daily life, they chose in fact to collaborate.

But state violence was one of the foundational pillars of the new European order and it is important to bear this in mind when we assess people's behaviour. This is especially the case when we examine the daily lives of women. An over-emphasis on the individual agency of women, and an under-emphasis on the structures of institutional power that governed women's lives, has twisted the general appreciation of women's experiences in Hitler's empire. In reality, the extent to which women had the freedom to exercise agency was negligible in many circumstances. The idea of women's bodies as 'combat zones' is relevant here.[62] Hundreds of thousands of women from Central and Eastern Europe were rounded up or kidnapped and sent to work in Germany. They suffered terrible

---

[60] Lambert, 'Third Reich', 42, 48ff.

[61] Timothy Snyder, 'Collaboration in the Bloodlands', in 'Review Forum: Timothy Snyder, *Bloodlands: Europe between Hitler and Stalin*', *Journal of Genocide Research*, 13/3 (2011), 313–352, 348.

[62] Anette Warring, 'Intimate and Sexual Relations', in Gildea et al., *Surviving Hitler*, 88–128.

conditions and were subjected to violence, including rape. Tens of thousands were forced into prostitution as a 'social service' for Wehrmacht and SS personnel. Moreover, agency diminished the lower down the racial hierarchy one found oneself. So, for example, Polish women were extremely vulnerable and Jewish women were even more so.[63]

Ordinary people were not 'free agents'. The violence of Nazi and collaborationist rule shaped their lives in obvious and less obvious ways. One did not need to be touched directly by the terror for one's life to be dominated by fear of it. The greater the degree and arbitrariness of state violence, the less need there was for a large body of 'enforcers'.[64] An overarching racist ideology, supported by state power and state violence, framed the context in which people exercised their agency and made their choices. Moreover, these factors shaped people's perception of their agency and their perception of the choices before them. The collapse of the totalitarian paradigm has reinforced the hierarchical view of resistance and collaboration. In turn, this has led to the over-simplification of the understanding of daily-life responses to Nazi rule.

The compulsion to label and to judge skews our understanding of daily life in Hitler's empire

Consciously or unconsciously, historians judge the behaviour of non-combatants in terms of the good and bad choices they made. Blamelessness and culpability are embedded in the hierarchies of resistance and collaboration. However, the people whom historians judge to be culpable did not always have the freedom, opportunity or capacity to choose the path that would render them blameless in the eyes of historians.

From about the 1980s, French historians, in particular those researching women in the war, began to recognise that this dichotomous approach

---

[63] Christa Paul, *Zwangsprostitution: Staatlich errichtete Bordelle im Nationalsozialismus* (Berlin: Edition Hentrich, 1994); Katherine R. Jolluck, 'The Nation's Pain and Women's Shame: Polish Women and Wartime Violence', in Nancy M. Wingfield and Maria Bucur (eds), *Gender and War in Twentieth-Century Eastern Europe* (Bloomington, IN: Indiana University Press, 2006), 193–219; Robert Sommer, 'Sexual Exploitation of Women in Nazi Concentration Camp Brothels', in Sonja M. Hedgepeth and Rochelle G. Saidel (eds), *Sexual Violence against Jewish Women during the Holocaust* (Waltham, MA: Brandeis University Press, 2010), 45–60.
[64] Lambert, 'Third Reich', 48.

was simplistic and led to inconsistencies. Any participation in public life whatsoever – no matter how basic – entailed a degree of accommodation with collaborators or the occupying regime. Earlier in the chapter we noted that, for many people, living with the enemy meant living a double life. Outside the intimate confines of the home, people could not make negative statements publicly about the political situation. They did not say plainly what they thought. Within homes where there were young children, there was still more pressure outwardly to conform. Children were incapable of 'double-think' and could easily 'betray' parents, family members and family friends inadvertently because of their inability to behave duplicitously. In the absence of mass resistance, and due to the tendency to interpret actions from the perspective of the military victory of the Allies, it was necessary for historians to find a word to describe politically or militarily indeterminate behaviours. For French historians the word was 'ambiguous'. We can see the advantage of such a term, but it blurs and does not address the root problem, which is the blanket application of the resistance/collaboration paradigm to everyday life.

Much empirical research on the 'ambiguities' in the choices made in daily life relates to cultural outputs. This research demonstrates how changing patterns in the analysis of culture and the arts reflect, or are governed by, changing patterns in the understanding of daily-life resistance and collaboration. The example of literary works published with approval from the censor in France is instructive. Medieval texts and poems, politically anodyne in themselves, proved extremely popular with the public when they broached the themes of conquest, imprisonment, 'resistance' of some kind, liberation and salvation.[65] After the war, the publishers of such material often claimed that their goal had been to subvert the enemy by saying in coded form what it was not possible to say overtly. However, it was difficult to prove this. Nor was it possible to establish precisely how the material was received. Hence its meaning in the context of occupation remains 'ambiguous' or open to interpretation. Jean Anouilh's rendering of Sophocles' *Antigone*, written and staged in Paris during the occupation, is a case in point. Its main characters can be seen as both defiant

---

[65] See, for example, Roy Rosenstein, 'Resistance Literature and the Exilic Imagination: Wartime Readings in Medieval Poetry for Occupied Europe', *Journal of Medieval and Early Modern Studies*, 27/3 (1997), 521–557.

and accommodating and, therefore, again, 'ambiguous'.[66] Ambiguity, a potentially useful concept, in practice becomes another means by which the narrowly prescribed resistance/collaboration paradigm is reinforced. We are left with no clearer sense of how to understand either daily life or resistance and collaboration.

The example of music demonstrates how this compulsion to judge can be unhelpful. Music, in certain contexts, has been interpreted as a vehicle to express defiance and resistance in daily life. Jews and Christians alike described musical performance in concentration camps as a form of spiritual resistance. In prisoner-of-war camps, music was important for maintaining morale. The French Catholic composer, Olivier Messiaen, wrote his now famous work 'Quartet for the End of Time' as a prisoner-of-war in Stalag VIIIA. Encouraged by his anti-Nazi German guard, Messiaen created a piece which he performed with three of his fellow prisoners who were accomplished musicians.[67] Partisans sang as they trooped through snow-covered mountain passes or after their meetings. Singing was important to them for many reasons, not the least of which was to inspire a sense of community. Lyrics were politically highly charged. Jazz and jazz clubs were seen by the Germans as subversive. Django Reinhardt, the virtuosic Roma guitarist, drew crowds, including Germans, to the Hot Club in Paris. The Hot Club was also the meeting-place of resisters.[68] Young people in Germany and elsewhere embraced jazz and, in doing so, rejected publicly and rebelliously the prevailing stereotypes of clean-cut, conformist youth. The so-called 'Swing Youth', who were distinguishable by their general appearance, defiantly embraced the 'seedy' world of clubs and clubbing.[69]

Yet music has also been identified as a kind of complicity. The prominent German conductors, Kurt Furtwängler and Herbert von Karajan, performed 'for the devil', apparently unconcerned that Jewish musicians

---

[66] Patrick Marsh, 'The Theatre: Compromise or Collaboration?', in Gerhard Hirschfeld and Patrick Marsh (eds), *Collaboration in France: Politics and Culture during the Nazi Occupation, 1940–1944* (Oxford: Berg, 1989), 142–161. See also Roderick Kedward and Roger Austin (eds), *Vichy France and the Resistance: Culture and Ideology* (London: Croom Helm, 1985).

[67] Rebecca Rischin, *For the End of Time: The Story of the Messiaen Quartet* (Ithaca, NY: Cornell University Press, 2006).

[68] John D. Pelzer, 'Django, Jazz and the Nazis in Paris', *History Today*, 51/10 (2001), 33–39.

[69] See Detlev Peukert, 'Youth in the Third Reich', in Richard Bessel (ed.), *Life in the Third Reich* (Oxford: Oxford University Press, 1987), 25–40.

were excluded or that the repertoire was being 'Aryanised'.[70] Furtwängler's career has been shrouded in controversy. He is variously described as self-interested, a closet Nazi, or someone who was against the system and tried, through his position and standing, to protect those (including Jews) over whom he exercised some authority. Maurice Chevalier, the immediately recognisable voice of popular French music, was bright and chipper when, in the presence of Pétain, he sang 'Ça sent si bon, la France' (France Smells/Feels so Good).[71] The much-loved Edith Piaf was not silent either. She delighted her adoring French and German audiences all through the occupation. Did the fact that she occasionally belted out some patriotic lyrics and had fleeting brushes with resisters, whom she protected, make her less of a Vichy stooge than Chevalier? Historians ask how we should judge individuals who composed, conducted, sang and danced their way through the war, while others ate grass and bark before starving to death.[72] The responses have not been altogether satisfactory, and many have complicated matters further still with their recourse to melodramatic 'conversion narratives'.

We have noted that, when resistance and collaboration are seen as deliberate choices, people are judged as having made 'good' or 'bad' choices as (relatively) free individuals. If one made a bad decision or choice, one's fate was more or less fixed, though redemption was possible following either of two eventualities: (1) a cynical turnaround or (2) a genuine 'conversion'. So, for example, in Western European historiography, the 'choice' to move from complicity to resistance can be depicted as self-interested (rats scurrying off a sinking ship) or as an about-face based on some kind of 'epiphany' regarding the true nature of National Socialism or collaboration. But the conceptual framework resting on choice and counter-choice imposes a false dichotomy between good and

---

[70] Michael H. Kater, *The Twisted Muse: Musicians and Their Music in the Third Reich* (New York: Oxford University Press, 1997). See also Richard Osborne, *Herbert von Karajan: A Life in Music* (London: Pimlico, 1999). See Richard J. Evans, *The Third Reich in Power* (London: Penguin, 2006) on the appropriation of the arts (particularly music) during the consolidating years of Nazi power, 187–218.

[71] See Brett Bowles, '"Ça fait d'excellents montages": Documentary Technique in *Le Chagrin et la pitié*', *French Historical Studies*, 31/1 (2008), 117–158.

[72] See, for example, Frederic Spotts, *The Shameful Peace: How French Artists and Intellectuals Survived the Nazi Occupation* (New Haven, CT: Yale University Press, 2008); Alan Riding, *And the Show Went On: Cultural Life in Nazi-Occupied Paris* (New York: Knopf, 2010).

bad choices. In changed circumstances, one's normal behaviour (the choices one made daily) could take on a new and different meaning. The melodramatic 'conversion narrative', also a familiar trope in films about the war, does not explain this process adequately.

The search for 'conversions' masks the significance of a dogged commitment to behaviours that blocked the penetration of Nazi and collaborationist ideology. Seemingly apolitical and, at first, acceptable and/or 'ambiguous', some activities nonetheless directly countered National Socialist dogma. In the Protectorate of Bohemia and Moravia, Czech schools were closed, teachers were harassed and sent to concentration camps and the university system was attacked. Anti-Nazi demonstrations in universities in late 1939 elicited a strong reaction and 1,200 students were interned in concentration camps. Nine were executed.[73] The period of intense persecution of teachers and the dismantling of Czech educational structures was then halted. In large part this was due to the introduction of a programme involving the absorption of the existing youth associations (Sokols) into the new Curatorium for Educating Children and Youth, which was the brainchild of a collaborator. The wholesale attack on Czech culture in the schools could only be countered in small ways to begin with. But a critical mass, refusing to surrender their cultural identity, reinforced it through education, and so the Curatorium became a site for banned activities and, finally, resistance.[74] A similar scenario obtained in France at Vichy's elite leadership school, L'École des Cadres d'Uriage. An initiative of the state, the institution's mission was to train new leaders for a new France. It became, instead, a 'training ground' for future resisters and was closed down in 1942.[75]

Non-conformism in many areas of daily life was regarded by the authorities not just with suspicion, but as a real threat to ideological hegemony. According to Pavla Vošahlíková, Bénédicte Rochet and Fabrice Weiss, 'culture wars' were a feature of daily life under occupation in many places and, often, it was teachers who were in the front line.[76] These 'culture wars' varied in intensity from place to place but they never abated,

---

[73] Pavla Vošahlíková, Bénédicte Rochet and Fabrice Weiss, 'Schooling as a Cultural Interface', in Gildea et al. *Surviving Hitler*, 129–152, 132.

[74] Vošahlíková et al., 'Schooling as a Cultural Interface', 138–141.

[75] Bernard Comte, *Une utopie combattante: L'École des cadres d'Uriage, 1940–1942* (Paris: Fayard, 1991).

[76] Vošahlíková et al., 'Schooling as a Cultural Interface', 140.

demonstrating the paramount importance of resilience and *Resistenz*, especially where the welfare of children and young people was in question. Teachers, parents, their dependants, and young people were under huge pressure to conform. Yet teachers also had the potential to intertwine the curriculum and traditional civic values as a means of blocking Nazification. So, for instance, Norwegian teachers tried to protect boys from having to leave for the Reich labour service and refused to follow directives to replace existing textbooks with Nazified materials.[77] It was not a dramatic about-turn or conversion that determined the course of the 'culture wars'; it was the resolute pursuit of 'normality' and the continuity of patterns of ethical behaviour pre-dating the war that, in many instances, countered the corrupting influence of occupation and collaboration.

Examples from the lives of women further illustrate the importance of continuities and 'normality' in daily life. Many women resisters did not go underground or flee to the forests. One's identity as a resister co-existed with one's 'day-job' of being a mother, a shopkeeper, a laundress, or a teacher. This, by definition, entailed accommodations of some kind. But the 'discovery' of women's daily-life resistance coincided with the first phase of the unravelling of the 'resistance myth' and was thus never fully integrated into the broader resistance narrative. The changing perceptions of collaboration as a mass phenomenon led to further marginalisation of the idea of women expressing opposition in daily life, highlighting once more the double standards in interpreting women's behaviour.

Women's survival is seen to be 'complicity' in some instances and defiance in others. It depended on which side 'one's men' were fighting. German women who did not resist in the conventional sense, who loved and nurtured their families and maintained norms of behaviour in family life are accused of having sustained and supported Nazism by acting in this basically humane way. Women in France who did the same were less culpable because their 'wait and see' attitude enabled them to jump on to the resistance bandwagon (or to 'convert') at the propitious moment. British women who loved and nurtured their families were just short of heroic and positively Churchillian. With their stiff upper lip and their firm resolve to carry on regardless (especially during the Blitz), they showed Hitler that 'Britain can take it'.

---

[77] Tessa Dunseath, 'Teachers at War: Norwegian Teachers during the German Occupation of Norway 1940–1945', *History of Education*, 31/4 (2002), 371–383.

The compulsion to label and to judge obscures an essential paradox in the relationship between interpretations of resistance and collaboration and the daily life of non-combatants. In France in the 1950s and 1960s, as we have seen, the prevailing view of resistance was based on the idea that it articulated the general will (or, as Charles de Gaulle put it, the spirit of 'true France'). From this perspective, resisters who blew up trains or assassinated German soldiers were embodying the national struggle against the occupier. By the 1970s and 1980s, however, historians were deconstructing the 'myth of the resistance' and portraying the mass of the population as apathetic and/or complicitous. The way that high-profile resistance was described – masculine, epic, heroic and individualistic – remained the same throughout. But, in the new historiographical climate, it was resistance 'without the people', a manifestation of the will of an elite who had not been corrupted by the occupation.

These two versions of the relationship between 'the resistance' and 'the people' (resistance as the expression of the people's will, and resistance despite the people) might seem to be saying different things. But they are both built on similar assumptions. In the traditional, celebratory narrative of the resistance, the people are no more than an abstraction. The resisters may be representing the general will, but the social matrix that bound the 'active resistance' to the population is ignored and the false distinction between active and passive resistance is reinforced. In the counter-narrative of the 1970s and 1980s, by contrast, 'the people' are still depicted in abstract terms – only now, the men with guns or explosives are no longer the embodiment of the general will, but the antithesis thereof. According to the counter-narrative, resistance was the marginal work of an elite, and most people in most places were either culpable through their 'non-action', or collaborated outright in some way with the Nazis. The social history of Hitler's empire has gone through various phases. It was over-theorised in some respects early on, but it is now so under-theorised that discrepancies such as those we have begun to highlight here go unchallenged. This is illustrated by the third of the problems that we identify in the historiography.

Privileging outcomes over process leads to teleological interpretations

A stumbling block to understanding resistance and collaboration in daily life is the fact that the dominant interpretative framework seeks to connect social behaviours with certain outcomes, even though there is no demonstrable causal link between them. Normally, a fundamentally (and narrowly) political or military question is transposed on to social behaviour and on to complex social processes, according to the following logic: if the war was fought against fascism, then people were either for it (and collaborated) or against it (and resisted). This approach, which defines resistance and collaboration by measuring social behaviour against the military and political objectives of the belligerent powers, has persisted through all the phases of the historiography.

The outcomes-focused approach is teleological and cannot accommodate one of the most elementary findings of daily-life studies: different people experienced the war differently. Any single event, no matter how significant it appears retrospectively, did not have the same effect everywhere. Moreover, the usual periodisation of the war and the linear interpretative framework, both of which shape the narrative arcs of all tales about resistance and collaboration, are generally incompatible with the personal or communal chronologies of the majority of the European population. This was apparent in our analysis of armed resistance and collaboration.

The dominant Western European chronology of highs, lows and turning points in the war cannot be made to stand for highs, lows and turning points in all non-combatant lives. For example, the Normandy landings of June 1944 were of monumental significance and heavy with symbolism for those involved. The operation was recorded on film and in photographs from the moment of the embarkation. But how people lived this moment varied across Europe and within France itself. The civilian population of the north-western departments became embroiled in a hard-fought campaign which gave many an opportunity to take a stand for the first time.[78] Some resisters, much farther away, and believing liberation was imminent, prematurely rose up against the German occupiers, who retaliated with harsh reprisals. Elsewhere, there was no one to fight and nothing to be done in terms of the military campaign until such time as the war drew

---

[78] Robert Gildea, *Fighters in the Shadows: A New History of the French Resistance* (London: Faber and Faber, 2015), Chapter 13. See also Mary Louise Roberts, *D-Day through French Eyes: Normandy 1944* (Chicago, IL: University of Chicago Press, 2014); and Hilary Footitt, '"Meeting Private Ryan": A Franco-American Liberation Community', in Hanna Diamond and Simon Kitson (eds), *Vichy, Resistance, Liberation: New Perspectives on Wartime France* (Oxford: Berg, 2005), 115–127.

nearer or Allied troops made their way towards Berlin. Even then, the (military) war might have bypassed one completely.

The linear approach idealises or treats as exceptional the heroic 'resisters of the first hour' who acted with 'foresight'. It leads us to think of the motives of 'converts' or 'eleventh-hour resisters' as somehow less heroic. With the benefit of hindsight, historians embrace the 'as late as' school of historical thinking. For example, in April 1944 Pétain, visited Paris and was welcomed by a large crowd when he attended mass at Notre Dame. Because Paris was liberated only four months later, the enthusiasm of the crowd, captured in photographs and on film, is seen to be a sign that, 'as late as' 1944, many French people still had illusions about the Vichy regime. In other words, they should have known better. This is in spite of the fact that detailed studies of opinion in wartime France have demonstrated that the Vichy regime lost credibility and legitimacy long before mid-1944.[79] Alternatively, the crowd is simply seen to be mindless or 'fickle'; not four months later those very same Parisians joyously greeted de Gaulle as their liberator and threw their posters of Pétain into the bin. These superficial assessments are made on the assumptions that people's behaviour is one-dimensional, that they experienced the war in the same way simultaneously, and that they had the same understanding of its nature in all its military, moral and ethical dimensions as it unfolded.

Conclusion

In this chapter we have shown that labelling people's behaviour in daily life as either resistance or collaboration is not straightforward. How restrictive were the controls under dictatorships and under occupation or collaborationist regimes? What were the options that were available to ordinary people, and how much freedom remained to them to choose between those options in their daily lives? Did Hitler's New European Order have a revolutionary thrust that dislodged existing patterns of sociability and connectedness? If we know how historians will answer these broad, general questions about social control, social agency and social revolution, we will usually be able to predict whether they will label

---

[79] Pierre Laborie, *L'Opinion française sous Vichy* (Paris: Seuil, 1990).

someone a resister or a collaborator in daily life. The point is that interpretative paradigms rather than empirical research have provided the key to understanding and assessing people's behaviour. Indeed, the same behaviour is labelled differently in different contexts, and it has become difficult to come up with a coherent narrative of daily life in Hitler's empire. This is not because of the diversity of people's experiences, but because of the very nature of the resistance/collaboration paradigm and its evolution since the war.

The loose application or definition of complicity and collusion in daily life trivialises all collaboration. Normally, the historian's concern is to avoid trivialising resistance or 'diluting' its definition. It is unacceptable to label both someone who did not risk death (a low-level dissenter) and someone who did (an arms-bearing hero) as resisters. But historians have no reservations about placing radically different behaviours on the continuum of collaboration. The study of many daily-life activities and routines within the generally accepted conceptual models of resistance and collaboration thus highlights their deficiencies and points to the need for a different paradigm.

Historians have set out to measure resistance and collaboration in everyday life. This is problematic at two levels. Firstly, the process of measuring can lead all too easily to judging inappropriately because the concepts of resistance and collaboration are so heavily value-laden. Secondly, the criteria that historians use to measure resistance and collaboration are often applied selectively and unevenly, without due regard for the concrete circumstances in which people found themselves. These tendencies are also present in the historiography of complicity in, and resistance to, the Holocaust, as we shall see in the next chapter.

5 Genocide and Rescue

During World War II, between 5.5 and 6 million Jews were killed by the Nazis and their local agents.[1] In the immediate aftermath of the war, the Allies were horrified by what they had discovered in the camps, and they were aware that Jewish people had been specifically targeted by the Nazi regime. But the victims were usually described in terms of their nationality rather than their Jewishness.[2] It was not until the 1960s that historians began to stress the central role of anti-Semitism in Nazi crimes. Two new words began to be widely used to describe what had happened: Holocaust (from the 1960s) and Shoah (from the 1980s).

In this chapter, we explain how ascribing responsibility for this genocide has been incorporated into narratives of resistance and collaboration. It is impossible to consider resistance and collaboration without also discussing the Holocaust. This is because establishing responsibility for the Holocaust has raised the stakes in describing people's actions as resistance or collaboration. We begin with a brief overview of the history of the Holocaust and then discuss how historians have attempted to address the question of responsibility. Finally, we discuss three ways in which this historiography amplifies our understanding of resistance and collaboration as social processes.

The fate of Jews in Hitler's empire

The Third Reich was the most virulently anti-Semitic regime in history. The mass murder of Jewish people began in 1941, at the time of the German invasion of the Soviet Union. The conflict on the Eastern Front

---

[1] Statistics in Michael Shermer and Alex Grobman, *Denying History: Who Says the Holocaust Never Happened and Why Do They Say It?* (Berkeley, CA: University of California Press, 2001), 174.
[2] Donald Bloxham, 'The Genocidal Past in Western Germany and the Experience of Occupation, 1945–6', *European History Quarterly*, 34/3 (2004), 305–335, 313–317.

descended into a totalising ideological war that was fought with particular ferocity. The territories which the Soviets and the Nazis had divided between themselves in the Molotov-Ribbentrop Pact of August 1939 became the sites where the greatest carnage of World War II – including the Holocaust – took place. Hitler's quest for more land in the east, which would be ethnically cleansed to make way for the super ('Aryan') race, was eventually halted by the Red Army at Stalingrad in 1942. But, in the meantime, the number of Jews falling within the orbit of the Third Reich had expanded dramatically. First, Jews were murdered in large numbers in mass shootings, and from 1942 in purpose-built extermination camps, most of which were located within the present-day borders of Poland and Belarus (see Map 5). The Nazis referred to their plan to kill the entire Jewish population of Europe as the 'Final Solution' (*Endlösung*).[3]

The Nazi seizure of power in 1933 led to the implantation of radical and, ultimately, annihilationist racial thinking in the key institutions of the state. This was evident not just within the SS, but also among medical and welfare professionals and educationalists. The Jews were deemed to be racially 'unfit' to participate in the life of the national community (*Volksgemeinschaft*). Whereas traditional anti-Semitism had defined Jewishness in religious terms, the Nazis articulated their anti-Semitism in racial terms. From the Nazi perspective, Jewish people who converted to Christianity and assimilated into German culture remained Jewish by blood, and therefore a threat to racial purity.

Nazi anti-Semitism was entangled with theories about the 'racial hygiene' of the nation and drew on eugenicist thinking, which had been popularised since the late nineteenth century. The flawed premise of eugenics is that it is possible to 'breed out' complex human traits, as well as diseases and disabilities, while increasing the occurrence of 'desirable characteristics'. It became common in nationalist circles to speak of 'fit and unfit' nations, 'strong and weak' nations, as well as racial hierarchies. In German eugenicist writing, people with inherited mental or physical disabilities

---

[3] This historiography is vast. Classic texts include: Gerald Reitlinger, *The Final Solution: The Attempt to Exterminate the Jews of Europe, 1939–1945* (London: Vallentine, Mitchell, 1953); Raul Hilberg, *The Destruction of the European Jews* (Chicago, IL: Quadrangle Books, 1961, rev. edn, 3 vols, New York: Holmes & Meier, 1985); Gerald Fleming, *Hitler and the Final Solution* (Berkeley, CA: University of California Press, 1984); Martin Gilbert, *The Holocaust: The Jewish Tragedy* (London: Collins, 1986). For a useful bibliography see Timothy Snyder, *Black Earth: The Holocaust as History and Warning* (New York: Tim Duggan Books, 2015).

were regarded as 'unworthy of life' and disposable. Furthermore, in this writing, social problems such as unemployment, poverty and crime were interpreted in biological or 'racial' terms. So-called 'asocials' – alcoholics, the 'work-shy', the homeless, delinquents, and homosexual people – could all be classified as being of lesser racial value. 'Asocials' thus came to constitute yet another loosely defined category of racial outcasts.[4] This biological explanation for social difference became an important form of social control in Nazi Germany.

Anti-Semitism in the Third Reich and elsewhere was also informed by anti-Communism. Anti-Semites associated Jews with revolutionary ideas of the Left, especially after the Russian Revolution. The identification of Jews with Communism (and hence the Soviet Union) was one of the main reasons for their persecution and murder in what Timothy Snyder has called the 'bloodlands' of East-Central Europe. Communism was regarded by the Nazis – and by many other European nationalists – as an international movement which could not be contained by borders, and which had been created to serve the interests of the 'anational' and 'unassimilable' Jews. The idea of the 'Jewish-Bolshevik menace' provided a lingua franca for extreme nationalists throughout Europe, and was usually an important ideological component of collaborationist movements. It is difficult to overestimate the significance of the fact that, for many of those responsible for killing Jews in World War II, the labels 'Jew' and 'Bolshevik' were interchangeable.[5]

The first massacres of Jews were carried out by special groups of SS, called Einsatzgruppen (task forces), which followed in the rear of the German armies as they entered the USSR in 1941. The Einsatzgruppen were mobile killing units, the 3,000 members of which had been deeply socialised in Nazi racial thinking.[6] The task of the Einsatzgruppen was to organise the liquidation of the 'racial enemies' of the Third Reich. At some point in the second half of 1941, a systematic, bureaucratised plan

---

[4] Paul Weindling, 'German Eugenics and the Wider World: Beyond the Racial State', in Alison Bashford and Philippa Levine (eds), *The Oxford Handbook of the History of Eugenics* (Oxford: Oxford University Press, 2010), 315–331; Henry Friedlander, *The Origins of Nazi Genocide: From Euthanasia to the Final Solution* (Chapel Hill, NC: University of North Carolina Press, 1995).

[5] Michael Burleigh, *The Third Reich: A New History* (Basingstoke: Pan Macmillan, 2001), 37–38.

[6] Donald L. Niewyk, 'Holocaust: The Genocide of the Jews', in Samuel Totten and Paul R. Bartrop (eds), *The Genocide Studies Reader* (New York: Routledge, 2009), 157–180, 158.

for the industrialised mass murder of Jews was adopted. The programme was laid out at the Wannsee Conference in January 1942. Top Nazis present at the meeting in Wannsee, a suburb of Berlin, outlined in detail how the Jewish 'problem' would 'finally' be solved. Their plans involved transporting Jews from all over Europe to camps designed expressly to kill people by gassing them. The circumstances that led to this policy included the very large number of Jews coming under German jurisdiction, the inefficiency of the mass shootings of Jews on the Eastern Front, and the negative psychological impact of the massacres on the German soldiers who carried them out.[7]

The historiography and the question of responsibility

As complicity in the Holocaust is one of the key markers of collaboration, it is essential to understand how the historiography of responsibility for the genocide has evolved. There have been vigorous debates about who drove the decision-making process that led to the Final Solution and about who was responsible for the implementation of that policy. Often the debates about origins and implementation have overlapped.

The first historians who dealt with this topic naturally focused on the role of Hitler and other Nazi leaders, whose culpability for mass murder had been established in post-war trials at Nuremberg and elsewhere. What became known as the 'Hitler-centric' or 'intentionalist' interpretation of responsibility for the Holocaust prevailed. The 'intentionalist' interpretation of the Holocaust posits that, from the very beginning, it had been Hitler's intention to destroy the Jewish people. There was thus a straight line from Hitler's anti-Semitic ravings in *Mein Kampf* through the anti-Jewish boycotts of 1933, the Nuremberg Laws of 1935, the anti-Semitic pogrom of November 1938 (*Reichskristallnacht*), the Wannsee Conference of 1942, to the gas chambers. Each measure was implemented as a step in a deliberate policy that culminated in genocide.[8] This top-down approach

---

[7] Christopher R. Browning and Jürgen Matthäus, *The Origins of the Final Solution: The Evolution of Nazi Jewish Policy, September 1939–March 1942* (Lincoln, NE: University of Nebraska Press and Yad Vashem, 2004). See also Christopher R. Browning, 'The Decision-Making Process', in Dan Stone (ed.) *The Historiography of the Holocaust* (Basingstoke: Palgrave Macmillan, 2004), 173–196.

[8] The classic study in this vein is Lucy S. Dawidowicz, *The War against the Jews, 1933–1945* (New York: Holt, Rinehart and Winston, 1975).

to explaining the Holocaust was in keeping with the totalitarian paradigm, which was still dominant at that time.

Before the advent of the social history movement in the 1960s and 1970s, the guilt or otherwise of ordinary Germans was not a focus. However, from the 1960s onwards, an increasing number of historians challenged the intentionalist view because they saw it as one-dimensional and deterministic. An alternative functionalist – or structuralist – position was put forward by scholars such as Martin Broszat, Kurt Pätzold, and Karl Schleunes. They argued that the decision to embark on the Final Solution was a more complex phenomenon involving the broader Nazi leadership and elite Nazi structures, including the SS.[9] Such historians pointed out that Hitler had rarely given direct and unambiguous orders in matters relating to the so-called Jewish question. For instance, it had been Joseph Goebbels, not Hitler, who had orchestrated *Reichskristallnacht*.[10] Functionalists also noted that the National Socialist leadership elites were being formed from the time of the establishment of the Nazi party in 1920 and more comprehensively after 1933. When the Einsatzgruppen massacred large numbers of Jews who had fallen under their control as the front moved eastwards, these men were behaving as exemplary Nazis. They knew instinctively what to do in order to fulfil the racial aspirations of the racial state. It was these Nazified and militarised men, responding to circumstances on the ground, who precipitated the Final Solution.

This argument derived from the functionalists' investigation of the perpetrators of the first mass killings of Jews and the chronology of events culminating in the Final Solution. Hans Mommsen contended that members of the Einsatzgruppen and similar bodies translated a 'utopian objective' (the fantasy of a Jew-free Reich) into 'hard reality'. Broszat concluded that the practice of liquidation on the ground led to the 'programme' of institutional killing and that the massacres were given 'retrospective sanction "from above"'. In Broszat's view, the fact that the first death camps were constructed in Poland following these massacres, that is between December 1941 and mid-1942, supports his thesis.[11] The initiatives in the large-scale massacring of Jews constituted examples of what historians

---

[9] Ian Kershaw, *The Nazi Dictatorship: Problems and Perspectives of Interpretation*, 4th edn (London: Arnold, 2000), 99–102.

[10] Kershaw, *Nazi Dictatorship*, 109–110.

[11] Summarised in Kershaw, *Nazi Dictatorship*, 99–100.

have described evocatively as 'working towards the Führer' or 'anticipating the will of the Führer'.[12]

Thus, according to the functionalists, the road from the Nazi seizure of power to the Holocaust was 'twisted' rather than 'straight'. The functionalists never questioned the centrality of anti-Semitism in Hitler's worldview, or the centrality of Hitler himself in the implementation of the Final Solution. The fact that Hitler was not present at the Wannsee Conference, and that there was no 'Führer order' sanctioning or outlining the programme of extermination, did not mean that he was not in control. But the functionalists did conclude that the decision to embark on the systematic annihilation of Europe's Jews was contingent. The functionalists thus noted that, while the Final Solution was not an accident of war, it was a product of the circumstances of the war and its nature. In other words, it was the result of a series of events and decisions by which racial policy was cumulatively radicalised in places where the war was most violent.

Eventually the debate between intentionalists and functionalists subsided because it became evident that the two perspectives were not mutually exclusive.[13] Without Hitler there would not have been a Holocaust. But Hitler could not have been solely responsible. The debate was important nonetheless, because it revealed a great deal about how different historians understood the nature of the Nazi regime and the nature of responses to and agency within that regime. The emphasis in this debate, however, was still on elite, Nazified individuals and structures, and on National Socialism as the force that drove the genocidal policies of the racial state.

A new phase of research on the Holocaust began when historians started to explore the role of local populations in the implementation of the Holocaust. The shift in emphasis away from the centre (Berlin), towards the periphery, was incremental. In France, for example, up to the early 1980s, the argument had been that, for the most part, French collaborators in the Holocaust had responded to the bidding of the Germans. The German authorities had given commands and the Vichy

---

[12] For an explanation of the origins of the idea of 'working towards the Führer' in the work of Ian Kershaw, see Dan Stone, *Histories of the Holocaust* (Oxford: Oxford University Press, 2010), 106.

[13] Christopher R. Browning, 'Beyond "Intentionalism" and "Functionalism": A Reassessment of Nazi Jewish Policy from 1939 to 1941', in Thomas Childers and Jane Caplan (eds), *Reevaluating the Third Reich* (New York: Holmes and Meier, 1993), 211–233.

state and French policemen had carried them out.[14] However, from the late 1980s, it became standard practice to focus on the responsibility and the anti-Semitic initiatives of non-Germans.[15] When responsibility for the Holocaust was thus broadened to include non-Germans, the effect on conceptualisations of resistance and collaboration was more dramatic.

The cooperation and direct involvement of non-Germans ensured that the industrial killing which came to epitomise the transnational genocidal enterprise proceeded relatively smoothly. For example, collaborationist regimes throughout occupied Europe had enacted their own racial policies and had begun the process of registering and isolating Jews, thereby laying the groundwork for their subsequent removal and elimination. On the Eastern Front, the work of the Einsatzgruppen had been facilitated by local militias who had helped them to round up Jews, transport them to the killing sites, murder them and bury the corpses. As Jan Gross and others have demonstrated, there were incidents where Jewish populations were massacred without any direct command from the Germans.[16] In many such cases, Jewish people were killed by their neighbours.[17] The integration of non-Germans into the interpretative framework to explain complicity thus necessitated ascribing responsibility for the Holocaust across the board, from the top down and the bottom up, from the centre to the periphery, and back again.

One of the challenges of this transnational methodological approach was to establish the relationship between the apparently unprompted massacres of Jews by non-Germans and the planning that went into the Final Solution. Some historians suggested that perhaps it was time to speak of two genocides.[18] Others claimed that a preoccupation with the

---

[14] Michael R. Marrus and Robert O. Paxton, *Vichy France and the Jews* (New York: Basic Books, 1981) deconstruct this argument.

[15] See Stone, *Histories of the Holocaust*, Chapter 1.

[16] Jan Tomasz Gross, *Neighbors: The Destruction of the Jewish Community in Jedwabne, Poland* (Princeton, NJ: Princeton University Press, 2001).

[17] David Bankier, *Expulsion and Extermination: Holocaust Testimonials from Provincial Lithuania* (Jerusalem: Yad Vashem, 2011); Delphine Bechtel, 'De Jedwabne à Zolotchiv: Pogromes locaux en Galicie, juin–juillet 1941', *Cultures d'Europe Centrale 5*; *La destruction des confins* (Paris: Centre Interdisciplinaire d'Études Centre-Européennes, 2005), 69–92.

[18] See Omer Bartov, 'Eastern Europe as the Site of Genocide', *Journal of Modern History*, 80/3 (2008), 557–593, for a discussion on the specific characteristics and motivations behind what he refers to as 'communal genocide' (571ff.).

death camps left much of the actual killing out of Holocaust histories.[19] As blame was spread across ever-widening circles of people and ethnicities, another problem that emerged was the fragmentation that came in the wake of the multitude of regional studies.[20] The sheer weight of the discussion in books and articles in the new specialised journals militated against the creation of an integrated narrative that could make sense of the phenomenon beyond the circle of academia.

Given that the genocide was the result of the actions of a wide range of groups and individuals, identifying degrees of culpability became a priority for historians. In 1961, Raul Hilberg suggested the Holocaust trichotomy of perpetrators, victims and bystanders.[21] But he did not fully develop the concept of the bystander until his 1992 publication, *Perpetrators, Victims, Bystanders: The Jewish Catastrophe 1933—1945*.[22] Both perpetrators and bystanders (or silent witnesses) were responsible, but to different degrees. The term bystander now overlaps with the term perpetrator. In witnessing and not acting, one became a perpetrator by default. We can see a parallel in the slippage between the concepts of functional collaboration and active collaboration, which pre-dated the conflation of the perpetrator and the bystander. Significantly, the term bystander may be applied to people who did not witness anything directly or even tangentially related to the Holocaust and were not in a position to make decisions that had any consequences, positive or negative, relating to it. Some historians refer to the Allies as bystanders based on their behaviour prior to the war, including their reluctance to accept Jewish refugees, and then their failure to halt the killing of Jews by not bombing the death camps and their transport networks.[23]

The publication in 1992 of Christopher Browning's *Ordinary Men: Reserve Police Battalion 101 and the Final Solution in Poland* led (possibly inadvertently) to the widening of responsibility for the Holocaust.[24]

---

[19] For a discussion of this, see Stone, *Histories of the Holocaust*, 90ff.

[20] Stone, *Histories of the Holocaust*, 90ff.

[21] Hilberg, *Destruction*.

[22] Raul Hilberg, *Perpetrators, Victims, Bystanders: The Jewish Catastrophe 1933–1945* (New York: Aaron Asher, 1992).

[23] Victoria J. Barnett, *Bystanders. Conscience and Complicity during the Holocaust* (Westport, CN: Greenwood Press, 1999); David Cesarani and Paul A. Levine (eds), *'Bystanders' to the Holocaust: A Re-evaluation* (London: Frank Cass, 2002).

[24] Christopher R. Browning, *Ordinary Men: Reserve Police Battalion 101 and the Final Solution in Poland* (New York: Aaron Asher, 1992).

This was in part because of the great receptivity to Browning's description of the involvement of 'ordinary men' in the extreme violence in the east. He argued that the soldiers in Battalion 101 were not young and fanatical Nazis. Nor had they been socialised in the values of the regime. He suggested that there was little to differentiate these soldier-murderers from ordinary men anywhere in Germany. They participated in the slaughter not because they were Nazi fanatics, but because they were psychologically unable to resist peer pressure. The idea of perpetrators as 'ordinary men', rather than 'brainwashed' or Nazified individuals, took hold. It chimed with the increasing focus of social historians on individual agency in the Third Reich, as well as with critiques of the totalitarian paradigm.

Daniel Goldhagen refashioned this concept, focusing on the premise that in Germany a special kind of anti-Semitism had emerged over the centuries that was fanatical, annihilationist and endemic.[25] According to Goldhagen, it was 'ordinary Germans', rather than 'ordinary men', who had imbibed this brand of anti-Semitism from childhood and who thus became Hitler's 'willing executioners'. Goldhagen's thesis provoked intense controversy, but it did not alter the direction of the historiography. This was not just because Goldhagen's argument was polemical. It was also because it did not call into question what was becoming the received wisdom, namely, that ordinary men (and women) from different classes and different ethnicities were responsible for the Holocaust on different levels.

The rationale for the generalisation of blame was that, once the Final Solution was in train, it proceeded unimpeded: many more people than those actually engaged in the killing facilitated the genocide by not preventing it. There were men with enormous power who planned and directed the camps. There were others who were engaged in the running of camp life, from overseeing work teams to disposing of the victims' bodies. For these people the work became routine or, in Arendt's words, 'banal', as we saw in Chapter 4. The burgeoning historiography of the Holocaust was reshaping ideas about collaboration.

The 'discovery' of more and more collaborators in – or perpetrators of – the genocide also had the effect of undermining national resistance

---

[25] Daniel Jonah Goldhagen, *Hitler's Willing Executioners: Ordinary Germans and the Holocaust* (New York: Knopf, 1996). In the afterword to the 2001 edition of *Ordinary Men*, Browning took some of Goldhagen's assertions to task.

narratives. Partly this was because, even in those places where there had been strong resistance movements, there was nonetheless complicity in the Holocaust. The Polish, Yugoslav, and French resistance movements were among the strongest and the most successful in the traditional sense. Yet Jews from Poland, Yugoslavia and France were persecuted and perished either *in situ* or after having been deported to death camps. Poland was the site of most of the killing in the Holocaust. By far the largest number of Jews were Poles and the largest number of Jews killed were Polish Jews. No more than 10 percent of the roughly 3 million Polish Jews survived the Holocaust.[26] In post-war Yugoslavia, as in Poland, the resistance heritage was celebrated. Marshal Tito (Josip Broz) was hailed as the great leader of the Yugoslavs' courageous and triumphant anti-fascist struggle and became an international celebrity, especially after his break with Stalin in 1948. Yet the percentage of Yugoslav Jews who perished was very high.[27] The French resistance was also renowned, and the armed militants of the Maquis came to stand for resistance in its purest form. But, as we have seen, in the 1980s new research revealed the extent of the Vichy regime's initiative in the deportation of Jews to certain death. The percentage of victims from France (25 percent) was much lower than in most European countries. Nonetheless, the deportations were difficult to reconcile with the narrative that France had been a 'nation of resisters'.[28]

While the historiography of the Holocaust is highly developed and highly theorised, a few stock phrases dominate popular perceptions of the perpetrators. Thus we have the image of 'willing executioners'[29] as 'ordinary people'[30] who did not baulk at killing their 'neighbours'.[31] At face value, the idea of 'willing executioners' is not problematic. There

---

[26] Jan T. Gross, *Fear: Anti-Semitism in Poland after Auschwitz: An Essay in Historical Interpretation* (Princeton, NJ: Princeton University Press, 2006), 4.

[27] Of the pre-war population of 80,000, 66,000 (82.5%) Yugoslav Jews perished. See 'Yugoslavia', Shoah Resource Center, The International School for Holocaust Studies [website]: <www.yadvashem.org/odot_pdf/Microsoft%20Word%20-%206379.pdf> (accessed 8 January 2017).

[28] Marrus and Paxton, *Vichy France and the Jews*.

[29] Goldhagen, *Hitler's Willing Executioners*.

[30] Browning, *Ordinary Men*.

[31] Gross, *Neighbors*.

were plenty of executioners. If they were not all enthusiastic, they were not dragooned, and many of them were more than willing. Moreover, a large number of perpetrators seemed to have lived otherwise normal or 'ordinary' lives even as they killed their 'neighbours'. But did all non-resistance to the Holocaust signal willing acceptance and participation by default (functional collaboration) in the genocide? Many historians would answer yes. Norman Naimark writes that 'tens of millions' of Europeans were knowingly indifferent to the fate of Jews in Hitler's empire, thereby implying much more widespread responsibility than even the term 'bystander' suggests.[32] This is one step short of declaring that all Europe and the non-European Allies were collectively responsible for the Holocaust.

The Holocaust and the resistance/collaboration paradigm

For the remainder of this chapter we will consider in more detail three ways in which the historiography of the Holocaust can refine our understanding of resistance and collaboration.

Realigning the balance in the relationship between centre and periphery

Holocaust historiography recalls to us the importance of situating collaboration and complicity within the context of a Nazified Europe. We are not arguing that everyone in Europe was a Nazi. We are, however, suggesting that National Socialism and its clients and lackeys dominated power relations in Hitler's empire. It was the interaction between a totalising war and the ideology of the racial state which determined the nature of public life in the racial empire. Our argument here builds on points developed earlier regarding the insularity of national or regional studies and agency inflation deriving from the under-emphasis on ideology and state violence.

Dan Stone has remarked that the significant increase in the number of local or regional studies of complicity in the genocide of Europe's Jews

---

[32] Norman M. Naimark, 'Foreword', in István Deák, *Europe on Trial: The Story of Collaboration, Resistance, and Retribution during World War II* (Boulder, CO: Westview Press, 2015), xiv.

led to a fragmentation in the Holocaust narrative. This was especially the case in Central and Eastern Europe after the collapse of Communism. Fragmentation in studies of complicity in the Holocaust resulted in a false dichotomy between the massacres in the field and the industrial killing, and between the 'committed ideologue' and the 'banal bureaucrat'.[33] Genocide is not a chaotic or spontaneous historical 'event' but a process with an inner logic which develops in stages. The mass killings of Jews in the field after the invasion of the Soviet Union were not the result of frenzied anti-Semitic outbursts. Rather, they were premeditated and targeted attacks. Einsatzgruppen officers instructed their men to kill Jews and (where possible) instigate local pogroms. While there are different opinions about the extent of Reinhard Heydrich's direct involvement in the decision to embark on this campaign of killing Jews in the field, there is no doubt that it was a campaign and that those involved felt sufficiently empowered to embark on it. They were also sufficiently confident in their actions to keep records of their 'success' and to communicate these back to the centre.[34] The killing of close to 2 million Jews in this manner was integral to the genocidal process, the next phase of which was the conceptualisation and implementation of the Final Solution.[35]

In explanations of collaboration and complicity, the balance shifted away from Nazi ideology and state structures to individual agency. In Chapter 4 we looked at the reasons for this shift and its implications, which are also relevant here. This is apparent in the changing face of perpetrators in Holocaust historiography. Perpetrators are less likely now to be depicted as fanatical ideologues or psychopaths.[36] Rather, they are portrayed as 'ordinary men' of various nationalities who were not even necessarily Nazified but who, for a variety of reasons, played a role in mass murder.

This understanding of perpetrators diminishes the transformative capabilities of the ideology underpinning the structures that governed and sustained the Nazi state and empire at war. Often this approach seems to rest

---

[33] Stone, *Histories of the Holocaust*, 102.
[34] Kershaw, *Nazi Dictatorship*, 117.
[35] Kershaw, *Nazi Dictatorship*, 117ff.
[36] Jürgen Matthäus, 'Historiography and the Perpetrators of the Holocaust', in Stone, *Historiography of the Holocaust*, 197–215, 210.

its case with pre-existing anti-Semitism. But, as we have noted, the racial imperative of Nazism permeated all state and military structures. The reason that 'peer pressure' led to the large-scale and systematic killing of Jews is that the state sanctioned, promoted and rewarded this behaviour. In his testimony at Nuremberg, Rudolf Höss, the commandant at Auschwitz, spoke as the quintessential perpetrator who had a clear sense of what had been expected of him. He explained how he fulfilled that expectation. His main preoccupation was to do his job well because he was ambitious. Höss was remorseless. Indeed, he did not even recognise the need for remorse. It is reasonable to suggest that he had not faltered in the 'work' he undertook at Auschwitz because he did not consider Jews to be human beings. Höss's actions were informed by Nazi ideology, whether or not he understood this.[37]

The move away from a focus on the totalitarian paradigm and powerful state structures as determinants of behaviour, towards a focus on individuals or individual agency, was also evident in the studies of local communities in the farthest reaches of the empire. But, in fact, little could occur on the periphery that was not condoned at the centre. Martin Dean has shown that, if local massacres were not always the result of German influence, the incidence of spontaneous attacks on Jewish people has been exaggerated. Dean argues that those locals involved in such attacks were generally mobilised into auxiliary units and that the instances of anti-Semitic violence or intimate killing of Jews by their neighbours, though shocking, were not representative. Moreover, such outbursts were not in the Germans' interest, indicating as they did that things were out of their control.[38] According to Dean, Gross has overstated his case regarding 'ordinary' civilian Poles massacring their Jewish neighbours. In eastern Poland, pogroms were relatively unusual. In the mainly Ukrainian provinces of Galicia and Volhynia, they were more common. There is no question that many thousands of Ukrainian nationalists and collaborators played an active role in the anti-Jewish outbursts of the summer of 1941.

---

[37] Rudolf Höss, 'Testimony on Auschwitz, April 15, 1946', in Michael R. Marrus (ed.) *The Nuremberg War Crimes Trial, 1945–1946: A Documentary History* (Boston, MA: Bedford Books, 1997), 202–207.

[38] Martin Dean, 'Local Collaboration in the Holocaust in Eastern Europe', in Stone, *Historiography of the Holocaust*, 120–140, 124ff.

But the presence on the ground of German troops was an essential precondition for the violence. Significantly, in those parts of western Ukraine that were occupied by Hungarian troops, there were no pogroms.[39]

Stone makes the point that two notable trends have emerged in the scholarly writing on the Holocaust as a result of the torrent of intensive local research. The first is a realignment in perceptions of the chain of command from the centre to the periphery. The second is the renewed focus on ideology as a key variable. These trends are important when ascribing responsibility for the Holocaust. They restore a physical and ideological Nazi or Nazified presence on the periphery, and recognise that this presence shaped power relations. These trends also bring to the forefront the fact that the Nazis and their accomplices regarded 'Jewish-Bolshevism' both as a racial and as a political threat.

Collaborators were not working in an ideological vacuum. It is true that massacres of Jews were, at times, the result of individual, collective and administrative initiatives on the ground, and that the Germans might not have overseen some of those initiatives. But collaborators were negotiating their way in a context that was Nazified. Even if self-interest rather than ideology motivated them, what collaborators did was determined by the circumstances in which the National Socialist worldview and government by domination had become the norm. There was some 'room for manoeuvre' on the periphery, but it was firmly contained within ideological boundaries. The 'will of the Führer', actual or anticipated, determined power relations in the empire. The ideological priorities of the Nazi state and its methods of war shaped the parameters of complicity and collaboration at the centre and at the periphery.[40]

If there was no direct 'Führer order' to kill Jews in the field, that does not mean that these massacres were outside the purview of National Socialism. There did not need to be such a direct order. Consciously or unconsciously, the SS death squads, 'ordinary' German soldiers in the Wehrmacht, and policemen, were the vanguard of the master race. The Nazis sought racial purity. They also sought living space for the master race. The state first endorsed then demanded murder in pursuit of that purity and in pursuit of extra territory. Massacring Jews was consistent

---

[39] Per Anders Rudling, 'Dispersing the Fog: The OUN and Anti-Jewish Violence in 1941', in *Yad Vashem Studies*, 44/2 (2016), 227–245, 238.

[40] Stone, *Histories of the Holocaust*, Chapter 2.

with this policy. Moreover, those working in the camps and the so-called 'desk killers' who planned them were not dissociated from each other or from those who perpetrated the massacres in the field, but were part of what emerged as an integrated process of genocide.[41] When the state sanctioned murder, and the perpetrators of massacres went unpunished or were rewarded, as was the case on the Eastern Front, the genocidal process unfolded. In the conditions of a total (or in some cases a civil) war, it was unlikely to be arrested, let alone reversed.

Resistance and collaboration are not universally applicable categories

We have observed that the resistance/collaboration paradigm has limitations and can be an impediment to understanding how the war was lived and fought. Jewish responses to persecution illustrate with particular force why this is the case and why the universal application of the paradigm is inappropriate. We have noted that some historians suggest that anyone living in Hitler's Europe may be said to have accommodated National Socialism in some way unless they fought it or were its victims. Jews were the chief victims in the racial empire but, while their responses to persecution were shaped by circumstances over which they had no control, they did not all behave in the same way.

Jewish reactions to mounting persecution were often determined by the prevailing conditions. One of the most visible Jewish responses was emigration or flight. For example, some Jews tried to flee Nazi Germany and were successful. But the overwhelming majority of Jews did not have the option or the means to emigrate, especially if they had families. The approximately 400,000 Jews who left Germany between 1933 and 1939 might have had foresight,[42] but they did not know that there was going to be a Holocaust. It was more difficult for Jews to leave Europe during the war and almost impossible without some support from non-Jews. Nonetheless, there are famous stories of successful flight after the onset of war. (Raphael Lemkin, the Polish-Jewish lawyer who coined the

---

[41] Stone, *Histories of the Holocaust*, 94–95 and passim; Eric Katz, 'On the Neutrality of Technology: The Holocaust Death Camps as a Counter-Example', *Journal of Genocide Research*, 7/3 (2005), 409–421; and Eric Katz (ed.), *Death by Design: Science, Technology, and Engineering in Nazi Germany* (New York: Pearson Longman, 2006).

[42] Richard J. Evans, *The Third Reich in Power* (London: Penguin, 2006), 599.

term 'genocide', fled Poland after the German invasion in 1939, and ended up in America.) Once they were forced into ghettoes or incarcerated in camps of one kind or another, Jews were further constrained, not just because of heavy surveillance but because of the consequences for others if they attempted to escape. The policy of collective punishment meant that hundreds of Jews could be executed in retaliation for any act of refusal or resistance or an escape.[43]

Normally, where Jews were assembled into ghettoes and camps, the Germans required Jewish community leaders to be involved in the management of day-to-day business. At times this became the work of the designated elders in the Jewish councils (Judenräte). Their duties ranged from supervising food rationing to ensuring that work schedules were met and that directives from the Germans were acted upon. Jews forced to undertake some of the work in camps, including in the gas chambers, were organised in Sonderkommandos (special detachments). Jewish kapos were engaged in 'policing' the camps in what the Nazis bureaucratically referred to as 'prisoner self-administration'. The kapos' responsibilities included anything from keeping track of prisoners to assisting with the killing process. Often kapos were afforded some privileges, such as private rooms.[44] The Nazis did not depend on the 'complicity' of Jews for the smooth running of the ghettoes or for the implementation of their plans for mass murder and, for obvious reasons, we would not regard Jews as having 'collaborated'. While most Jews eschewed positions of authority that involved negotiating in any way with their oppressors, this was not always an option.

The example of a 'compliant' Jew interviewed in Claude Lanzmann's remarkable film, *Shoah* (1985), reveals that involving the victims in the running of the camps and ghettoes was just one of the perverse ways in which the Nazis exercised their total domination over their victims. *Shoah* draws primarily on people's recollections of Treblinka and other death camps. Lanzmann's interview with Abraham Bomba, a Polish-Jewish barber, illustrates what 'complicity' meant for Jews in the dire circumstances of a death

---

[43] Nikolaus Wachsmann, *KL: A History of the Nazi Concentration Camps* (London: Little, Brown, 2016), 530–536.

[44] Wachsmann, *KL*, 512–527; Tuvia Friling, *A Jewish Kapo in Auschwitz: History, Memory, and the Politics of Survival* (Waltham, MA: Brandeis University Press, 2014); Adam Brown, 'Beyond "Good" and "Evil": Breaking Down Binary Oppositions in Holocaust Representations of "Privileged" Jews', *History Compass*, 8/5 (2010), 407–418; Piotr Wróbel, 'The *Judenräte* Controversy: Some Polish Aspects', *Polish Review*, 42/2 (1997), 225–232.

camp. Bomba, together with a friend from the same town who was also a barber, had the job of cutting the hair of Jewish women and children before they were gassed. Lanzmann persuaded Bomba to recall on film the day when neighbours from his town, including his friend's wife and sister, arrived in the camp. The women were relieved to see the men, whose familiar presence was comforting. Neither Bomba nor his friend revealed the fate that awaited the women after their hair was cut, not just because it was forbidden, but because they could not bear to do so. Bomba's description of his friend's last embrace with his wife immediately prior to her entering the gas chamber shows, with astonishing candour, the psychological trauma resulting from 'collusion' with the Nazis. There are recorded cases of corruption and self-interest in the camps where 'Jews policed Jews'. Overwhelmingly, however, as Lanzmann's interview with Bomba reveals, the Jewish people in this impossible situation were faced with a 'choiceless choice'.[45]

It was also the case that Jews actively defied their persecutors in a number of ways. There was a time when the notion of Jews going to their death in the Holocaust as 'lambs to slaughter' dominated. A reaction against this image of Jews meekly accepting their fate came with a new focus on Jewish redemption and self-assertion.[46] Jews played a disproportionate role in the armed resistance, sometimes as members of Jewish-only organisations, and sometimes as members of national movements.[47] The story of the Warsaw Ghetto Uprising (April–May 1943), whereby a band of about 750 armed fighters attacked and then held out against the Germans for almost a month, has always figured prominently in the Jewish resistance narrative. But there were Jewish armed rebellions in seven larger ghettos and 100 smaller ghettos, and there was armed Jewish resistance in 18 forced-labour camps and five death camps.[48] Studies documenting active

---

[45] Wachsmann, *KL*. Chapter 10 is titled 'Impossible Choices'.

[46] Thomas Rahe, 'Jewish Religious Life in the Concentration Camp Bergen-Belsen', *Journal of Holocaust Education*, 5/2–3 (1996), 85–121; Arnold Paucker, 'Resistance of German and Austrian Jews to the Nazi Regime 1933–1945', *Leo Baeck Institute Year Book*, 40 (1995), 3–20.

[47] Konrad Kwiet, 'Problems of Jewish Resistance Historiography', *Leo Baeck Institute Year Book*, 24 (1979), 37–57.

[48] 'Jewish Uprisings in Ghettos and Camps, 1941–1944', *Holocaust Encyclopedia* (Washington, DC: United States Holocaust Memorial Museum) [website]: www.ushmm.org/wlc/en/article.php?ModuleId=10005407 (accessed 12 January 2017); John M. Cox, 'Jewish Resistance against Nazism', in Jonathan C. Friedman (ed.), *The Routledge History of the Holocaust* (Abingdon, Oxon: Taylor and Francis, 2011), 326-336, 331.

Jewish resistance in a broad sense, and in accordance with the hierarchies of opposition that we have already described, became more common from the 1980s. These works often celebrated the armed Jewish resistance.[49] Films like *Defiance* (2008), mentioned in Chapter 3, which tells the story of the Bielski brothers' resistance and rescue of approximately 1,100 Jews in the forests of Belorussia, attest to the ongoing tendency in the public sphere to represent the Jews' response to persecution in this way.

The radicalisation of young Jews and the spread of Zionism in ghettoes and camps resulted in active resistance, even in the face of near certain failure.[50] Jewish elders were often sceptical about the wisdom of armed revolt. They feared that the immediate consequences would be devastating for the whole community, which they generally were, and advocated a less conspicuous form of defiance or cooperation. But experiences varied from place to place. There is evidence that armed rebellion was more likely in instances where Jews were aware of the fate that awaited them. In Warsaw, this was the case. In the Lodz ghetto, while there was no knowledge of the death camps, armed rebellion was not countenanced because hope had not been entirely crushed.[51] For Jews in Vilna, the situation was different again. There was some hope to begin with, but by the time their fate became known there was no longer the option or the opportunity to resist.[52]

Jewish resistance took many forms. The focus on militancy in Jewish resistance can obscure the significance of prosaic acts of refusal. The challenge in Jewish resistance studies lies in balancing competing claims: of the quest for survival on the one hand, and the call for militancy on the other. Survivor testimony has confirmed over and again the importance and effectiveness of Jewish resistance in daily life. Privileging survival over militancy (or regarding survival as a kind of militancy) was a self-conscious strategy for many Jewish victims of Nazism. It was not simply a default position

---

[49] See, for example, Isaac Kowalski (ed.), *Anthology on Armed Jewish Resistance 1939–1945*, 3 vols (Brooklyn, NY: Jewish Combatants Publishers House, 1984–1991).

[50] Moshe Arens, 'The Jewish Military Organisation (ŻZW) in the Warsaw Ghetto', *Holocaust and Genocide Studies*, 19/2 (2005), 201–225; Anika Walke, 'Jewish Youth in the Minsk Ghetto: How Age and Gender Mattered', *Kritika*, 15/3 (2014), 535–562.

[51] Larissa Z. Tiedens, 'Optimism and Revolt of the Oppressed: A Comparison of Two Polish Jewish Ghettos of World War II', *Political Psychology*, 18/1 (1997), 45–69.

[52] Rachel L. Einwohner, 'Leadership, Authority, and Collective Action: Jewish Resistance in the Ghettos of Warsaw and Vilna', *American Behavioral Scientist*, 50/10 (2007), 1306–1326.

based on a feeling of helplessness, but an active choice based on a recognition of what was possible and effective, given the abject circumstances.

In Chapter 4, we considered the importance of 'holding on' or 'keeping the faith' in the general and metaphorical sense. This discussion is relevant to the case of resistance in the daily life of Jews. Nonetheless, we must not essentialise such experiences. Primo Levi, the Italian Holocaust survivor who famously went on to write about his incarceration in Auschwitz, was among those whose Jewish identity was formed in the war as a response to persecution. He did not consider himself Jewish until his persecutors gave him that label.[53] For others, familiar routines and practices, including religious rituals, took on new meanings in changed circumstances and constituted spiritual resistance. While spiritual resistance can be difficult to define, and while a number of historians do not even accept it as a concept, it was a form of daily defiance in the eyes of those who practised it.[54] Religious holidays (Yom Kippur, Passover and Hanukkah) could be invested with even greater symbolic significance when observed in secret or underground, and provided the opportunity for collective action in a situation where the very humanity of Jews was denied.[55]

All manner of cultural traditions and activities had an impact on Jewish victims' capacity to endure. For instance, there was a concerted effort to encourage musical and literary activities in Theresienstadt. Speaking and writing in Hebrew or Yiddish were important mechanisms for preserving Jewish identity in the face of all efforts to expunge it. Story-telling was a way of withstanding the brutalisation of daily life for children and adults alike. Humour (especially in languages one's guards did not understand), like allegory, as we saw in Chapter 4, enabled one to broach painful subjects openly.[56] Jewish musicians were forced to perform for their incarcerators

---

[53] Primo Levi, *The Drowned and the Saved* (London: Abacus, 1989).

[54] Eliyana R. Adler, 'No Raisins, No Almonds: Singing as Spiritual Resistance to the Holocaust', *Shofar*, 24/4 (2006), 50–66; Shirli Gilbert, *Music in the Holocaust: Confronting Life in the Nazi Ghettos and Camps* (Oxford: Clarendon Press, 2005).

[55] Rahe, 'Jewish Religious Life in the Concentration Camp Bergen-Belsen'.

[56] Ernst Simon, 'Jewish Adult Education in Nazi Germany as Spiritual Resistance', *Leo Baeck Year Book*, 1/1 (1956), 68–104; Aaron Kramer, 'Creative Defiance in a Death-Camp', *Journal of Humanistic Psychology*, 38/1 (1998), 12–24; Miriam Intrator, 'The Theresienstadt Ghetto Central Library, Books and Reading: Intellectual Resistance and Escape during the Holocaust', *Leo Baeck Institute Year Book*, 50/1 (2005), 3–28; Anselm Heinrich, 'Germanification, Cultural Mission, Holocaust: Theatre in Łódź during World War II,' *Theatre History Studies*, 33 (2014), 83–107.

and were filmed doing so for propaganda purposes. But Jews also performed music of all genres for themselves, and survivor testimony indicates that this behaviour became an unambiguous expression of defiance in daily life.[57] One Holocaust survivor, Alice Herz-Sommer, was a pianist and teacher. She said that music was 'like food' for those incarcerated in Theresienstadt, and that it kept her and those in her care, including her young son, alive.[58]

Keeping spiritually and intellectually active was a deliberate strategy of Jewish musicians, artists, writers and teachers, among others. But measuring the success of this strategy on the basis of outcomes (rates of survival) cannot reflect the significance of the acts themselves. Success in that limited understanding of the word was determined not by the strategy enlisted to withstand the attack, but by the powerful external factors that governed the victims' fate. This alerts us to the problems that arise when historians attempt to define resistance according to its perceived effectiveness and when they focus more on outcomes and impact than on motives and process. The identification of five levels of Jewish resistance by Werner Rings, discussed in Chapter 2, is particularly relevant here.

There was a time when the Warsaw Ghetto Uprising would have been the main focus of any study of Jewish resistance. Recent historiography is more attuned to everyday acts of Jewish refusal, non-compliance and defiance. Jewish survival was a form of resistance. Obviously, that does not mean that those who did not survive did not resist. A resistance hierarchy that places militancy at the pinnacle is always problematic, as the case of Jewish resistance attests. Writing daily-life resistance out of the historical narrative turns Jewish victims into faceless statistics. It does the same for non-Jews.

The impact of social cohesion and social fragmentation

In the context of the Holocaust, one of the most discussed forms of resistance is rescue. Whether or not non-Jews took action to rescue Jewish people depended on a range of factors, one of the most important of

---

[57] Kramer, 'Creative Defiance in a Death-Camp'; Stephen Powitz, 'Musical Life in the Warsaw Ghetto', *Journal of Jewish Music and Liturgy*, 4 (1981/1982), 2–10.
[58] Carol L. Schnabl Schweitzer, 'A Music Lesson on Resilience: Alice Herz-Sommer, Her Piano, and the Capacity to Survive', *Interpretation: A Journal of Bible and Theology*, 71/1 (2017), 50–63; Caroline Stoessinger, *A Century of Wisdom: Lessons from the Life of Alice Herz-Sommer, the World's Oldest Living Holocaust Survivor* (London: Two Roads, 2012).

which was the degree of social cohesion and social fragmentation. Where communities cohered under the stress of total war, large-scale rescue was more likely. Where communities fragmented, it was less likely. The crucial significance of the survival or collapse of civil society, clear from the example of responses to the Holocaust, can also be applied to other forms of resistance.

Conceptualising rescue as resistance entails considering it like other kinds of resistance: something that was possible only under certain circumstances. Some rescuers were paid. Some rescue was the result of acts of kindness imparted if the opportunity presented itself. Famous stories of rescue often involve rural populations responding spontaneously to requests for assistance by providing short-term shelter and/or supplies for the next leg of the journey. In terms of the overall numbers of Jews saved, rescue was most successful when it involved pre-existing and stable structures or institutions (like churches and schools), where there was a high degree of social cohesion, and where populations did not suffer state collapse or retributive communal violence. Whether resistance networks were solely organised for rescue was also an important variable. Particular conditions on the ground facilitated large-scale rescue operations. These included close proximity to neutral or liberated territory and the prospect of relatively safe passage across terrain that was not in zones of combat or under the direct oversight of the Germans.[59]

Military invasions and occupations, the redrawing of maps by the Germans and the Soviets, and the losing and retaking of land, created the preconditions for the massacres of Jews and for armed collaboration. Snyder and other historians have pointed out that the worst of the violence was in the east. It was here, Snyder tells us, that 14 million people were killed between 1933 and 1945.[60] Ordinary people were subjected to the destructive forces of what Christian Gerlach has referred to as 'extremely violent societies', resulting in greater and greater bloodshed.[61] Snyder also

---

[59] Michael L. Gross, 'Jewish Rescue in Holland and France during the Second World War: Moral Cognition and Collective Action', *Social Forces*, 73/2 (1994), 463–496; Leonid Smilovitsky, 'Righteous Gentiles, the Partisans, and Jewish Survival in Belorussia, 1941–1944', *Holocaust and Genocide Studies*, 11/3 (1997), 301–329.

[60] Timothy Snyder, *Bloodlands: Europe between Hitler and Stalin* (New York: Basic Books, 2010), 409–414.

[61] Christian Gerlach, 'Extremely Violent Societies: An Alternative to the Concept of Genocide', *Journal of Genocide Research*, 8/4 (2006), 455–471.

notes that Jews were most vulnerable in the east, and we know that it was in the east that almost all the victims of the genocide perished. According to Snyder, one of the most important factors determining the extent of the killing of civilians was the collapse of state structures.[62] The examples of Denmark, France, Poland and Yugoslavia support this thesis. A greater percentage of Jews survived in Denmark and France, where many state structures, especially at the level of local government, remained largely intact, than in Poland and Yugoslavia, where they did not.

The political experiences and memories that populations carried through to the war also shaped responses to state collapse. Snyder makes this observation in relation to how Ukrainians lived the war, in particular their response to scarcity. Evoking the Holodomor, the Soviet-induced famine in Ukraine in the 1930s, Snyder writes that 'mass participation in the murder of millions of people was already an everyday reality in eastern Europe at the moment when the Nazis were building their first concentration camp'.[63] Similarly, their inter-war history had a bearing on how Poles and Yugoslavs behaved in the war and on their capacity to withstand its ravages. Both Yugoslavia and Poland were products of the Great War and the disintegration of empires. As ethnically heterogeneous states, they comprised sizeable and multiple minorities who felt their rights were infringed by the dominant national groups. Poland and Yugoslavia were also carved up after the Nazi invasion and experienced complete state collapse.

The example of Yugoslavia merits further investigation as it illustrates well why we cannot make generalisations about collaboration and complicity based simply on ethnicity or political preferences pre-dating the war, or even state collapse. In Yugoslavia, there was a direct link between state collapse and social fragmentation on the one hand, and the limited structural and geographical capacity for large-scale rescue on the other. The south Slavs were not poised to embark on an orgy of genocidal violence on the eve of war. We have seen that, under the conditions created by the Axis invasion, the moderate politicians went into hibernation and the radical extremes of Yugoslav politics moved to centre stage, supported initially by those who felt that they themselves were victims of a national or political enemy of some kind. Ante Pavelić was installed as leader of

---

[62] Snyder, *Black Earth*, Chapter 9.

[63] Timothy Snyder, 'Collaboration in the Bloodlands', in 'Review Forum: Timothy Snyder, *Bloodlands: Europe between Hitler and Stalin*', *Journal of Genocide Research*, 13/3 (2011), 313–352, 343.

the Independent State of Croatia (NDH) because the head of the most popular Croatian political party – the Croat Peasant Party – declined the 'invitation' to lead Croatia in collaboration with the new German and Italian overlords. But in spite of the imperviousness of the general population in the 1930s to *Ustašism*, and the absence of an indigenous Croatian fascist party, the Ustaša regime in Zagreb enjoyed a degree of legitimacy for a period of time. This was due to the absence of tolerable options for Croats and because of the regime's nationalist, staunchly anti-Yugoslav rhetoric. The pre-war governments of Yugoslavia were repressive (a royal dictatorship was declared in 1929), Serb-dominated and ethnically divisive.[64] For the Ustaša regime, Yugoslavism stood for the gradual extinction of Croatian national identity and was indistinguishable from Serbdom. Hence Serbs were the enemy within. Most of the extreme violence of the NDH was directed towards Serbs, but Jews were victims too.[65] The regime was at its most lethal in the early stages and before resistance (which was Communist-led and initially alienating to many for that reason) had a mass following among women and men in Croatia and across all the constituent nationalities and all the Yugoslav territories.[66]

If we look to France and Denmark, we note that a different set of variables influenced how people responded to war and occupation. There was less ethnic tension in France and Denmark because they were less ethnically diverse and because of their long-established liberal and democratic institutions and traditions. France and Denmark were also far from the worst of the fighting, and their administrative apparatuses were not under the same degree of German control or surveillance as those of Poland and Yugoslavia. Moreover, French and Danish resisters involved in rescue could direct those in flight to safe destinations close to their state borders. Finally, the total number of Jews residing in France and Denmark was much lower than in the eastern regions of Hitler's empire, and there was less direct interest from the Germans in the deportations of

---

[64] Christian Axboe Nielsen, *Making Yugoslavs: Identity in King Aleksandar's Yugoslavia* (Toronto: University of Toronto Press, 2014).

[65] Sabrina P. Ramet, *The Three Yugoslavias: State-Building and Legitimation, 1918–2005* (Washington, DC: Woodrow Wilson Center Press and Indiana University Press, 2006), Chapter 4.

[66] Stanley G. Payne, 'The NDH State in Comparative Perspective', *Totalitarian Movements and Political Religions*, 7/4 (2006), 409–415.

French and Danish Jews. Virtually all Denmark's 7,200 Jews were rescued in one of the most famous acts of collective non-violent resistance during the war. Danes from every walk of life took part in the rescue operation. In October 1943, the Jews were taken on boats to safety in Sweden. This was a coordinated act of civil disobedience, indicating a blanket refusal to hand over the state's Jewish population for deportation.[67] By contrast, the Germans declared that they would make Serbia 'Jew-free', a goal they realised with assistance from local collaborators.[68] Thus, as Snyder attests, an explanation of the behaviour of populations under conditions of state collapse must refer to the pre-existing social and political dynamic, and to the contingencies of war.

We have already noted the many variables that determined the extent to which rescue was, first, likely, and then likely to succeed. According to Renée Poznanski, another factor that facilitated rescue was the existence of a collective identity that encompassed both the rescuers and the persecuted.[69] We referred to this idea in Chapter 4 in terms of the 'universe of obligation'. An incident in France illustrates its significance. The roundup of Jews in Paris in July 1942 shattered whatever illusions remained with regard to the Vichy regime and Pétain's promise to provide a shield to protect France. In a single night, French police rounded up 12,850 Jews in the capital and took them to the enclosed winter velodrome, where they were forced to remain in unspeakable conditions prior to their removal to the transit camp at Drancy, situated 10 kilometres north-east of Paris. The roundup highlighted the vulnerability of Jews in France, and marked a turning-point for French resistance and rescue.[70] But there is more to this story. The target for this roundup was

---

[67] Leni Yahil, 'The Uniqueness of the Rescue of Danish Jewry', in Yisrael Gutman and Efraim Zuroff (eds), *Rescue Attempts during the Holocaust*, Proceedings of the Second Yad Vashem International Historical Conference, 8–11 April 1974 (Jerusalem: Yad Vashem, 1977), 617–625.

[68] Christopher R. Browning, 'The Final Solution in Serbia: The Semlin Judenlager – A Case Study', *Yad Vashem Studies* 15 (1983), 55–90.

[69] Renée Poznanski, 'Reflections on Jewish Resistance and Jewish Resistants in France', *Jewish Social Studies*, 2/1 (1995), 124–158.

[70] Robert Gildea, *Fighters in the Shadows: A New History of the French Resistance* (London: Faber and Faber, 2015), 230; Limore Yagil, *Chrétiens et Juifs sous Vichy (1940–1944). Sauvetage et désobéissance civile* (Paris: Cerf, 2005), 533ff; François and Renée Bédarida, 'La persécution des Juifs', in Jean-Pierre Azéma and François Bédarida (eds), *La France des années noires*, Vol. 2, *De l'Occupation à la Libération* (Paris: Seuil, 1993), 129–158, 158.

the 28,000 Jews known to be residing in Paris. Police tip-offs enabled groups and individuals already engaged in resistance on behalf of Jews, or those who acted spontaneously, to warn and rescue the 15,000 people who subsequently escaped arrest that night.[71] At the very least, there had to have been a critical mass of active resisters, and a considerable degree of *Resistenz* based on social cohesion, for this to have been possible in a city occupied by the Germans and run with the support of fawning collaborationists.

Where there was pluralism in resistance (or 'resistances'), there was more likely to be large-scale rescue. Where resistance networks undertook different but complementary tasks, religiously and politically divergent groups expressed a solidarity based on the fact that they were fighting a common (foreign or ideological) enemy or engaging in a common enterprise (the restoration of democracy). In France, civil disobedience involved people from across the political spectrum but was, generally speaking, the product of an identification with the Republic and the values it enshrined. Mutual solidarity combined with the existence of a critical mass who refused to seek personal gain through collaboration were the preconditions for successful rescue in France. We have noted that 75 percent of France's Jews were saved. The Vichy government had enacted anti-Semitic legislation soon after coming to power. Whether this legislation was annihilationist in intent is questionable, but it left Jews, especially refugees, exposed. From a population of approximately 330,000 Jews residing in France in 1939, 75,000 were deported, mostly to Auschwitz. Only 2,500 survived. Those who were saved were mostly French citizens: over two thirds of the victims were refugees.[72] The French government, in an effort to protect its citizens, deported foreign Jews first. As foreign Jews did not have established networks, either within French Jewish communities or more generally, they were less likely to have access to rescue operations mounted by French resisters in moments of crisis such as the July 1942 roundup. French rescuers saved 45,000 Jewish children under the age of 15 by spiriting them across the country to safety in an operation involving thousands of people from all walks of life, linked by a 'chain of silent

---

[71] Marrus and Paxton, *Vichy France and the Jews*, 252, 270–279.

[72] Charles Sowerwine, *France since 1870: Culture, Politics and Society* (Basingstoke: Palgrave, 2001), 210; Marrus and Paxton, *Vichy France and the Jews*, 343.

solidarities'.[73] A Protestant village in the south of France (Le Chambon-sur-Lignon) was the site of an extraordinary community-based action that resulted in the shelter and rescue of 5,000 Jews.[74]

In stark contrast, the examples of Yugoslavia and Poland demonstrate that rescue was much less likely in those places where the war had caused or exacerbated social fragmentation. Ukraine provides us with another instance of this phenomenon. After more than 20 years of Communism, civil society in the Ukraine had been virtually destroyed even before the arrival of the German army. In addition, the Germans made it clear that any attempt to help Jews would be punished ferociously. As a result, rescue was very difficult. It was most likely to take place either in small, isolated communities where individuals were well known to each other, or amongst Protestant minorities. Protestant communities had been persecuted in the USSR and were bound together by strong personal ties, as well as a sense of religious obligation to help those in need.[75] We can see some parallels with the action of the French Protestants of Le Chambon-sur-Lignon.

Genocides do not generally occur in peaceful, stable and established democracies. If Jews were not an integral part of the prevailing conception of the 'universe of obligation' or members of a community of citizens prior to 1939, it was unlikely that things would change for the better during the war. In fact, the opposite was more likely to be the case. Even if Jews had legal citizenship before the war, that was to change with the Nazi invasion: they were now 'uncitizens'. What the 'universe of obligation' signified for non-Jews before the war also helps us to understand better the non-German perpetrators and the collaborators. Even had the killers stopped to ask 'who is my neighbour?', it is likely that if they had experienced discriminatory and violent inter-war regimes – or if they were experiencing extremely violent conditions in the war – their answer to that question would have been shaped by their self-perception as

---

[73] François and Renée Bédarida, 'La persécution des Juifs', 158. See also Yagil, *Chrétiens et Juifs sous Vichy*.

[74] Patrick Henry, *We Only Know Men: The Rescue of Jews in France during the Holocaust* (Washington, DC: Catholic University of America Press, 2007); Richard Unsworth, *Portrait of Pacifists: Le Chambon, the Holocaust, and the Lives of André and Magda Trocmé* (Syracuse, NY: Syracuse University Press, 2012).

[75] Karel C. Berkhoff, *Harvest of Despair: Life and Death in Ukraine under Nazi Rule* (Cambridge, MA: Belknap Press of Harvard University Press, 2004), 71–88.

victims. Where there had been a history of various combinations of political violence, dictatorship, discrimination, displacement and exclusion, a host of 'victims' were contemplating their own existential battles in Hitler's racial empire.

Conclusion

Holocaust historiography teaches us that there is no simple explanation for the extent of resistance and collaboration in Hitler's empire. Further, it reveals that, if we were to rely solely on the accepted definitions of either resistance or collaboration, we would have a very limited understanding both of the Holocaust and of resistance and collaboration themselves. Holocaust historiography provides us with important insights into the nature of power relations in occupied Europe and the way in which Nazi ideology determined or shaped those relations. War and occupation shifted the balance of power, creating new classes of haves and have-nots. Rapid change and destabilisation provided opportunities for career advancement and profit, as the various levels of collaborationism attest. The extent to which the collapse of societal norms resulted in fragmentation affected a population's capacity to withstand the downward spiral of persecution and communal violence. The collapse of the rule of law also led to a sense of helplessness.

Debates about establishing responsibility for the Holocaust are important because they uncover layers of complicity from the centre to the periphery. They are also important because they reveal the barrenness of ethnicised arguments and of arguments that, in effect, evoke collective guilt without using the term. To understand complicity and collaboration, we must take account of historical context, the experiences that people brought to the war, and the experience of the war itself. The study of rescue highlights the structural and social preconditions necessary for successful resistance and shows that these preconditions were contingent. It also highlights the fallacy in the approach that separates active and passive resistance and separates both from the social fabric from which they emerged.

6 Beyond Resistance and Collaboration

So far in this book we have identified many of the limitations of the resistance/collaboration paradigm. The purpose of this chapter is to outline what might lie beyond it. To this end, we begin by summarising the key points that we have made about European society under Nazi rule. We then discuss an alternative way of approaching the history of this period, which we call the 'social history of politics'. Finally, we give an example of what this approach might look like in practice by applying it to a specific topic, namely, the Catholic Church.

Seven maxims

For convenience, we have brought together all the observations that we have made into seven overarching maxims which we believe are helpful to the study of social behaviour in Hitler's empire, including resistance and collaboration.

1. *Resistance and collaboration were social processes.*
The resistance/collaboration paradigm has its uses but it does not have to be our only analytical tool. There were many, varied behaviours which were important to people's experience of the war but which cannot easily be labelled as either resistance or collaboration. All these behaviours, regardless of the labels that we attach to them, were interconnected. Both resistance and collaboration were thus fundamentally social in nature, and neither can be understood in isolation from a wider matrix of social behaviours and relationships. The rigid application of the

resistance/collaboration paradigm, which does not take account of this matrix, is thus an obstacle to the study not only of society in general but of resistance and collaboration as well.

2. *The analysis of social behaviour (including resistance and collaboration) must take into account the interaction between pre-existing conditions and the nature of Nazi rule.*

The structures and character of Nazi rule varied considerably from place to place. But the territories over which the Nazis ruled were also varied. A key factor was the presence or absence of a strong civil society. Where pre-existing community ties were long-established and inclusive, civil resistance (including rescue) was more likely. Where community ties during the inter-war period had been eroded by civil and/or ethnic conflict, or by authoritarian government, social fragmentation and violence were more likely to occur. People's behaviour in the war was thus shaped by the interaction of two key variables: the ferocity of Nazi rule and the degree of pre-existing social cohesion.

3. *When analysing social behaviour in Hitler's empire, we must bear in mind the extreme conditions of the time.*

Not everyone in Hitler's empire was directly touched by violence. However, almost all Hitler's subjects lived in a violent world under a terroristic state apparatus. During the later years of the war, orderly government and the rule of law collapsed across large parts of the continent. Food became scarce. Crime and the black market flourished. As the state became both more ruthless and more ineffectual, a process of paramilitarisation intensified the violence and the lawlessness. Meanwhile, at the centre of the empire, the driving energy of Nazi ideology sought increasingly radical solutions to the problems which had been created by its own remorseless radicalism. Under these conditions, most Europeans had choices but little genuine agency.

4. *Gender must be fully incorporated as a category of analysis.*

The way that gender has been factored into the resistance/collaboration paradigm has been uneven. Approaches to the study of collaboration have been broadened and feminised, whereas approaches to the study of resistance have not. Moreover, collaboration or complicity in private life is deemed to have had high impact, whereas resistance in private life is not. These are just two of the double standards that have become embedded in the dominant paradigm due to the insufficient regard for gender as an analytical tool. Therefore, it is not enough simply to write more about women and gender within the existing paradigm. The paradigm itself needs to be rethought in such a way that it fully incorporates gender.

5. *Resistance and collaboration are best understood in a comparative and transnational context.*

Nazi rule varied greatly over time and place, as did people's responses. Yet there were also underlying structural and ideological commonalities. Only comparative history can untangle patterns which were local and contingent from those which were structural and pan-European. Similarly, as the example of the Holocaust demonstrates, only transnational approaches can explore the relationships between the centre of the empire and the periphery, and between different parts of the periphery. None of this means that the historian of World War II must try to study everything all at once. But historians of specific places or events must remain sensitive to the transnational forces that were at work, and willing to make comparisons where they are appropriate.

6. *Resistance and collaboration should be studied within flexible chronological parameters.*

Most histories of social behaviour under Nazi rule are written within a chronological framework that is determined by events of significance from the perspective of Allied and Axis governments, for instance the invasion of Poland and the outbreak of World War II (September 1939), the fall of France (June 1940), the invasion of the USSR (June 1941), the D-Day landings (June 1944) and the German capitulation (May 1945). But these dates did not necessarily have much significance for ordinary people in Hitler's empire and, even if they did, they did not necessarily mean the same thing. If we wish to understand social behaviour, we must investigate it within chronological parameters that are appropriate to the communities which we are studying.

7. *Students of resistance and collaboration should read the secondary literature with an awareness of the political context within which it was written.*

There is a dialectical relationship between the history and the historiography of Hitler's empire. On the one hand, the war itself gave birth to a series of concepts (such as resistance and collaboration) which have framed the understanding of historians ever since. On the other hand, the way that historians have written the history of the war has constantly changed in line with political developments. Because the historiography has always been so politicised, the student must be sensitive to the context in which it was produced. Claims that are made by historians about the nature of Hitler's empire should be evaluated in this light, and never taken at face value.

Towards a 'social history of politics' in Hitler's empire

What, then, might lie beyond the resistance/collaboration paradigm? In answering this question, we do not wish to imply that there is one 'correct' way to approach the social history of Hitler's empire. The dominance of one paradigm should not be exchanged for the dominance of another. The approach we put forward here is simply intended as an illustration of one possible alternative way of conceptualising social responses to Nazi rule.

Our starting point is the observation that both the Nazi regime and the war which it unleashed were totalising in the sense that they tended to break down the barriers between social domains. The distinction between the 'fighting front' and the 'home front' was blurred almost everywhere, and in some parts of Europe it disappeared altogether. As a result, politics, the economy, and social life were all militarised. At the same time, the radical force of Nazi ideology meant that all economic, social, and military activity became highly politicised. In Hitler's empire, there was no social space that remained autonomous from politics. This is true even where the motives that lay behind certain behaviours were largely or purely personal. All choices were made in a politicised environment and had (often unforeseen) political implications beyond the personal and the local. Survival itself was a political act, and the will to survive generated activism of a political nature. Food riots initiated and led by women are a case in point. Historians who have studied women's activism in this seemingly narrow sphere of domestic politics have demonstrated that the impact of such behaviour was felt well beyond the community in which it was situated.[1]

---

[1] Mary Elizabeth Reed, 'Croatian Women in the Yugoslav Partisan Resistance, 1941–1945', PhD Thesis, University of California, Berkeley (1980), Chapter 3; Donna F. Ryan, 'Ordinary Acts and Resistance: Women in Street Demonstrations and Food Riots in Vichy France', *Proceedings of the Annual Meeting of the Western Society for French History*, 16 (1989), 400–407; Jane Slaughter, *Women and the Italian Resistance, 1943–1945* (Denver, CO: Arden Press, 1997).

In place of the resistance/collaboration model, we need a more holistic framework of analysis. This, in turn, requires interdisciplinarity. Unlike traditional historical methodology, which focuses on specific domains (for example, military history, economic history, political history, social history), interdisciplinary history explores the connections between them. Attempting to study Hitler's empire from a holistic and interdisciplinary perspective means that we need to ask new questions, to broaden our focus and to adopt a more fluid approach when we address old questions. As the historian of memory Pieter Lagrou has argued, the breaking down of inappropriate national, disciplinary, and chronological boundaries (*Entgrenzung* – the removal of conceptual borders) is a 'central challenge' facing historians of this period.[2]

To move beyond the resistance/collaboration dichotomy, we therefore need a model that (1) emphasises the interrelationships between the political, the social, the economic, and the military in Hitler's empire and (2) recognises the pervasiveness of politics. We illustrate this in Figure 6.1. Unlike the models of Kershaw and Peukert, this way of conceptualising European society under Nazi rule does not focus specifically on resistance, though resistance can be incorporated into it. The model uses the terms 'political history', 'social history', 'economic history', and 'military

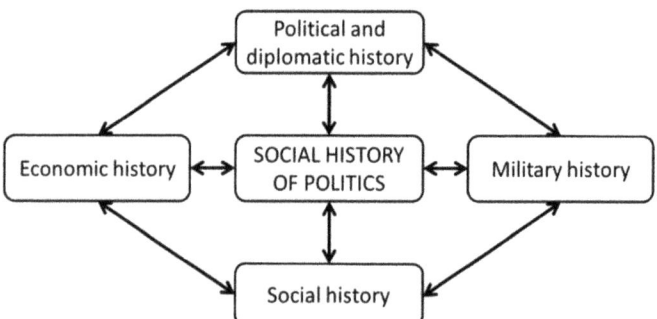

Figure 6.1 A social history of politics approach.

---

[9] Pieter Lagrou, 'Between Europe and the Nation: The Inward Turn of Contemporary Historical Writing', in Konrad Hugo Jarausch and Thomas Lindenberger (eds), with Annelle Ramsbrock, *Conflicted Memories: Europeanizing Contemporary Histories* (New York: Berghahn, 2007), 69–77, 73–74.

history'. However, it does not conceptualise these as separate domains but, rather, as linked components of an integrated process. The concept of the 'social history of politics' is placed at the centre of the model because Nazi ideology and total war politicised European society in an unprecedented fashion. Gender history does not appear at any specific location in this model because it is embedded in all the connections. It is important to emphasise that our aim is not to replace the models of Kershaw and Peukert with another model. We are simply trying to present in diagrammatic form the basic point that it is necessary to focus not on specific categories such as economic, military, and political history but on the relationships between them. To put it another way, we believe that it is analytically helpful to focus not only on the boxes but also on the arrows which connect them.

Many of the most innovative works on World War II in Europe are interesting because they explore the interconnectedness of social domains. For example, Omer Bartov's theories about the barbarisation of warfare on the Eastern Front, though controversial, have stimulated debate for the very reason that he examines the Wehrmacht not just as a military organisation, but as a social and political one as well.[3] Tom Behan's monograph *The Long Awaited Moment* (1997) focuses on everyday life and material conditions in northern Italy between 1943 and 1948 and investigates the way that these influenced the politics of the resistance movement and the relationship of workers with their managers, the Fascist and Nazi authorities, and then the Allies.[4] Victoria Belco (2010), meanwhile, has written about local communities in central Italy between 1943 and 1948. She examines the interactions between local, regional, and national politics during this period of social dislocation, and she does so within chronological parameters that make sense in terms of the people whom she is studying.[5] Stathis Kalyvas, in his seminal monograph on the logic of violence in civil war (2006), systematically compares civil violence in wartime and post-war Greece with other irregular conflicts. In contrast to many traditional accounts of Greece in the 1940s,

---

[3] Omer Bartov, *The Eastern Front, 1941–45: German Troops and the Barbarisation of Warfare*, 2nd edn (Basingstoke: Palgrave, 2001).

[4] Tom Behan, *The Long Awaited Moment: The Working Class and the Italian Communist Party in Milan, 1943–1948* (New York: Peter Lang, 1997).

[5] Victoria C. Belco, *War, Massacre, and Recovery in Central Italy, 1943–1948* (Toronto: University of Toronto Press, 2010).

which concentrate on high politics and operational matters, Kalyvas drills down to the community level in order to theorise civil war as a sociological process.[6] Wendy Lower, in her study of the Holocaust in a specific region of Ukraine (2005), firmly locates her analysis of local events in the context of the imperial project of the Nazi empire, and the interactions between the centre and the periphery.[7] Though they work in different fields and put forward different arguments, what Bartov, Behan, Belco, Kalyvas, and Lower have in common is that they move beyond traditional disciplinary boundaries and they recognise the intensely political nature of their subject matter, even when they are discussing behaviours that other historians would regard as purely economic, social, or military.

The Catholic Church in Hitler's empire

In order to explore what a 'social history of politics' approach might look like, we shall now give a specific case study suggesting how the resistance/collaboration paradigm might be transcended: the Catholic Church in Hitler's empire. This is a vast and controversial topic, the comprehensive treatment of which is far beyond the scope of the chapter. Our aim is merely to consider how and why the historiography has been shaped by the resistance/collaboration paradigm and to suggest possible alternatives. There are some parallels with the treatment of other Christian churches, and there is plenty of room for studies which systematically compare Catholic, Orthodox, and Protestant responses to Nazi rule (maxim 5). But, again, we do not have the space to embark on such a study here.

A polarised historiography

The historiography of the Catholic Church in Hitler's empire provides us with one of the clearest illustrations of the way in which the resistance/collaboration paradigm has been applied rigidly and with limited success. Much of what we have observed already in the book is relevant to histories

---

[6] Stathis N. Kalyvas, *The Logic of Violence in Civil War* (Cambridge: Cambridge University Press, 2006).

[7] Wendy Lower, *Nazi Empire-Building and the Holocaust in Ukraine* (Chapel Hill, NC: University of North Carolina Press, 2005).

of the Church at this time. The literature is polarised and politicised, and historians are often categorised by their colleagues according to whether they appear to defend the Church or to criticise it.[8] The early historiography of the Church under Nazism was inward-looking and hagiographic. Since the 1970s, the view has become widespread that, the bravery of some individuals notwithstanding, the majority of Catholics from the Pope down either actively supported or passively accommodated the Nazi and collaborationist regimes.[9]

Regardless of whether they defend or condemn the Church, most historians who study it have applied a conventional methodological approach, with little regard for the principles which we have identified above. Four characteristics stand out in the existing historiography. Firstly, irrespective of the fact that the Church is the quintessential transnational institution, the national paradigm prevails. Secondly, unless they are concerned with Germany or Italy, works on the Church in Hitler's empire generally touch only fleetingly on the pre-war period. Thirdly, the literature is top-heavy and dominated by studies of Church–state relations, the role of the Vatican, and the response of the Church to the Holocaust. Overwhelmingly, the emphasis is on the Pope, Pius XII, and other high-ranking clergy.[10] Finally, most historians routinely apply the dichotomous framework of

---

[8] Examples of this literature include Guenter Lewy, *The Catholic Church and Nazi Germany* (London: Weidenfeld and Nicolson, 1964); John Cornwell, *Hitler's Pope: The Secret History of Pius XII* (London: Viking, 1999); Gerard Noel, *Pius XII: The Hound of Hitler* (London: Continuum, 2008); Patrick J. Gallo (ed.), *Pius XII, the Holocaust, and the Revisionists: Essays* (Jefferson, NC: McFarland, 2006); Ralph M. McInerny, *The Defamation of Pius XII* (South Bend, IN: St. Augustine's Press, 2001). For a good insight into how historians position themselves in these debates, see book reviews in journals such as *Church History, Catholic Historical Review, Journal of Church and State*, and *Contemporary Church History Quarterly*.

[9] See W.D. Halls, *Politics, Society and Christianity in Vichy France* (Oxford: Berg, 1995), Chapters 12–14 and 19; Donald J. Dietrich, 'Introduction', and Michael Phayer, 'Questions about Catholic Resistance', *Church History* 70/2 (2001), Special Issue on Churches and Resistance, 226–231 and 328–344.

[10] For example, Frank J. Coppa (ed.), *Controversial Concordats: The Vatican's Relations with Napoleon, Mussolini, and Hitler* (Washington, DC: Catholic University of America Press, 1999); Lieve Gevers and Jan Bank (eds), *Religion under Siege*, Vol. I: *The Roman Catholic Church in Occupied Europe (1939–1950)* (Leuven: Peeters, 2007); Gerhard Besier and Francesca Piombo, *The Holy See and Hitler's Germany* (Basingstoke: Palgrave Macmillan, 2007); Vincent A. Lapomarda, *The Catholic Bishops of Europe and the Nazi Persecutions of Catholics and Jews* (Lewiston, NY: Edwin Mellen Press, 2012); Jan Bank with Lieve Gevers, *Churches and Religion in the Second World War* (London: Bloomsbury, 2016).

interpretation within which Catholic activity is judged as either defiant or complicitous, resistant or collaborationist. Kevin Spicer, for instance, who is a leading expert on the Catholic Church in Nazi Germany, has written two books on German priests. The first, published in 2004, looks at the resistance of priests in Berlin. The second, published four years later, focuses on the small number of 'brown priests' who joined the Nazi Party.[11]

Given the dominance of the resistance/collaboration paradigm, this way of analysing and judging Catholic behaviour is unsurprising and, to a degree, understandable. Evidently there were Catholic resisters and, evidently, there were Catholic collaborators. In the immediate post-war years, the Church itself embraced the dominant paradigm in order to deflect attention away from the criticisms of Catholic collaboration. By adopting a defensive stance, the Church attempted to demonstrate that it, too, had 'resisted', and that Catholics had been victims of Nazism. Martyrdom was a word commonly used to describe the fate of Catholic men and women killed by the Nazis. Dioceses sponsored studies that documented assaults on the Church and clashes with the Nazi or collaborationist authorities. Books provided lists of lay Catholics, priests, and members of religious orders who had been incarcerated or liquidated.[12] And, indeed, the losses of the Church had been substantial. In Poland, for instance, the Nazis targeted and killed approximately 2,000 priests and 900 members of religious orders.[13] At the concentration camp at Dachau, crucifixion was just one of the forms of torture inflicted on priests.[14] It thus seemed fitting to speak of the 'martyred Church'.

Critics of the Church do not deny that individual Catholics resisted. Their argument is, rather, that there were not enough of such individuals.

---

[11] Kevin P. Spicer, *Resisting the Third Reich: The Catholic Clergy in Hitler's Berlin* (DeKalb, IL: Northern Illinois University Press, 2004); and *Hitler's Priests: Catholic Clergy and National Socialism* (DeKalb, IL: Northern Illinois University Press, 2008).

[12] See, for example, Paul Vergnet, *Les Catholiques dans la Résistance* (Paris: Les Éditions des Saints Pères, 1946).

[13] Jerzy Kloczowski, *A History of Polish Christianity* (Cambridge: Cambridge University Press, 2000), 300–301.

[14] See Volker Schlöndorff's film, *Der neunte Tag* (The Ninth Day, 2004). See also Paul Berben, *Dachau, 1933–1945: The Official History* (London: Norfolk Press, 1975); and Paul Bartrop, 'Portrayals of Christians in Holocaust Movies: Priests in Dachau and Volker Schlöndorff's *The Ninth Day*', *Shofar*, 28/4 (2010), 28–40.

In their view, this was because, institutionally, the Church failed to provide adequate guidance for the millions of Catholics who were left without moral leadership in the turmoil of the war.[15] Historians have attributed this weakness in Catholic leadership to the Church's seemingly opportunistic approach to fascism and parties of the far Right, which was in marked contrast to its trenchant anti-Communism. Some historians have applied the term 'clerical fascism' to what they regard as an alliance between the Catholic Church and European fascism.[16] The most visible examples of Catholic collaboration, for example in Slovakia and Croatia, were made to stand as emblematic of the deeply compromised Church.[17]

The historiography of the Church under Nazi rule has barely been touched by the social history movement which we discussed in Chapter 4. Consequently, the literature remains predictable. One reason for this is the difficulty that historians face when attempting to interpret specifically Catholic behaviour. The general perception is that Catholics, like almost everyone else, sought only to survive the ordeal rather than to fight fascism or Nazism. This view provides a way out of the conundrum of having to account for the myriad ways in which Catholics lived the war 'as Catholics', not as 'registered' resisters or collaborators. Instead of studying Catholics as Catholics, historians focus on institutional culpability.

---

[15] See, for example, Robert P. Ericksen and Susannah Heschel, 'The German Churches and the Holocaust', in Dan Stone (ed.), *The Historiography of the Holocaust* (Basingstoke: Palgrave Macmillan, 2004), 296–318.

[16] The focus has shifted slightly with the more recent emphasis on fascism as a 'political religion'. Richard J. Evans, 'Nazism, Christianity and Political Religion: A Debate', *Journal of Contemporary History*, 42/1 (2007), 5–7. See also Matthew Feldman and Marius Turda, Roger Griffin, Richard Steigmann-Gall, John Pollard and others in the special issue of *Totalitarian Movements and Political Religions*, 8/2 (2007), focusing on 'clerical fascism'.

[17] Richard J. Wolff, 'The Catholic Church and the Dictatorships in Slovakia and Croatia, 1939–1945', *Records of the American Catholic Historical Society of Philadelphia*, 88/1–4 (1977), 3–30; Mark Biondich, 'Religion and Nation in Wartime Croatia: Reflections on the Ustaša Policy of Forced Religious Conversions, 1941–1942', *Slavonic and East European Review*, 83/1 (2005), 71–116; 'Controversies surrounding the Catholic Church in Wartime Croatia, 1941–1945', *Totalitarian Movements and Political Religions*, 7/4 (2006), 429–457; and 'Radical Catholicism and Fascism in Croatia, 1918–1945', *Totalitarian Movements and Political Religions*, 8/2 (2007), 383–399; James Mace Ward, *Priest, Politician, Collaborator: Jozef Tiso and the Making of Fascist Slovakia* (Ithaca, NY: Cornell University Press, 2013).

In particular, historians have shown very little interest in the religious or spiritual lives of ordinary Catholics and of the faith communities of which they were members. There are almost no studies of 'Catholics in the pews'.[18] The Pope, the upper clergy, and, less frequently, the lower clergy are made to stand for the Church as a whole. The interlocking social networks at the level of the parish, and the responses of these networks to the experience of war and occupation, remain virtually unexplored. Nor have historians paid much attention to the numerous Catholic associations and charitable organisations which connected Catholic parishes to the wider community. These omissions mean that Catholic women, who during the war made up the majority of practising adult members of most parishes, are more or less invisible in the historiography unless they were involved in rescuing Jews or in some other oppositional activity.[19] This is especially the case for women in religious orders and for lay Catholic women who did not work outside the home, even though many of these women were deeply engaged in the associational life of their local churches and communities.

The tendency is to write this modern religious history with the religion left out.[20] Studies of the Church, therefore, take no account of the very thing which defines faith communities. Michael Phayer has explicitly stated that he is interested in the 'political Pope Pius XII', not the spiritual Pope Pius,[21] as if there can be a separation between the two.

---

[18] For an exception to this general rule, see Vesna Drapac, *War and Religion: Catholics in the Churches of Occupied Paris* (Washington, DC: Catholic University of America Press, 1998). See also Robert Gildea, *Marianne in Chains: In Search of the German Occupation, 1940–1945* (London: Macmillan, 2002), Chapter 9; and Jean-Dominique Durand, 'Clergé et paroisses: la vie religieuse dans une ville en guerre', in Isabelle von Bueltzingsloewen et al. (eds), *Lyon dans la Seconde Guerre mondiale: villes et métropoles à l'épreuve du conflit* (Rennes: Presses Universitaires de Rennes, 2016), 179–189.

[19] For example, Laura Gellott and Michael Phayer, 'Dissenting Voices: Catholic Women in Opposition to Fascism', *Journal of Contemporary History*, 22/1 (1987), 91–114; Michael Phayer, *The Catholic Church and the Holocaust, 1930–1965* (Bloomington, IN: Indiana University Press, 2000), 114–132; Lamore Yagil, *Chrétiens et Juifs sous Vichy (1940–1944). Sauvetage et désobéissance civile* (Paris: Cerf, 2005); Suzanne Vromen, *Hidden Children of the Holocaust: Belgian Nuns and Their Daring Rescue of Young Jews from the Nazis* (Oxford: Oxford University Press, 2008); Marína Zavacká, 'Crossing Sisters: Patterns of Protest in the Journal of the Catholic Union of Slovak Women during the Second World War', *Social History*, 37/4 (2012), 425–451.

[20] Brad S. Gregory, 'The Other Confessional History: On Secular Bias in the Study of Religion', *History and Theory*, 45/4 (2006), 132–149.

[21] Michael Phayer, *Pius XII, the Holocaust, and the Cold War* (Bloomington, IN: Indiana University Press, 2008), ix–x.

Where historians do take spiritual concerns seriously, they are accused of mounting the 'incense defense'.[22] Furthermore, historians rarely distinguish between observant and non-observant Catholics, but subsume both under the generic label 'Catholic'. Historians thus make generalisations about Catholics based on people who might have been baptised but who were otherwise not involved in religious life. There is no understanding of the characteristics that defined Catholic responses to the ordeal and what was distinctive about those responses other than from the perspective of Catholic elites, normally male resisters or collaborators.

This problem has been compounded by the inability of historians to distinguish between 'Catholic resistance' and 'Catholics in the resistance'.[23] According to those Catholics who participated in it, 'Catholic resistance' was motivated by Christian teaching, and it was this which set it apart from other kinds of resistance. Leaders of the 'Catholic resistance' often spoke of their action as constituting 'spiritual resistance', even though what they did (for example, producing underground papers) sits squarely within the accepted (and narrow) definition of 'resistance proper'. Catholics 'in the resistance', on the other hand, are discussed by historians as if their decision to resist was unconnected to their faith and Christian principles. The motives and behaviours of Catholics who resisted in contexts that were not explicitly Catholic remain unexplored.

Given all these gaps and anomalies, it will perhaps come as no surprise that double standards abound in studies of the Church in the war. Three examples are sufficient to make the point. Firstly, Catholic resisters are seen to be outside the mainstream (often Left-of-centre males bucking the system) while Catholics who did not resist are placed firmly in the mainstream as conservative and archetypal representatives of institutional accommodation.[24] In the depiction of Catholic resisters, their activity is not associated with the broader ideological and structural framework of the institutional Church. It is deemed the product of private or political

---

[22] Phayer, *Pius XII, the Holocaust, and the Cold War*, x.

[23] See, for example, Robert O. Paxton, 'France: The Church, the Republic, and the Fascist Temptation, 1922–1945', in Richard J. Wolff and Jörg K. Hoensch (eds), *Catholics, the State and the European Radical Right 1919–1945* (Boulder, CO: Social Science Monographs, 1987), 67–91.

[24] For a classic exposition of this line of thinking see Oscar L. Arnal, 'Catholic Roots of Collaboration and Resistance in France in the 1930s', *Canadian Journal of History*, 17/1 (1982), 87–110. See also Nicholas Atkin, '*Ralliés* and *résistants*: Catholics in Vichy France, 1940–1944', in Kay Chadwick (ed.) *Catholicism, Politics and Society in Twentieth-Century France* (Liverpool: Liverpool University Press, 2000), 97–118.

initiatives. Even though much Catholic resistance took place under the mantle of protection afforded by the Church, it is seen merely as the location where this behaviour took place. The fundamental connection between institutional presence and individual action or agency in Catholic resistance is therefore underplayed. Secondly, chaplains to the German army are seen – for example by Doris Bergen – to be supporting and enabling 'Nazi German slaughter' and helping to 'legitimate a war of annihilation' through their provision of spiritual support and emotional respite for 'killers'. This is regardless of the fact that the chaplaincy's work was 'coded as feminine' and, consequently, the object of derision among young Nazified soldiers.[25] On the other hand, chaplains to Allied servicemen are seen to be providing spiritual succour to deserving soldiers.[26] Thirdly, we learn that, privately, the Pope exhibited sound Christian qualities and sheltered Jews in the Vatican. But, in his public role, he fell short of the mark as the Church's moral leader due to his failure to condemn outright the mass murder of Jews. These and other contradictions spring from the dissociation of the behaviour in question from its social and ideological roots, and from the narrow interpretation of the political impact of behaviour not deemed public.

The overwhelming majority of works on the Church at war focus exclusively on the question of Catholic resistance and collaboration with regard to the Holocaust. There are hundreds of books on this topic. The goal of these works is to establish whether the Church 'resisted' the Holocaust by condemning it. Most historians arrive at the conclusion that the Catholic Church both could and should have done more to oppose Nazi genocide. Generally, they base their views on a close scrutiny of official Church statements issued by the Pope and various bishops. The goal is to ascertain whether these statements identify the Jews and their persecutors by

---

[25] Doris L. Bergen, 'German Military Chaplains in World War II and the Dilemmas of Legitimacy', *Church History*, 70/2 (2001), 232–247, 234 and 247.

[26] Yves Yvon J. Pelletier, 'Faith on the Battlefield: Canada's Catholic Chaplaincy Service during the Second World War', *Historical Studies*, 69 (2003), 64–84.

[27] A very small sample of works that have appeared since 2000 includes: Susan Zuccotti, *Under His Very Windows: The Vatican and the Holocaust in Italy* (New Haven, CT: Yale University Press, 2000); James Carroll, *Constantine's Sword: The Church and the Jews: A History* (Boston, MA: Houghton Mifflin, 2001); Carol Rittner and John K. Roth (eds), *Pope Pius XII and the Holocaust* (London: Continuum, 2002); Daniel Jonah Goldhagen, *A Moral Reckoning: The Role of the Catholic Church in the Holocaust and Its Unfulfilled Duty of Repair* (London: Little, Brown,

name (generally they do not) and, if they do, at what point.[27] Historians conclude that, while there were some 'impassioned denunciations' of the treatment of Jews,[28] what was lacking was a 'systematic' or 'comprehensive' defence of the Jewish victims of persecution from the top down. Significantly, historians also point out the deep historical roots of Christian anti-Semitism and its popular manifestations, especially in regions where violence against Jews was common during the war. Naturally, we would not expect there to have been a denunciation of genocide or the Holocaust as these terms had not yet been coined. But there was mass persecution and then mass murder of Jews. Theoretically, the Pope could have condemned anti-Semitism more openly, but instead remained 'silent'. The general critique of the Pope's 'silence' was first mounted by Polish Catholics because he never spoke out openly in their defence when they were subjected to invasion and relentless maltreatment by their occupiers.[29] The Pope's 'silence' is the recurring motif in most studies of the role of the Church in the Holocaust.[30]

While Catholic behaviour is normally judged according to the single criterion of its impact or otherwise on the protection of Jews, it would be unusual for a historian to argue that the Church or Catholics were responsible for the genocide or could have prevented it. Rather, the implication is that, had the Pope and others spoken out with more force, more

---

2002); David G. Dalin, *The Myth of Hitler's Pope: How Pope Pius XII Rescued Jews from the Nazis* (Washington, DC: Regnery, 2005); Kevin P. Spicer (ed.), *Antisemitism, Christian Ambivalence, and the Holocaust* (Bloomington, IN: Indiana University Press, 2007); Phayer, *Pius XII, the Holocaust, and the Cold War*; Frank J. Coppa, 'Between Morality and Diplomacy: The Vatican's "Silence" during the Holocaust', *Journal of Church and State*, 50/3 (2008), 541–568; and 'Pope Pius XII: From the Diplomacy of Impartiality to the Silence of the Holocaust', *Journal of Church and State*, 55/2 (2013), 286–306; Jacques Kornberg, *The Pope's Dilemma: Pius XII Faces Atrocities and Genocide in the Second World War* (Buffalo, NY: University of Toronto Press, 2015). See also note 10 above.

[28] Phayer, *Catholic Church and the Holocaust*, 93, quoting Lawrence Baron.

[29] Idesbald Goddeeris, 'The Catholic Church in Poland under Nazi Occupation (1939–1945) and the First Years of Communism (1944–1948)', in Gevers and Bank, *Religion under Siege*, 1–38. See also Phayer, *Pius XII, the Holocaust, and the Cold War*, Chapter 2.

[30] For background and a good summary of the literature of the 2000s see the review article by William Patch, 'The Catholic Church, the Third Reich, and the Origins of the Cold War: On the Utility and Limitations of Historical Evidence', *Journal of Modern History*, 82/2 (2010), 396–433. See also Phayer, *Pius XII, the Holocaust, and the Cold War*, Chapters 3 and 4 for his revised account of the Pope's 'silence'.

Catholics would have saved more Jews.[31] This seems persuasive because, as we have seen, institutional support was important for successful large-scale rescue. In 1998, Pope John Paul II, who had experienced the war in Cracow, issued a document entitled 'We Remember: A Reflection on the Shoah', in which he acknowledged and apologised for the inadequacy of the Church's response to the assault on Jews in World War II.[32]

The critique of the Church, however, does not simply rest on the question of its sin of omission, its 'silence'. The accusation of Catholic anti-Semitism and Catholic indifference to Jewish suffering is embedded in this narrative. We know that individual clerics did openly condemn some policies of the Nazi state, notably the murder of disabled people. In addition, bishops in Germany and across Europe, with varying levels of success, aimed to thwart the attempts of the Nazis and the collaborationists to curb Catholic associational life and religious practice.[33] The dominant view has thus become that, where its institutional 'interests' were directly threatened, the Church was forthright and unambiguous in its pronouncements. The accusation that the Church pragmatically defended and extended its own interests draws on the easily accessible documentation revealing negotiations between upper clerics and Fascists, National Socialists, and collaborationists. With regard to resistance against the Third Reich, Donald Dietrich writes that 'Churches themselves offered very little heroic sustenance to their members, but instead seemed to be satisfied with a very unfortunate, self-centered resistance bent on their survival as institutions'.[34] If one were to take this line of thinking to its logical end-point, which few historians seem willing to do directly, one would

---

[31] Phayer, *Catholic Church and the Holocaust*, 217.

[32] Randolph L. Braham, 'Remembering and Forgetting: The Vatican, the German Catholic Hierarchy, and the Holocaust', *Holocaust and Genocide Studies*, 13/2 (1999), 222–251; Patrick Henry, 'The Art of Christian Apology: Comparing the French Catholic Church's Apology to the Jews and the Vatican's "We Remember"', *Shofar*, 26/3 (2008), 87–104; Adam Gregerman, 'Interpreting the Pain of Others: John Paul II and Benedict XVI on Jewish Suffering in the Shoah', *Journal of Ecumenical Studies*, 48/4 (2013), 443–466.

[33] Michael Burleigh, 'Between Enthusiasm, Compliance and Protest: The Churches, Eugenics and the Nazi "Euthanasia" Programme', *Contemporary European History*, 3/3 (1994), 253–264. For an insight into disputes at a local level, see Ian Kershaw, *Popular Opinion and Political Dissent in the Third Reich: Bavaria 1933–1945* (Oxford: Clarendon Press, 1983), Chapter 5.

[34] Dietrich, 'Introduction', 229.

have to conclude that, for example, Bishop Clemens August von Galen of Münster, renowned for condemning the killing of disabled 'Aryans' in the 'euthanasia' programme in 1941, was later unperturbed by and indifferent to the killing of Jews.[35]

It is impossible here to deal with all the questions raised by these deeply ingrained perceptions of the Church at war. But if we take into consideration just some of the maxims outlined above, a different story comes into focus. This story is told by the kinds of Catholics whose voices are rarely heard because they are rarely sought out.

By looking at Catholics 'as Catholics', rather than as resisters or collaborators, we can gain an understanding of how their faith communities responded to the crisis, and of how the various levels of the Church interacted with each other. We also get a sense of the concerns and daily tribulations of ordinary people (maxims 1–4 and 6). Moreover, when we study the Church as a transnational institution, we catch a glimpse of the beliefs and behaviours that bound people of different nationalities together, even when their homelands were at war (maxim 5). If we adopt a broader time frame, we can observe continuities and overarching patterns in Catholic association. We can also observe the extent to which the totalitarian aspirations of the Nazi empire, and total war, challenged or undermined or strengthened community life (maxims 3 and 6). When we view the Church from outside the resistance/collaboration paradigm, a whole range of people and activities emerges from the shadows. As we have noted, most of these people and behaviours have been ignored by historians. But it is impossible to understand Catholic responses to the ordeal, including resistance and collaboration, without understanding the social processes that underpinned Catholic life and practice (maxim 1).

The 'politics of presence': Catholic faith communities in Hitler's empire

The Church in occupied France declared openly that it was engaged in the 'politics of presence'. This term relates to the prudential considerations of the institution of the Church during 'the ordeal'. Catholic clerics everywhere in Europe were engaged in the same behaviour and had the same priorities, even if they did not use the same expression to describe

---

[35] Beth A. Griech-Polelle, *Bishop von Galen: German Catholicism and National Socialism* (New Haven, CT: Yale University Press, 2002).

them. The need for continuity in the sacramental and associational life of the Church, throughout the crisis, underpinned the politics of presence: the priest's duty was to be with his people, to abide in his parish, and to make the sacraments available.[36] In some places, maintaining the basic sacerdotal functions of the Church was not straightforward and led to wrangles with the occupying or collaborationist forces. In other places, religious practice was forced underground and involved the risk of arrest, incarceration and execution. Elsewhere again, maintaining these functions did not incur risk. Indeed, in parts of the empire – such as France, Croatia, and Slovakia – collaborationist regimes actively courted Catholic opinion by claiming that they represented traditional Catholic values. At least at first, many French, Croatian, and Slovak Catholics embraced the new regimes and took them at their word. But, even here, sooner or later there were clashes between Church and state. Catholics, like others, became disenchanted. By definition, the politics of presence necessitated negotiation with the ruling authorities and varying degrees of accommodation (maxims 2, 3 and 6). But the same basic drive to be present is evident wherever Catholics lived (maxim 5).

Thus, the Church did indeed pursue a course of action designed to extend its interests in the sense that it attempted, as it always does in any circumstances, to widen its spiritual and social reach. Fundamental to the self-understanding of Catholicism is the idea that the Church's spiritual and social missions are connected. This often created tensions with the German authorities, who insisted that Catholics were to desist from engaging in communal activities unless they were of a 'purely religious' nature. Catholics, in turn, defined 'purely religious' activities as broadly as possible. Disputes over the demarcation between 'religious' and 'social' activities sometimes led to confrontations.[37]

In fact, the lines between social, civic, and religious activity were blurred (maxim 1). This became apparent in any 'politics of presence' that was negotiated between the Church and the authorities in Hitler's empire. Parish life in France incorporated a number of different activities, or 'works' (*œuvres*), catering to a number of different interests and

---

[36] Drapac, *War and Religion*, passim. See also Martin Conway and Peter Romijn (eds), *The War for Legitimacy in Politics and Culture 1936–1946* (Oxford: Berg, 2008), especially Chapter 4 by Nico Wouters on the broader context linking the stability of institutions and social cohesion.

[37] Halls, *Politics, Society and Christianity in Vichy France*, Chapters 12, 15, 16 and 17.

capabilities. In some parishes in Paris, there were between 20 and 30 locally based spiritual, social, educational, and welfare initiatives. There were sodalities and devotional works for men and women, boys and girls.[38] There were charitable works, as well as the new groups based on the principles of Catholic Action which had been developed in the inter-war years as a strategy for sustaining and extending Christian values in an increasingly secularised world (maxim 6). The specialised Catholic Action structures comprised the 'lay apostolate' and drew together people with similar interests and in similar professions. The most well-known of these organisations involved young people and included the Jeunesse Ouvrière Chrétienne, the Jeunesse Étudiante Chrétienne, the Jeunesse Indépendante Chrétienne and the Jeunesse Agricole Chrétienne. There were also women's organisations such as the Ligue Féminine d'Action Catholique and men's groups, for example Groupe Diocésain d'Action Catholique and Mouvement Ingénieurs et Chefs d'Industrie d'Action Catholique. The motivating premise of Catholic Action was, precisely, to incorporate religion into the civic life of the nation (maxim 1).[39] In some ways it could be understood as the Catholic equivalent of 'energising the everyday' (see Chapter 4) and a means of extending Catholic sociability. During the occupation, meetings of these groups and other parochial associations were normally held in churches or on Church property in order to conform to the regulation regarding 'purely religious' activity. In practice, therefore, the delineation between the temporal and the spiritual was never clear-cut, and much religiously inspired social action had its roots in the continuation of Catholic associational life (maxim 1). This action remained the same but assumed a new significance under the harsh conditions of German occupation (maxims 2 and 3).

Catholic associational life and activism directed at young people were among the most important concerns – or 'interests' – of the Church in Hitler's Europe. In France, the Church flatly refused to collapse its youth groups into a single state-run organisation because it had witnessed the negative impact of this policy in Nazi Germany

---

[38] Drapac, *War and Religion*, Chapters 5 and 6.

[39] A.M. Crofts, *Catholic Social Action: Principles, Purpose and Practice* (London: Catholic Book Club, 1936). See also the encyclical of Pius XI, *Non abbiamo bisogno* (29 June 1931) on Catholic Action and the Fascist government's attempts to curb it. Vatican [website]: <w2.vatican.va/content/pius-xi/en/encyclicals/documents/hf_p-xi_enc_29061931_non-abbiamo-bisogno.html> (accessed 22 January 2017).

(maxims 5 and 6).[40] Having noted these struggles from a distance in the 1930s, the Catholic hierarchy in France rejected the Vichy regime's attempt to establish a state monopoly of all youth associations, and retained jurisdiction over Catholic scouting and youth structures.[41] The curé of the parish of St-Nicolas-du-Chardonnet, in the fifth *arrondissement* of Paris, took a particular interest in his parish's scouts, who were called the Chevaliers (knights) du Chardonnet because Catholic scouting was technically banned. Throughout the occupation, the curé attended the troop's special ceremonies and spoke to the boys on occasions of national significance, including Armistice Day (11 November). At a time when these boys, like all French schoolchildren, were saturated with propaganda about Pétain as the new 'Chef de l'État', the scouts at St-Nicolas-du-Chardonnet were reminded that they had only one *Chef*, Christ, and were answerable to him alone. The curé told the boys that, even if they were suffering now, the victory of 1918 was always a source of hope, and that on 11 November they were to remember that the *patrie* would triumph once again. The worst thing that they could do was to despair.[42]

The microcosm of parish life reveals that there were multiple ethical, non-combatant Catholic responses to total war which varied according to local conditions and people's standing (maxims 2–5). To label these responses as complicitous or defiant, according to the hierarchies of collaboration and resistance, can be problematic. This point is evident in the example of the parish-based groups (conferences) of the charitable association, the Society of St Vincent de Paul.[43] In Paris alone, over 5,000 men were involved in the work of the Society. For the most part, this action entailed relieving the burden of shortages and rationing on the poor. The conferences were able to do their work relatively freely in Paris and were highly regarded by the municipal authorities because of their experience, local knowledge, and integrity. The state entrusted the Society with the distribution of public money, food, and other necessities – such as shoes for children – in the knowledge that the goods would be fairly apportioned

---

[40] Halls, *Politics, Society and Christianity in Vichy France*, Chapters 16 and 17.

[41] For a study of Vichy's youth policy, see W.D. Halls, *The Youth of Vichy France* (Oxford: Clarendon Press, 1981).

[42] Archives Historiques de l'Archevêché de Paris: St-Nicolas-du-Chardonnet (fifth *arrondissement*).

[43] Drapac, *War and Religion*, Chapter 7.

and that they would not find their way on to the black market. In the sense that they cooperated with the authorities in this work, members of the society in Paris could be seen to be 'collaborating'. In Strasbourg, however, which was located in territory that had been contested ground between the Germans and the French for centuries, and which fell in the annexed zone (see Chapter 1), Catholic association was banned. There was an intense campaign of Germanisation and Strasbourg cathedral was closed for services.[44] Here, the conferences had to meet underground in order to continue their charitable work. The religiously motivated activity of the local groups thus constituted a transgression (and, hence, potentially, in the traditional paradigm, 'resistance') and was a punishable offence (maxims 1–3). Among prisoners-of-war, the situation was different again. Conferences of the Society were established in the POW camps and the General Council of the Society, located in Paris, supported them. Through this support, Parisian Catholics became part of a network of solidarity with the approximately 1,580,000 French POWs.[45] In the camps, French Catholics shared what they received from home and created an even wider network of mutual aid and trust by drawing into their circles fellow prisoners, not just Frenchmen and not just their co-religionists (maxim 5).[46]

Normally, Catholic women only find their way into the narrative of the Church in Hitler's empire if they were involved in activity that incurred obvious risk (maxim 4). Samuel Oliner notes that historians tend to focus much more on highly visible, individual rescuers than on community-driven rescue,[47] but we do have some insights into female religious communities in Belgium, Poland, France and elsewhere that sheltered Jews.[48] The French Sisters of Notre-Dame de Sion in Grenoble,

---

[44] Jean-Pierre Azéma, *From Munich to the Liberation, 1938–1944* (Cambridge: Cambridge University Press, 1984 [1979]), 107–108; Halls, *Politics, Society and Christianity in Vichy France*, 179–181.

[45] There were still 940,000 French POWs in 1944. See Sarah Fishman, *We Will Wait: Wives of French Prisoners of War, 1940–1945* (New Haven, CT: Yale University Press, 1991), xv.

[46] Vesna Drapac, 'The Devotion of French Prisoners of War and Requisitioned Workers to Thérèse of Lisieux: Transcending the "Diocese behind Barbed Wire"', *Journal of War and Culture Studies*, 7/3 (2014), 283–296.

[47] Samuel P. Oliner, reviewing Vromen, *Hidden Children*, *Shofar*, 28/3 (2010), 197–199.

[48] See note 19 above.

in south-eastern France, hid Jewish children and young people, as well as over 800 Jewish families. The nuns obtained false identity papers and provided crucial assistance to the local resistance involved in rescue.[49] Theirs was a significant record of shelter which merits a special place on the resistance honour roll. However, the participation of the nuns in resistance was predicated on an accident of geographical location. The convent where they lived happened to be situated in a region where there were escape lines to Switzerland. Other nuns, in other convents, who lived far from the escape lines, are almost never discussed. Their lives and experiences are invisible in the historiography or, worse, these faceless women are accused of passivity. It is important to note also that the actions of Sisters of Notre-Dame de Sion were not just the result of geographical location. That there were still functioning convents in the region in the first place was itself decisive (maxims 1–4), since the Nazis had suppressed convents elsewhere. Put simply, had there been no convent, the nuns could not have provided assistance on such a scale. As we will suggest below, it would seem that the 'politics of presence', combined with the less ferocious occupational policies towards the Church in occupied France, created the convergence of circumstances that made large-scale Catholic rescue possible.

Catholic women were also engaged in what one would generally consider more prosaic social work in a range of contexts (maxims 3–5). Due to its seemingly negligible public (or political) impact, such behaviour would probably not be plotted on Peukert's graph. The long-established association, the Dames de Charité, functioned effectively in almost every parish in Paris and worked side-by-side with the conferences of the Society of St Vincent de Paul to alleviate the suffering of the local poor, notably the elderly who lived alone and families without fathers. Catholic women collected money and goods for care parcels for men in POW camps as well as for requisitioned workers.[50] They provided support and material assistance for people in need, especially other

---

[49] Limore Yagil, 'Résistance et sauvetage des Juifs dans le département de l'Isère (1940–1944)', *Guerres mondiales et conflits contemporains*, 212 (2003), 51–74; and *Chrétiens et Juifs sous Vichy*.

[50] Fishman, *We Will Wait*, passim; Drapac, *War and Religion*, 165–167; and 'The Devotion of French Prisoners of War and Requisitioned Workers to Thérèse of Lisieux'. On social problems arising from extended absences of POWs, see Gildea, *Marianne in Chains*, Chapter 4.

women, from the beginning of the ordeal to the end, and then beyond that (maxim 6). The teleological, outcomes-focused approach, which is one of the foundation-stones of the resistance/collaboration paradigm, has no allocated space for these women. But when we look still more closely at their actual behaviours, we can see that the traditional labels and taxonomies which disregard social context and gender are misleading (maxims 1 and 4).

The example of a young Catholic woman living in the north-west of France illustrates with particular clarity why this is a problem for historians of the Church under Nazi rule. We have noted already that, at the time of the Normandy landings, the choices before some people changed almost overnight. This was the case for Huguette Courcier (1920–1944), who until June 1944 was engaged unspectacularly in the associational life of the Church through membership of the Jeunesse Indépendante Chrétienne and other activities. In October that year, she died of typhoid which she had contracted while ministering to the wounded.[51] Though her brother was a resister, she was not, and so her place in the grand narrative of the liberation of France is marginal at best. But the point about Courcier is not where we ought to place her on the resistance/collaboration continuum, or even the fact of her untimely death. The point about Courcier is the life that she led. It is through the study of such lives that we discover the connections between the institutional presence of the Church and its works, civilian behaviour, social cohesion, and the master narrative of resistance and collaboration (maxim 1).[52] Those who commemorated Courcier's life noted the links between her faith, her willingness to volunteer to do what it was in her power to do when the opportunity presented itself (maxims 4 and 6), and her commitment to fulfilling her civic duty. When we transcend the resistance/collaboration paradigm, the lives of women like Courcier come into focus and enable us to consider Church 'interests' at the most basic level of faith communities, and from multiple perspectives. A detailed examination of the experiences of such women also enables us to approach long-standing questions about Catholic resistance and collaboration with greater precision.

---

[51] *Ce n'est qu'un au revoir: Huguette Courcier JICISTE (1920–1944)* (Paris: Lethielleux, 1948).

[52] See Conway and Romijn, *War for Legitimacy*, Chapter 4 by Nico Wouters, and Chapter 5 by Mary Vincent and Erica Carter, for a discussion of the factors contributing to resilience and cohesion.

Transnational Catholic connections

What we also see, when we look at Catholic communities from the inside-out and when we move away from the resistance/collaboration paradigm, is that these communities cohered both in terms of their internal congregational life and in terms of transnational connections (maxim 5).

Catholics in concentration camps created transnational faith communities based on shared beliefs and an attachment to core principles. This was also the case in the barracks for requisitioned workers and in POW camps.[53] By building chapels and altars and organising religious discussion groups, as well as worshipping together, Catholics from countries that were at war with each other established bonds of friendship. In Dachau, where 2,579 Catholic priests from over 20 countries were incarcerated, there was at first some difficulty in overcoming national divisions. However, priests were soon involved in communal worship and secretly helped the Polish clergy, who had been singled out for especially sadistic treatment by the guards.[54] Catholics in the vicinity of Dachau, together with German Catholics farther afield, offered charitable assistance to the priests who had been incarcerated. In Paris, it was a German priest, Franz Stock, who ministered to French hostages and resisters facing execution.

There were other examples of transnational faith communities that grew out of trust and mutual respect. John Delaney has shown that Polish forced labourers in (overwhelmingly Catholic) rural Bavaria were not as vulnerable as, and fared better overall than, those sent to larger towns or industrial centres. Of the 1.7 million Poles working in Germany, 70,000 ended up in Bavaria. Delaney notes that local Catholics and their priests provided the Poles with a degree of protection and support. The Polish workers attended mass in the village churches and, for the most part, they sat alongside the German members of the congregations. Mass at this time was celebrated in Latin, the universal language of the

---

[53] Drapac, 'The Devotion of French Prisoners of War and Requisitioned Workers to Thérèse of Lisieux'; Yves Durand, *La Vie quotidienne des prisonniers de guerre dans les Stalags, les Oflags et les Kommandos, 1939–1945* (Mesnil-sur-l'Estrée: Hachette, 1987), Chapter 11; Pierre Flament, 'La vie religieuse d'un Oflag', *Revue d'histoire de la Deuxième Guerre mondiale*, 7/25 (1957), 47–65.

[54] Guillaume Zeller, *La Baraque des prêtres: Dachau, 1938–1945* (Paris: Tallandier, 2015); John M. Lenz, *Christ in Dachau or Christ Victorious: Experiences in a Concentration Camp* (Vienna: Missionsdruckerei St Gabriel, 1960).

universal Church, but all Catholic communities had local customs as well as devotions and hymns in the vernacular. Police reports noted disapprovingly that Polish workers were encouraged to remain in the churches after mass to sing Polish hymns. Meanwhile, the German priests praised the Poles as exemplary Catholics. Some priests invited the newly arrived workers into their rectories and gave them cigarettes and warm clothes. Villagers emulated their priests and offered the Polish workers extra food and took them to dances and fairs. All this occurred, Delaney writes, despite the 'utilisation of threats and terror' against the local population. Charitable actions towards the Polish workers were closely monitored and could (and did) lead to arrest and incarceration. Reports compiled by the secret police referred to these actions under the heading *Gegner* (opponents). The behaviour of these German Catholics was not intended to bring down the regime, but it went against the state's directives. According to Delaney, it was motivated by 'entrenched faith' and 'pre-existing values' that ran counter to Nazi teaching and ideology (maxims 2, 3 and 5).[55]

International Catholic unity around devotion to a modern French saint helps us to imagine different kinds of transnational links, fragile as they became in time of war. Thérèse of Lisieux (1873–1897) was the most popular saint of the twentieth century. She was canonised in 1925 and her appeal crossed national, class and generational boundaries.[56] Thérèse's intense 'spirituality of the ordinary', or her 'little way', was an important source of her appeal in uncertain times and was explained in her writings. Following the example of Thérèse meant seeking out the opportunity to do good daily in the course of one's normal life. It meant seeking the heroic (spiritually speaking) in the anti-heroic (maxims 4 and 6). Thérèse's 'little way' was the ordinary Catholic's path to sanctification.[57] Devotion to Thérèse 'took off' in the early twentieth century, leading to a deluge of correspondence to the Carmel of Lisieux from Catholics from all over the world.

---

[55] John J. Delaney, 'Racial Values vs. Religious Values: Clerical Opposition to Nazi Anti-Polish Racial Policy', *Church History*, 70/2 (2001), 271–294.

[56] For a study of Thérèse's life see Thomas R. Nevin, *Thérèse of Lisieux: God's Gentle Warrior* (Oxford: Oxford University Press, 2006); and *The Last Years of Saint Thérèse: Doubt and Darkness, 1895–1897* (Oxford: Oxford University Press, 2013).

[57] See John Clarke (ed.), *Story of a Soul: The Autobiography of St Thérèse of Lisieux*, 3rd edn (Washington, DC: ICS Publications, 1996).

At this time of international conflict, Thérèse was a model for Catholics of a simple life well lived. She also served as a vehicle for creating and extending transnational Catholic connections. The correspondence to Lisieux from the 1930s and 1940s can teach us a great deal about Catholic faith and practice in a period of crisis, but there is only space to consider two themes: the isolation felt by German Catholics under Nazism and the anxiety brought on by war.[58] In contrast to the optimistic tone of letters sent to Lisieux in the 1920s, especially after Thérèse's canonisation, the correspondence from the late 1930s hints at some of the difficulties that German Catholics were enduring (maxim 6). It was becoming more and more difficult for German Carmelites to send gifts and donations for the Basilica which was being built in honour of Thérèse in Lisieux. They regretted that they were now unable to pay for the relics, holy cards and other mementos that arrived from Lisieux.[59] They were burdened with higher taxes and the customs duties were beyond their means. All this forced them to be 'as parsimonious as possible'.[60] But there was still not enough money to support their missionaries in Japan who were now in 'dire straits' (maxims 2–6).[61] Collectively, the sisters were relying on Thérèse's intercession on that score.

When the state treated the powerless with disdain, and at a time of heightened anxiety brought on by their fears for the future, Catholics on opposite sides in the war continued to reach out to each other. In February 1940, an Austrian Jesuit who was living in exile in Switzerland wrote to Lisieux on behalf of the Carmel of Innsbruck, and provided some of the background to his own difficult situation. He asked for prayers and 'the intercession of [the] holy sisters' for the international seminary, the Canisianum, which the Nazis had expelled from Austria.[62] A year later, in February 1941, a retired priest from Trier wrote to Lisieux. He had heard from the Central Post Office that letters were arriving in the department of Calvados 'with no difficulty', and so took the opportunity to make contact again: 'I have been thinking upon your

---

[58] Drapac has drawn on some of the wartime correspondence in 'The Devotion of French Prisoners of War and Requisitioned Workers to Thérèse of Lisieux'.

[59] Archives of the Carmel of Lisieux (ACL). Letters to the Carmel of Lisieux from the Carmel in Aachen dated 19 January 1937, 26 October 1938 and 14 March 1939.

[60] Letter to the Carmel of Lisieux from the Carmel of Cologne-Lindenthal dated 4 April 1938, in ACL.

[61] Letter to the Carmel of Lisieux from the Carmel of Cologne-Lindenthal dated 4 April 1938, in ACL.

[62] Letter to the Carmel of Lisieux from Michael Hofmann SJ in Sion, Switzerland dated 27 February 1940, in ACL.

pious intentions daily and I have been praying for you throughout the period during which it has been impossible to reach you by mail.' He continued: 'It is my profound hope that ... the completion of the great Basilica is progressing smoothly. May this magnificent Sanctuary, consecrated by our Holy Father the current Pope, become a place of sacrifice and grace for true reconciliation of peoples and a blessed and lasting peace' (maxims 2, 3 and 5).[63] All these examples demonstrate the degree to which many Catholics continued to regard themselves as part of a transnational faith community.

Prayers for international peace and justice were a constant feature in worship at all levels in the Church, before, during and after the war (maxim 6). We should think of the union of prayers and intentions in a similar way to our diagram of the 'social history of politics'. Transmission belts of ideology, moving up and down as well as back and forth across borders, inspired actions of different kinds, according to need and capacity. In Paris, the image of a prayerful community that transcended the nation was deliberately evoked. In their parishes, Catholics prayed for the universal Church, for Europe, for France, for their neighbourhoods, and for their families. Rome designated universal days of prayer for the world in crisis, for all victims of the war and for POWs. Private, familial, local, national, and international intentions melded in this communal action.[64]

The master narrative of resistance and collaboration has been an impediment to understanding social life in Hitler's empire. This is especially the case for the Catholic Church. The sheer diversity and plurality of 'purely Catholic' behaviours meant that, within churches, different people with different views about many things rubbed shoulders and negotiated the ordeal as best they could. Ethical and moral guidelines on first principles were invoked in countless ways in the churches. The 'politics of presence' was important not just for spiritually and intellectually well-formed Catholics, but also for the weak, the corrupt, the self-interested, the lukewarm, and for those who attended mass rarely or not at all. All these people were encouraged to participate in all manner of services and activities. How well Church structures could attend to such divergent needs and capabilities in Hitler's empire was determined by conditions that were outside the control of Catholics (maxims 2 and 3). There are many fronts in an ideological war, but brute force trumps prayerful action, at least in the short term.

---

[63] Letter from a retired priest in Trier, Germany, dated 21 February 1941, in ACL.

[64] Drapac, *War and Religion*, Chapter 8.

The question of Catholic complicity

It is beneficial to look more holistically at Catholic faith communities. This is not just because it allows us to see all kinds of people and behaviours that otherwise remain invisible, but because, as we have already intimated, it makes it possible for us to look at old questions in new ways. In Chapter 4 we noted that the social history movement made an important contribution to general understandings of resistance and collaboration. We suggest that drawing on a wider sample of Catholic behaviours can also shed new light on ideas about Catholic complicity. Our intention here is not to contribute to debates in which Catholic behaviour is relativised, defended or excoriated (maxim 7). Rather, we would like to bring into the discussion the plurality of Catholic experiences and consider whether the 'social history of politics' approach enables us to look at important and enduring questions in a more nuanced fashion.

We have seen that one of the central premises on which the assessment of Catholic complicity rests is that, had the Pope and other high Churchmen given stronger directions to the millions of Catholics in Europe, more Jews would have been saved. Yet one of the best-known examples of Church leaders speaking out against the persecution of Jews did not have that positive result. Under the leadership of the Primate of the Netherlands, Archbishop Johannes de Jong of Utrecht, the Dutch Church issued statements in July 1942 and again in February 1943 opposing directives from the Germans for the roundup of local Jews. These statements were unambiguous. They provide evidence of the fact that in certain circumstances the Church did indeed speak out 'courageously' against Jewish deportations. Yet, soon after the July statement was circulated, 40,000 Dutch Jews were deported. Overall, out of a population of 140,000 Dutch Jews, 102,000 perished in the Holocaust. This was by far the highest percentage of victims of the Holocaust in Western Europe.[65]

After the war, the leadership of the Church in France and ordinary believers were seen to have compromised the faith and 'the nation'. A number of Catholic individuals and groups stood out and were praised. But the Archbishop of Paris, Cardinal Emmanuel Suhard, who

---

[65] Of an estimated Jewish population of 140,000 in the Netherlands in 1941, 73 percent perished. See Marnix Croes, 'The Holocaust in the Netherlands and the Rate of Jewish Survival', *Holocaust and Genocide Studies*, 20/3 (2006), 474–499, 474.

represented the compliant majority, was in the firing line after the liberation of the capital. De Gaulle, for instance, did not allow him to celebrate the thanksgiving mass in Notre Dame.[66] However, in the 'dark years' of occupation, Suhard's pastoral letters and his sermons touched on many of the practical, ethical, and moral issues challenging Parisian Catholics daily: the black market, the need for charity, the importance of forgiveness, and respect for one's neighbour. In the weeks before and after the July 1942 roundup of Jews in Paris discussed in Chapter 5, the organ of the Church in the capital, *La Semaine religieuse de Paris*, broached the subject of persecution based on race and religion in the coded – some would call it 'ambiguous' – language disparaged in the dominant strand of the historiography.[67] Suhard spoke and wrote about the pervasiveness of institutionalised violence. He also invoked the equality and solidarity of races and nations.[68] We do not suggest that Suhard's pastoral letters and sermons that were openly reproduced in *La Semaine religiuese de Paris* constituted resistance, still less a 'comprehensive' condemnation of the persecution of Jews. But it is not unreasonable to speculate on the relationship between the 'politics of presence' and social cohesion on the one hand, and the rescue of 15,000 Jews on the night of the July 1942 roundup, as well as other examples of large-scale Catholic rescue in France, on the other.

One of the greatest stories of rescue in the war was of 50,000 (mostly British) POWs escaping south towards the advancing Allies, or north towards Switzerland, after the fall of the Fascist regime in Italy in 1943. Incredible as it seems, it was only decades after the war that historians began to explore this topic.[69] What they discovered was that, almost without exception, the

---

[66] See André Latreille, *De Gaulle, la Libération et l'Église catholique* (Paris: Cerf, 1978).

[67] Richard H. Weisberg, *In Praise of Intransigence: The Perils of Flexibility* (Oxford: Oxford University Press, 2014).

[68] See, for example, *La Semaine religieuse de Paris*, 6 June 1942, 288; 13 June 1942, 294–295; 8 August 1942, 359; 22 August 1942, 374. See also Vesna Drapac, 'Catholic Resistance and Collaboration in the Second World War: From Master Narrative to Practical Application', in Sabine Rutar (ed.), *Beyond the Balkans: Towards an Inclusive History of Southeastern Europe* (Vienna: Lit Verlag, 2014), 279–322 (Studies on South East Europe, Vol. 10).

[69] Roger Absalom, 'Allied Escapers and the *Contadini* in Occupied Italy (1943–5)', *Journal of Modern Italian Studies*, 10/4 (2005), 413–425. See also Roger Absalom, 'Escape into the Other Italy (1943–45): Some Reflections on a Use of Oral History', *Oral History*, 19/2 (1991), 49–54; and 'Hiding History: The Allies, the Resistance and the Others in Occupied Italy 1943–1945', *Historical Journal*, 38/1 (1995), 111–131.

escapers found safe shelter in the homes and barns of peasants, and in churches and presbyteries. Peasant communities and the local clergy protected the foreigners and shared what little they had with them. There was nothing to connect the rescuers to the rescued other than the fact that the latter were in need and the former were in a position, and willing, to help. It is not entirely clear why this 'great escape' elicited so little interest from academics for so many years, but we would suggest that it was at least in part because it was difficult to label. The mass concealment of POWs by peasants was subversive and those providing shelter recognised this. But without slogans and without arms it could not be interpreted as specifically political or militant anti-Fascist action. It therefore had no place in the master narrative of Italian resistance, in spite of the many thousands of people and the hundreds of communities involved. The interesting question to ask about this rescue is not how we should label it, but why it was possible. One explanation is that the ties that connected the rescuers to each other and to those whom they rescued were based on values that were counter-cultural in the context of the totalising war and the totalising dictatorships. Peasant traditions of social solidarity, which were deeply rooted in Catholicism, were one of the key variables in this instance (maxims 1, 2, 3, and 6).

The near obsessive quest to label and to judge behaviour within the resistance/collaboration paradigm leads to inconsistencies, distortion, errors, revisions, and sweeping generalisations about large numbers of people at the top and at the bottom of Catholic hierarchies. The Archbishop of Zagreb, Alojzije Stepinac, deemed by some as the most criminally complicitous of Catholic leaders, is regarded by others as an outspoken critic of persecution and genocide in Hitler's empire.[70] Whether or not this man should be seen as a collaborator or as a kind of resister is not, in itself, an invalid question. But it is not the only question, and the answer to that

---

[70] Sabrina P. Ramet, *The Three Yugoslavias: State-Building and Legitimation, 1918–2005* (Washington, DC: Woodrow Wilson Center Press and Indiana University Press, 2006), 120–128; Jure Krišto, 'The Catholic Church in Croatia and Bosnia-Herzegovina in the Face of Totalitarian Ideologies and Regimes', in Gevers and Bank, *Religion under Siege*, 39–92; Phayer, *Pius XII, the Holocaust and the Cold War*, 10–15; Drapac, 'Catholic Resistance and Collaboration in the Second World War'; Esther Gitman, *When Courage Prevailed: The Rescue and Survival of Jews in the Independent State of Croatia 1941–1945* (St. Paul, MN: Paragon House, 2011); and 'Archbishop Alojzije Stepinac of Zagreb and the Rescue of Jews, 1941–45', *Catholic Historical Review*, 101/3 (2015), 488–529. See also note 17 above.

question does not tell us much about his behaviour (maxims 2, 3, and 6). This is especially the case given the background of the polarised historiography of collaboration in Yugoslavia (maxim 7). As we have shown so many times throughout the book, the raft of unacknowledged and entrenched double standards in the historiography alerts us to the need for a different perspective. Church presence seemed to amount to 'complicity' in some instances and 'defiance' in others. But the nature, intention, consequences, and wider context of that presence are hidden behind those labels. It is also instructive to ask what it was actually in the power of people – not just the able-bodied and not just men – and institutions to achieve in the social milieu in which they were operating and in response to Nazi rule and persecution.

Conclusion

The resistance/collaboration paradigm is an obstacle to understanding Catholic life under Nazi rule. By placing the Catholic Church itself at the centre of our analysis, many behaviours, hitherto ignored or dismissed, come into focus. These include private and collective acts of piety, charitable activities and associational life, and a dense nexus of local, national, and transnational interactions that connected Catholics to each other and to wider society. Moreover, all sorts of people who regarded themselves as Catholics, and whose Catholicism was important to their experience of Nazi rule, but who have never been studied 'as Catholics', step out of the shadows. This is particularly true of Catholic women. What all these behaviours and people had in common, irrespective of the labels which we might want to attach to them, is that they were rooted in community and in the Catholic faith. Therefore, to make sense of Catholics and Catholic behaviour in Hitler's empire, we must see them within their historical, theological, political, and economic context, which in turn is only possible if our approach is interdisciplinary.

This is where a 'social history of politics' approach can be useful. Rather than concentrating on any single domain of Catholic life (for example, the 'high politics' of the Vatican and senior clergy, Catholic rescuers, the 'social history' of Catholics in the pews, or the experiences of Catholics in the army and POW camps), it is more useful to explore the connectedness

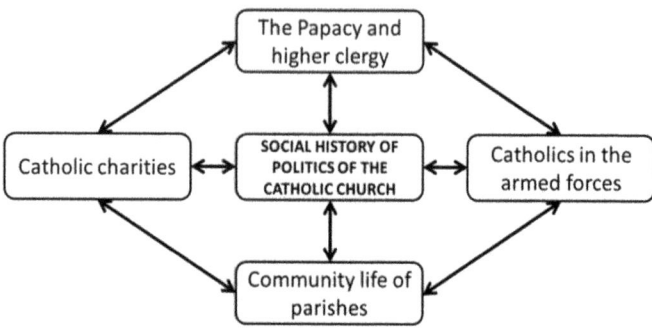

Figure 6.2 A social history of politics approach to the Catholic Church.

of these domains. Furthermore, we must take account of the fact that, in the context of a total war waged by a totalising dictatorship, all these behaviours were of political significance (Figure 6.2).

Viewed from this perspective, it is striking that Catholic communities were able to preserve a high degree of social coherence during the great crisis of the 1940s, even in countries such as Poland where the test had been particularly brutal. Up to a point, and depending on location, the social power of Catholic communities proved highly resistant to the attempts of Nazis and collaborationists to penetrate them ideologically. The transnational social cohesion of the Catholic Church created a space for acts of rescue and overt resistance in many contexts. However, there were also limits to the agency of Catholic individuals and faith communities. When the brute power of the Nazi empire intervened directly in the life of communities, Catholics were powerless. They could not prevent the Nazis from implementing specific policies, as the example of the Dutch hierarchy attests. The hard power of Hitler's empire overwhelmed the social power of Catholic communities. But, in the longer term, neither the Nazis nor the catastrophe of war broke down the nexus of values and relationships at the heart of the universal Catholic community of faith.

7 Resistance and Collaboration in Official and Public Memory

Although historians have always been in the forefront of constructing the public memory of World War II, other groups have also played an important role, including politicians, political activists, lawyers, public intellectuals, school teachers, museum curators, sculptors, authors, playwrights, and filmmakers. Moreover, millions of ordinary Europeans harboured personal memories of resistance and collaboration that were often different from, and sometimes incompatible with, public narratives. In this final chapter, we shall look at the public and official memory of resistance and collaboration. Our focus here is not on the work of historians, but on other types of public discourse.

World War II and the 'memory boom'

In recent years there has been a surge of scholarly interest in the relationship between memory, history and identity. This trend has been evident in the disciplines of history, art history, philosophy, literary studies, psychology, sociology, and political science. University programmes and academic journals have been established that focus on the emerging, interdisciplinary field of 'memory studies'.

One of the most important figures in the field of memory studies is the French sociologist and philosopher, Maurice Halbwachs (1877–1945), who was himself a victim of Nazi oppression. A socialist with a Jewish father-in-law, Halbwachs was arrested by the Gestapo in 1944 and died the following year at Buchenwald concentration camp. During his scholarly career, Halbwachs developed the theory of 'collective memory'. According to Halbwachs, the way human beings process their memories is always influenced by social context. Rather than being fixed immutably like a tape-recording, memory is continually reconstructed by individuals in interaction with those around them. Memories, in short, can be collective as well as individual, and they are shaped by the present as well as the past.[1] These ideas have been very influential in the field of memory studies.[2]

Another significant figure in the field is the French historian Pierre Nora (born 1931) who, between 1984 and 1992, published a series of edited volumes entitled *Les Lieux de mémoire* (The Sites of Memory). Bringing together the work of leading French scholars, *Les Lieux de mémoire* provides a compendium of how memory is embodied in architecture, street names, statues, objects, public ceremonies, music, folk heroes, and national symbols.[3] According to Nora, memories in traditional societies are passed on organically from one generation to the next. In modern, mass society, by contrast, memory has become artificial. He calls this 'prosthesis-memory'. Artefacts stockpiled in museums and documents in archives serve as a substitute for organic memory.[4] The sites where this prosthetic memory is constructed include physical spaces, literary sites (the pages of books), and, more recently, the internet. Though not all scholars accept Nora's assessment of the role of sites of memory in the construction of public narratives about the past, the term *lieux de mémoire* is now an established point of reference in memory scholarship.[5]

All these developments are highly relevant to the study of wartime resistance and collaboration. World War II has been central to public commemorative practices in almost all the countries that fell under Nazi rule. Controversies about different understandings of resistance and collaboration are fought out, not just in the history books, but also in debates about street names, state holidays, public monuments, school textbooks, and many other *lieux de mémoire*.

---

[1] Maurice Halbwachs, *On Collective Memory*, ed. and tr. Lewis A. Coser (Chicago, IL: University of Chicago Press, 1992).

[2] Jeffrey K. Olick, Vered Vinitzky-Seroussi and Daniel Levy (eds), *The Collective Memory Reader* (New York: Oxford University Press, 2011), Introduction.

[3] Pierre Nora and Lawrence D. Kritzman, *Realms of Memory: Conflicts and Divisions* (New York: Columbia University Press, 1996).

[4] Pierre Nora, 'Between Memory and History: *Les Lieux de mémoire*', *Representations*, 26, Special Issue: Memory and Counter-Memory (1989), 7–24.

[5] Michael Rothberg, 'Introduction: Between Memory and Memory: From *Lieux de mémoire* to *Noeuds de mémoire*', *Yale French Studies*, 118–119 (2010), 3–12.

The intersection between memory and national identity is another issue that is relevant to the study of resistance and collaboration. Many theorists have argued that collective memories constitute the core of national identity. In other words, national identity is nested within a shared history which is reaffirmed and reproduced in rituals and symbols. Collective memory is thus seen by scholars as a powerful integrative force that is used to demarcate the boundary between 'us' and 'them'.[6] Peter Sahlins, for instance, argues that: 'National identity is a socially constructed and continuous process of defining "friend" and "enemy".'[7] In a similar vein, Homi Bhabha claims that the nation is a text that is continually rewritten. National narratives, however, can be incompatible with each other, and this may result in conflict. From this perspective, the history of nationalism is the history of conflicts over competing narratives.[8]

Such an analysis of the role of memory in national identity is germane to the study of resistance and collaboration because the history and memory of both are entwined with the project of nation-building. Ever since the end of World War II, stories about resistance and collaboration have been central to the national narratives of many European countries. This is why the historiography has been so politicised. The emergence of the Holocaust as a central issue in the historiography of twentieth-century Europe has rendered the subject of resistance and collaboration even more politically sensitive. Indeed, the Holocaust has also become a central issue in the field of memory studies. As Nora himself has pointed out: 'Whoever says memory, says Shoah.'[9]

The *lieux de mémoire* of resistance and collaboration

The importance of resistance and collaboration in public discourse is clear from even a cursory overview of the many sites where their memory is invoked. As popular perceptions of resistance and collaboration have shifted, so have there been corresponding changes in commemorative

---

[6] Duncan S.A. Bell, 'Mythscapes: Memory, Mythology and National Identity', *British Journal of Sociology*, 54/1 (2003), 63–81.

[7] Quoted in Lloyd Kramer, 'Historical Narratives and the Meaning of Nationalism', *Journal of the History of Ideas*, 58/3 (1997), 525–546, 526.

[8] Homi K. Bhabha, *Nation and Narration* (London: Routledge, 1990).

[9] Quoted in Jay Winter, 'The Memory Boom in Contemporary Historical Studies', *Raritan*, 21/1 (2001), 52–66, 52.

practice. Here, we only have space to cover a handful of the most significant 'sites of memory' where public understandings of resistance and collaboration are negotiated, contested, or enforced.

The first *lieu de mémoire* of resistance and collaboration was the street. Immediately after the departure of the Nazis, the spontaneous punishment of collaborators took place across Europe. In France and Italy, thousands of (mainly male) collaborators were rounded up by resistance fighters, taken away, and executed.[10] Women who were accused of having slept with German soldiers were subsequently denounced as 'horizontal collaborators'. In front of jeering crowds, they were stripped, publicly humiliated, and their heads were shaved.[11] In the Sudetenland, ethnic Czechs physically attacked their German-speaking neighbours, whom they accused of having collaborated with the Nazis.[12] Underlying these carnivals of retribution were deeply gendered attitudes both to resistance and to collaboration. To resist had been courageous, manly and virile, whereas to collaborate had been weak and effeminate. In the words of Luc Capdevila, the ritual of head-shaving 'was tantamount to saying that masculinity, and the virility of the nation itself, required the restoration of male domination over women's bodies'.[13] As we saw in Chapters 3 and 4, this gendered resistance/collaboration paradigm became a salient feature of the historiography.

Though the mob violence that took place in the days and weeks after liberation was dramatic, of greater long-term significance in terms of the memory of resistance and collaboration was the role of the state. In the territories that had been liberated, the new governments that came to power struggled to impose their authority. To bolster their legitimacy, they took ownership of the public memory of World War II. They initiated a vast sifting process to evaluate how people had behaved under Nazi rule, to identify and punish collaborators and war criminals, and to reward

---

[10] Antony Beevor and Artemis Cooper, *Paris after the Liberation: 1944–1949* (London: Penguin, 1994), 98–107; Jonathan Dunnage, *Twentieth Century Italy: A Social History* (London: Longman, 2014), 131–133.

[11] Keith Lowe, *Savage Continent: Europe in the Aftermath of World War II* (London: Penguin, 2013), Chapter 14.

[12] Giles MacDonogh, *After the Reich: The Brutal History of the Allied Occupation* (New York: Basic Books, 2007), Chapter 4.

[13] Luc Capdevila, 'The Quest for Masculinity in Defeated France, 1940–1945', *Contemporary European History*, 10/3 (2001), 423–445.

resisters. The state took a leading role in defining who was a collaborator and who was a resister, thereby establishing hierarchies of villainy and heroism.

One of the most important sites where the state attempted to control the public memory of resistance and collaboration was the courtroom. The trials of collaborators began in the Soviet Union as early as 1943 in territories that had been liberated from the Germans after the Battle of Stalingrad. In Krasnodar in southern Russia, those found guilty of collaboration were hanged in public before cheering crowds. Ilya Bourtman claims that the purpose of the trial was not just to punish traitors, but also to ease the culpability of the majority by pinning the blame on a small number of collaborators. This in turn cleared the ground for the construction of a narrative of a people in revolt. The Krasnodar trial was thus a cathartic ritual. It drew a veil over uncomfortable facts and permitted a symbolic reconciliation to be played out between the state and the mass of the population, now reunited behind a myth of mass resistance.[14]

What began in Krasnodar was repeated many times across Europe in the years to come. The trials of Philippe Pétain (July/August 1945), Pierre Laval (October 1945), Vidkun Quisling (August 1945), Draža Mihailović (June/July 1946) and other high-profile collaborators attracted media attention, not just in the countries concerned, but internationally. Even the British government participated in the public ritual of punishing collaborators. In September 1945, the pathetic figure of William Joyce ('Lord Haw-Haw') was brought to trial at the Old Bailey, accused of having made radio broadcasts for the Germans. Though there were doubts about whether Joyce was even a British subject, he was found guilty and executed. From one end of Europe to the other, tens of thousands of lesser collaborators were likewise brought before trials and tribunals and punished with execution, prison sentences or loss of civil rights. In Norway, a country with just 3 million inhabitants, nearly 100,000 people were put on trial, of whom 17,000 were given prison sentences and 25 were executed. In the Netherlands, 200,000 people were investigated, nearly half of whom were imprisoned, sometimes for minor offences such as giving the Nazi salute.[15]

---

[14] Ilya Bourtman, '"Blood for Blood, Death for Death": The Soviet Military Tribunal in Krasnodar, 1943', *Holocaust and Genocide Studies*, 22/2 (2008), 246–265.

[15] Tony Judt, *Postwar: A History of Europe since 1945* (London: Pimlico, 2007), 45–46.

The most famous post-war trials took place at Nuremberg in Germany. Though the prominent Nazi officials in the dock cannot properly be regarded as collaborators, the Nuremberg trials did establish an international precedent for the prosecution of war crimes and crimes against humanity.[16] In the following decades, there was a string of high-profile trials of Nazi officials and collaborationists, each of which prompted a re-examination of the narratives of collaboration, complicity, and guilt. As we saw, the trial of Adolf Eichmann in Jerusalem in 1961 provoked a great deal of discussion and had a significant impact on public awareness of the Holocaust.[17] Other high-profile trials have included those of John Demjanjuk (1986 and 2011), Klaus Barbie (1987), Paul Touvier (1994), and Maurice Papon (1997–98). In France, the cases of collaborators like Papon and Touvier led to a marked shift in how the French government dealt with the Vichy past. In 1995, Jacques Chirac became the first French president officially to acknowledge the complicity of the French state in the implementation of the Holocaust.[18]

As we have noted, the regimes that emerged in Europe in the aftermath of World War II were not just concerned with punishing collaborators; they also identified and rewarded resisters. Prizes and pensions were awarded to those whose contribution to the struggle against Nazism was seen as worthy of celebration. Streets and squares were named after heroes of the resistance, and monuments were erected in their honour. In Communist Croatia by the beginning of the 1970s, two-thirds of 2,700 registered public monuments were dedicated to the memory of fallen resistance fighters.[19] In many towns and cities in northern Italy, the main street or square is called '25 Aprile' in commemoration of the anti-Fascist uprisings of 1945, and 25 April was declared a national holiday.[20] In West Germany, streets, schools, and public buildings were named after heroes of the nationalist or religious resistance. For instance, Hans and Sophie Scholl, who had led the White Rose youth resistance group in Munich, and who

---

[16] Michael Biddiss, 'Victors' Justice? The Nuremberg Tribunal', *History Today*, 45/5 (1995), 40–46; Toby Thacker, *The End of the Third Reich* (Stroud: Tempus, 2006), 203–210.

[17] David Cesarani (ed.), *After Eichmann: Collective Memory and the Holocaust since 1961* (London: Routledge, 2013).

[18] David Art, 'Memory Politics in Western Europe', in Uwe Backes and Patrick Moreau (eds), *The Extreme Right in Europe: Current Trends and Perspectives* (Göttingen: Vandenhock & Ruprecht, 2011), 359–382.

[19] Ljiljana Radonic, *Krieg um die Erinnerung: Kroatische Vergangenheitspolitik zwischen Revisionismus und europäischen Standards* (Frankfurt: Campus Verlag, 2009), 113–115.

[20] Tom Behan, *Italian Resistance: Fascists, Guerrillas and the Allies* (London: Pluto Press, 2009), 1.

were executed in 1943, were (and are) widely commemorated.[21] In East Germany, by contrast, it was the memory of the Communist resisters that was celebrated in countless statues, plaques, and street names. The second Sunday of September was designated the Day of Remembrance for the Victims of Fascism, which in theory commemorated all those who had suffered under the Nazi dictatorship, but which in reality focused on the suffering of Communists.[22] Everywhere in Europe, the achievements of the resistance were celebrated in museums and school textbooks.

One common feature of state-sponsored narratives of resistance is that the experiences of individuals were subsumed into archetypes. Juliane Furst has noted how the lives (and often deaths) of female partisans were widely commemorated in the USSR. But the Soviet state showed little interest in these partisans as individual people. According to Furst: 'The intense glorification of partisan existence led to the muting of partisan girls' own voices under volumes of sentimental and conformist stories.'[23] Pieter Lagrou has described how, in the Netherlands, expressions of collective memory were homogenised. Every municipality had to centralise commemorative initiatives in one monument, rather than erect tributes to specific movements or individuals. Meanwhile, veterans' organisations, which represented the individuals who had served in the Dutch resistance, were marginalised.[24]

State-imposed narratives, even when they are hegemonic, are never uncontested. In post-war Italy, there was open competition between the Catholic Church and the Communist Party of Italy (PCI) over who should control public ceremonies that honoured the resistance and commemorated those killed by the Nazis.[25] In France and the Netherlands, the

---

[21] Douglas Peifer, 'Commemoration of Mutiny, Rebellion, and Resistance in Postwar Germany: Public Memory, History, and the Formation of "Memory Beacons"', *Journal of Military History*, 65/4 (2001), 1013–1052; Gavriel D. Rosenfeld, *Munich and Memory: Architecture, Monuments, and the Legacy of the Third Reich* (Berkeley, CA: University of California Press, 2010), 215–218.

[22] Peter Monteath, 'A Day to Remember: East Germany's Day of Remembrance for the Victims of Fascism', *German History*, 26/2 (2008), 195–218.

[23] Juliane Furst, 'Heroes, Lovers, Victims – Partisan Girls during the Great Fatherland War', *Minerva*, 18/3–4, (2000), 38–75.

[24] Pieter Lagrou, 'The Politics of Memory: Resistance as a Collective Myth in Post-War France, Belgium and the Netherlands, 1945–1965', *European Review*, 11/4 (2003), 527–549.

[25] Victoria C. Belco, *War, Massacre, and Recovery in Central Italy, 1943–1948* (Toronto: University of Toronto Press, 2010); Andrea Cossu, 'Commemoration and Processes of Appropriation: The Italian Communist Party and the Italian Resistance (1943–48)', *Memory Studies*, 4/4 (2011), 386–400.

Communists preserved a distinct memory culture, with its own *lieux de mémoire*, its own pantheon of heroes and rituals.[26] In Belgium, memories of resistance and collaboration were fragmented along ethnic lines. The Flemish-speaking population of northern Belgium nurtured memories of the war that were distinct from those of their French-speaking compatriots in the south. There was much resentment in Flanders at the punishments that had been inflicted by the post-war Belgian state on Flemish nationalists who had been charged with collaboration.[27] In Communist countries, meanwhile, the state exerted an almost complete control over the public memory of resistance and collaboration, but it was never able to eradicate the alternative memories of those who had lived through the war years. Passed down from one generation to the next in the private sphere – in particular in the family – these counter-memories rose to the surface during the 1980s and 1990s, and then coalesced into new, state-sponsored hegemonic narratives.[28]

The Communist narrative of the resistance was not just imposed from above by the states of the Soviet Bloc. In many places, including western Russia, Belorussia, Bulgaria, and Yugoslavia, the Communist-led partisan movements had enjoyed genuine popular backing. The women and men who had fought in them, or who had supported their activities, were proud of their wartime achievements. After the war, the local people who laid flowers on the memorials, or who participated in official ceremonies, did so out of conviction. They also created local, unofficial sites of memory. After the collapse of the Soviet Bloc, people continued to lay flowers and to participate in public rituals.

In the 1960s and 1970s, there emerged a new and important *lieu de mémoire* where narratives of World War II were both transmitted and renegotiated: television. In January 1979, for example, an American made-for-television series entitled *Holocaust* was screened over four successive nights in West Germany. The mini-series, which focused on the experiences of a German-Jewish family, was watched by half the adult

---

[26] Lagrou, 'Politics of Memory'.

[27] Olivier Luminet et al., 'The Interplay between Collective Memory and the Erosion of Nation States: The Paradigmatic Case of Belgium', *Memory Studies*, 5/1 (2012), 3–15.

[28] For overviews of memory politics in East-Central Europe since the 1980s, see Helmut Altrichter (ed.), *GegenErinnerung: Geschichte als politisches Argument im Transformationsprozess Ost-, Ostmittel- und Südosteuropas* (Munich: Oldenbourg, 2006); *Osteuropa: Geschichtspolitik und Gegenerinnerung: Krieg, Gewalt und Trauma im Osten Europas*, 6 (2008).

population of the Federal Republic and had a profound effect on public opinion. Each night, after the episode had finished, a panel of historians dealt with questions from members of the public. The response was overwhelming. Viewers were variously shocked, angry, or distraught. Why, they asked, had such things been possible in Germany, and why had they not learned about these dark pages of German history in their school lessons?[29] The Gesellschaft für deutsche Sprache (Society for the German Language) named 'Holocaust' as the German Word of the Year.[30] More recently, a French television series entitled *Un village français*, first aired in 2009, has attracted a cult following both in France and internationally. It is set in the fictional commune of Villeneuve, and the concepts of resistance and collaboration are the twin poles around which the story-arcs of the various characters are narrated. *Un village français* is another example of the enduring importance of the resistance/collaboration paradigm in popular perceptions about life in Hitler's empire.

A new ingredient in the memory politics of World War II is the internet, which is a *lieu de mémoire* unlike any other. Hitherto, debates about resistance and collaboration have been dominated by political, cultural, and educational elites (including historians). The 'voice of the people' was occasionally heard on the streets, or articulated passively through the purchase of books or cinema tickets. But popular discourse did not shape what was said and written in the public sphere about World War II. Ordinary people had no direct input into the content of the textbook at the local school or the plot of the latest World War II blockbuster.

In cyberspace, by contrast, the hegemony of elites over the articulation of public memory has been destabilised. Governments, political parties, and historians maintain an online presence, but they have almost no control over people's online behaviour. Anybody with access to a computer can post a video or write a comment on YouTube that might be seen by thousands or even hundreds of thousands of people. The internet is now a primary mechanism by which information and ideas about the past are disseminated in the public domain. The democratising potential of this new technology is difficult to exaggerate.

---

[29] Judt, *Postwar*, 811–812.
[30] Georg Stötzel and Martin Wengeler, *Kontroverse Begriffe: Geschichte des öffentlichen Sprachgebrauchs in der Bundesrepublik Deutschland* (Berlin: Walter de Gruyter, 1995), 576.

However, in an era of increasing political polarisation, the internet provides a fertile environment for the spread of misinformation that would still (for now) make little headway in other social domains. What this means, in terms of public discourse about Hitler's empire, is a rising tide of online anti-Semitism, Holocaust revisionism, and the whitewashing of war criminals and collaborators. The nature of the impact of the internet on memory politics is a topic that scholars are only just beginning to examine.[31]

Resistance and collaboration in cinema

One of the most important *lieux de mémoire* is cinema. Filmic narratives of resistance and collaboration have reached a wider audience than any other kind. For this reason, we shall look in a little more detail at the evolution of the resistance/collaboration paradigm in cinema, and its close relationship with the evolution of the historiography.

Many popular perceptions about the war in general, and resistance and collaboration in particular, have been shaped by film. School teachers routinely use film and fiction in history lessons and there are university courses devoted to the study of the war on film. Between 1945 and 1999, almost 800 films touching on themes related to the Holocaust alone were produced, mostly in the United States and Germany.[32] The number of studies of the war in film attest to the enduring impact of film on attitudes to the war.[33]

---

[31] See, for example, Ellen Rutten, Julie Fedor and Vera Zvereva, *Memory, Conflict and New Media: Web Wars in Post-Socialist States* (London: Routledge, 2013).

[32] Robert A. Rosenstone, *History on Film/Film on History* (Harlow: Pearson/Longman, 2006), 136.

[33] See, for example, Roger Manvell, *Films and the Second World War* (South Brunswick, NJ: A.S. Barnes, 1974); Jeanine Basinger, *The World War II Combat Film: Anatomy of a Genre* (Middletown, CT: Wesleyan University Press, 2003); Christopher Lloyd, *Collaboration and Resistance in Occupied France: Representing Treason and Sacrifice* (Basingstoke: Palgrave Macmillan, 2003); Leah D. Hewitt, *Remembering the Occupation in French Film: National Identity in Postwar Europe* (New York: Palgrave Macmillan, 2008); Margaret Atack and Christopher Lloyd (eds), *Framing Narratives of the Second World War and Occupation in France, 1939–2009: New Readings* (Manchester: Manchester University Press, 2012).

Filmmakers have evoked resistance and collaboration in ways that have both disturbed and reassured audiences. The French historian Henry Rousso famously theorised the entanglement of film, perceptions of the war and its historiography in his book, *The Vichy Syndrome* (first published in 1987).[34] According to Rousso, there was a pattern (or syndrome) in the way that public discourse about France's 'dark years' had evolved in response to the work of filmmakers. Resistance and collaboration, he claimed, were constantly being 're-staged' or reinterpreted in film. This occurred because filmmakers commonly do one of two things, or a combination of both. Some directors express their views about contemporary political problems by drawing on the familiar 'lessons' of resistance and/or collaboration. Others are moved to revisit the topic in the light of their engagement with contemporary problems and thereby project their presentist concerns on to the past.[35] So, for example, feminism has had an impact on the depiction of women in films about resistance and collaboration. More resistance films involving women, and more women-focused stories, were produced from the 1970s. However, it could not be said that the gendered understanding of what it meant to resist has been called into question. On the contrary, in films like *Lucie Aubrac* (1997), *Charlotte Grey* (2001), and *Les Femmes de l'ombre* (Female Agents, 2008), the conventional view of resistance has been reinforced.

Resistance is normally depicted on film in a narrow sense. As a general rule, the defining filmic trope of resistance has always been the heroic act of an individual or a small group embarking on a dangerous mission. Part of the problem of how best to convey the nature of resistance on film is the narrative convention of the medium. For the most part it only allows for a narrative arc in which a problem is resolved (the Nazis are thwarted), a measurable outcome has been reached (the train is blown up) and a lesson in moral integrity conveyed (a selfless man pays the ultimate sacrifice for the greater good). Commonly, this kind of film also shows heavy reliance on a small group of skilled individuals with different personal qualities. Films like *The Guns of Navarone* (1961) and *The Heroes of Telemark* (1965) are just two of the most popular examples of this format. However, early resistance films were less concerned with the outcomes of resistance than with what it entailed or what had made it possible.

---

[34] Henry Rousso, *The Vichy Syndrome: History and Memory in France since 1944* (Cambridge, MA: Harvard University Press, 1991 [1987]).

[35] See Rosenstone, *History on Film/Film on History*.

One of the changes in the story of resistance in popular film relates to the way in which the social context has been integrated into the narrative. During the war itself, Hollywood directly addressed the topic of resistance and projected it as an integrative, communal activity. For example, *Casablanca* (1942) was directed by Michael Curtiz, a Hungarian Jew who had emigrated during the political turmoil in the period after 1918. Although he was not a refugee from Nazism, many others involved in making the film were. The success of *Casablanca* has been attributed to the ethnic diversity of the cast and crew, who projected a positive image of the 'melting pot' of the filmic endeavour as a metaphor for resistance.[36] Similarly, the 'resistance myth' was founded on the idea that opposition against Hitler and the Nazis brought together people from many different backgrounds united around a common desire to defeat Nazism.

Another classic film about resistance produced in Hollywood during the war approached the subject differently, from the perspective of a close-knit homogenous community under occupation. *This Land Is Mine* (1943), directed by expatriate filmmaker Jean (son of Auguste) Renoir, focused on teachers. It considered the moral challenges facing those who were living with the enemy. Teachers in the film are the (sometimes reluctant) heroes of daily-life resistance. They do not engage in violent acts of sabotage but 'carry the flame' against total Nazi indoctrination. The daily-life transgression of the teachers entails risk because the children, unaware of the consequences of their actions, can and do inadvertently 'tell tales'. At the heart of this film is the dilemma that confronted those who were living with the enemy and trying to protect young people.

Early post-war films about resistance were more likely to feature active resisters engaged in direct attacks on the enemy, but community remained an important element.[37] Resistance was thus still seen to be the articulation of the general will. This focus on the military aspect of resistance has been explained by the need for states humiliated by defeat and occupation to reassert national pride. In countries behind the Iron Curtain there was an

---

[36] Ray Merlock, '*Casablanca* – Popular Film of the Century', *Journal of Popular Film and Television*, 27/4 (2000), 2-4.

[37] Suzanne Langlois, 'Images that Matter: The French Resistance in Film, 1944–1946', *French History*, 11/4 (1997), 461–485. See also Sylvie Lindeperg, *Les Écrans de l'ombre: la Seconde Guerre mondiale dans le cinéma français (1944–1969)* (Paris: CNRS Éditions, 1997); and Suzanne Langlois, *La Résistance dans le cinéma français, 1944–1994: De La Libération de Paris à Libera me* (Paris: L'Harmattan, 2001).

emphasis on the core of partisans and the sacrifices required by their stand against German occupation. Andrzej Wajda's trilogy, *Pokolenie* (A Generation, 1955), *Kanał* (1957), and *Popiół i diament* (Ashes and Diamonds, 1958), represents this genre at its height. The conservative Polish resistance features in Wajda's trilogy, but does not dominate. Nor do the Soviets. In this sense, his films were an expression of Polish nationalism at the time of the Communist implantation, which explains their resonance and enduring popularity.[38]

Films about resistance produced in Western European democracies were less political in the narrow party sense. Nonetheless, they also focused on small groups or communities to illustrate the solidarity necessary for successful resistance. *La Bataille du rail* (Battle of the Railways, 1946) exemplifies this in France. Actual resisters participated in the making of the film and are referred to in the credits by their resistance code names. This film was supported financially by the state, which had become the protector of the memory of the resistance, and de Gaulle attended the premiere. *La Bataille du rail* was filmed in the neo-realist style and celebrated the gritty determination of the railway workers to thwart the enemy. It shows how the men engaged in acts of sabotage, the risks involved, and the randomness of the punishment (execution) meted out for the high impact and visible transgressions.[39]

Perhaps the most iconic and most loved resistance film of this period is Roberto Rossellini's *Roma città aperta* (Rome, Open City, 1945). As is the case in *La Bataille du rail* and Wajda's trilogy, the heroes of Rossellini's film are working class. We see the way that different members of the community (including the children of the neighbourhood and the local priest) contribute to the resistance. It is not the outcome of resistance but the social setting that Rossellini brings to the fore. The Germans are ever-present and powerful. They try to block and rout out resistance through their cruelty, but they cannot penetrate the wall of integrity that protects the working people's Rome.[40] All these early resistance films were critically acclaimed and popular with audiences.

---

[38] Magdalena Saryusz-Wolska, 'The Transformation of National Memory in Polish Post-War Cinema', *Studia Universitatis Cibiniensis. Series Historica*, 11, Supplement (2014), 201–214.

[39] Martin O'Shaughnessy, '*La Bataille du rail*: Unconventional Form, Conventional Image?', in H.R. Kedward and Nancy Wood (eds), *The Liberation of France: Image and Event* (Oxford: Berg, 1995), 15–27.

[40] Mark Shiel, *Italian Neorealism: Rebuilding the Cinematic City* (London: Wallflower Press, 2006), 46–53; Millicent Marcus, *Italian Film in the Light of Neorealism* (Princeton, NJ: Princeton University Press, 1986), 33–53.

While the common themes of early resistance films – community, integrity, solidarity – never disappeared entirely, in due course there was more emphasis on the dark side of active resistance. This departure coincided with the demise of the resistance ideal or 'myth' in France and elsewhere, and the emergence of the new histories of collaboration. Directors began to look beyond archetypes of resistance and questioned the sanitised image. In *L'Armée des ombres* (Army of Shadows, 1969), the director, Jean-Pierre Melville – himself a veteran resister – demonstrated how lonely and isolating the life of the resister could be. Melville also showed how ruthless resisters were in the pursuit of their goals. In the film, one of the leaders of the resistance cell is a woman who is beyond reproach, but who becomes a liability due to a typically 'feminine' error of judgement.[41] Therefore, she is 'sacrificed' (assassinated) in the interests of the group as a whole. 'The people' are absent in *L'Armée des ombres*. In the kind of activity in which the cell specialised, large numbers simply could not have been involved due to the constant danger of infiltration and denunciation. So, if they were not resisting, what were all those 'absent people' doing? Collaborating, it would seem.

Collaborators had appeared in resistance films as moral weaklings, informers, or corrupt self-interested individuals in the pay of the Germans. But they were often marginal characters. From the 1970s, more and more filmmakers began to address collaboration as a central theme in their work. This change was the result of the convergence of different variables, including the fact that younger people were questioning their parents and grandparents about their wartime lives.

An important moment in the evolution of the public narrative of World War II in France was the release of *Le Chagrin et la pitié* (The Sorrow and the Pity). Directed by Marcel Ophüls, this documentary overturned many popular perceptions about France during the war. It first screened on German and Swiss television in 1969 and 1970 respectively. The director of the Office de Radio-Télévision Française refused to purchase the rights for French television, saying that the film 'destroys the myths that the French still need'.[42] The documentary was, however, shown in French cinemas, and it created an immediate stir.

---

[41] Sandy Flitterman-Lewis, '*Army of Shadows*', *Cineaste*, 31/4 (2006), 68–71.

[42] Brett Bowles, '"Ça fait d'excellents montages": Documentary Technique in *Le Chagrin et la pitié*', *French Historical Studies*, 31/1 (2008), 117–158, 118.

Using interviews, film footage, and newsreel from three different countries, Ophüls presented an uncomfortable image of cosy complicity. He did not deny the importance of resisters. There are interviews with 'salt-of-the-earth' peasants who did not accept Vichy's capitulation, with quixotic aristocrats who were involved in armed revolt, and with high-profile male resisters like Pierre Mendès-France, a Jew who had been close to de Gaulle and held key posts in his post-war governments. However, the scenes from the documentary that were most unsettling are of those men whose right-wing politics steered them towards support for Vichy's collaboration, or those who had simply accommodated the occupation and 'made do'. The message of the film was that there had been much collaboration in daily life and that this was most prevalent in the bourgeoisie and petit-bourgeoisie. In short, *Le Chagrin et la pitié* raised questions in the public domain about the 'true' history of the dark years in France, and many have claimed that it shattered the idea of France as the nation of resisters.[43]

Soon after the furore surrounding *Le Chagrin et la pitié*, Louis Malle's *Lacombe Lucien* (1974) famously depicted a slightly different and unfamiliar kind of collaboration. It de-emphasised the politicised elites and focused instead on the destabilisation that came with the overturning of power relations by the occupation. A young, uneducated peasant in the south of France, Lucien Lacombe seems to fall into collaboration by accident after being rejected by the local resistance leader. Bored and disconnected from the spiritually arid community from which he has emerged, Lucien is easy game for the rapacious French collaborationists who can give him money and power. Throughout the film, the Germans are mostly in the background and the conflict between the collaborators and the local resistance is depicted as a war of the French against the French. (This was also characteristic of the historiography at that time.) *Lacombe Lucien* has attracted much commentary on the absence of political motivation among collaborators. We have already become acquainted with the way that historians describe certain daily-life behaviours as 'ambiguous' or 'ambivalent'. Critics have used both terms in their appraisals of the politics of this film.[44]

---

[43] See Bowles, '"Ça fait d'excellents montages"', 117.

[44] Paul Jankowski, 'In Defense of Fiction: Resistance, Collaboration, and *Lacombe, Lucien*', *Journal of Modern History*, 63/3 (1991), 457–482; Richard J. Golsan, *Vichy's Afterlife: History and Counterhistory in Postwar France* (Lincoln, NE: University of Nebraska Press, 2000), 57–72.

While collaborationist archetypes can be as superficial as resistance archetypes, many films focusing on complicity rise above simple dichotomies. This is why they have been so popular and so engaging. There has been a tendency in films to show collaboration within the aspirational classes (the bourgeoisie or petit bourgeoisie) or among directionless and vulnerable young people like Lucien. Interestingly, however, films rarely convey the pervasiveness of Nazi ideology. Bearers of the ideology are brutal thugs and its influence or transforming capacity is barely touched upon in cinematic representations of complicity. It is as if collaborators were just born that way, not products of a particular set of circumstances or worldview. Lucien is a political imbecile and his understanding of what is occurring around him is rudimentary at best. But the war and the occupation, and the ideology underpinning them, are the making and unmaking of Lucien.

There are some exceptions to the general rule about the apolitical depiction of complicity on film. Bernardo Bertolucci's *The Conformist* (1970) and István Szabó's *Mephisto* (1981) are two films that adopt a more subtle approach. Both are based on novels, and show what Saul Friedlander has described as 'the actual mutation of behaviour' to which Fascism and Nazism gave rise.[45] *The Conformist* is about a politically ambitious man in Fascist Italy. It shows the corrupting potential of conformism: men were made, not born, Fascist. *Mephisto* tells the story of an actor involved with an avant-garde ensemble in Weimar Germany who, after the Nazi seizure of power, chooses to accept a post as director of an important theatre. He thereby makes his pact with the devil for earthly rewards. Both films were influenced by the political context in which they were made. *The Conformist* was produced at a time when radical 'New Left' politics posed uncomfortable questions about the complicity of elites during the 1930s and 1940s. *Mephisto* is a German story about culture and ideology, retold on film by a Hungarian living under Communism, where the parallels with regard to professional and artistic complicity and compromise under dictatorship would have been obvious.

The cinema has proven to be one of the most compelling sites of the memory of resistance and collaboration because filmic techniques provide directors with an unparalleled opportunity to condense complex situations

---

[45] Quoted in Robert Gellately, 'Between Exploitation, Rescue, and Annihilation: Reviewing *Schindler's List*', *Central European History*, 26/4 (1993), 475–489, 488.

and dilemmas. A mere look or brief exchange can communicate why someone chose one path rather than another at a particular moment. But the narrative conventions of feature films militate against complex analysis, and this deficiency has led to the reinforcing of particular images, especially gendered stereotypes. In pursuit of commercial success, big-budget feature films tend to follow a formula and include familiar tropes and symbols, which situate the drama and make the characters' predisposition evident. *Lucie Aubrac*, for example, is a film about the married couple Lucie and Raymond Aubrac, both of whom had leadership roles in the French resistance. Though in reality neither had been involved in armed resistance, the film begins with Raymond and his group blowing up a supply train. This departure from historical fact was dictated by the genre. The film must start with a recognisable act of subversion to demonstrate that it is about resistance. The attack establishes that the men being observed on film are indeed the 'good guys', even as they embark on an act of 'terror'.[46]

The subject of the Holocaust has become central to the filmic output about the war and, as a result, to perspectives of resistance and collaboration. Directors of films about the Holocaust have often been keen to communicate that their film is based on a 'true story' or 'actual events' and that they aim to depict these events realistically. In the first decades after 1945, many fiction films used wartime footage. Some imitated the documentary style with voice-overs establishing the scene and alerting the viewer to important historical facts about the setting and characters. Other films went further and attempted to reproduce the filmic techniques of documentaries to convey more dramatically the notion that what the audience is about to see is as objectively close to the truth as it gets. Famously, Steven Spielberg went to great pains to do this for his blockbuster *Schindler's List* (1993). The story of Oskar Schindler's rescue of 1,200 Jews who worked in his factory near Cracow became well known through the prize-winning novel *Schindler's Ark* (1982) by Thomas Keneally. The film, a huge commercial success, revealed an unconventional hero who was a member of the Nazi Party. Spielberg's Shoah Foundation, which was established subsequently, ensured that every high school in the United States, and every secondary school in Britain, had a copy of the film.

---

[46] Claire Gorrara, 'Reviewing Gender and the Resistance: The Case of Lucie Aubrac', in Kedward and Wood, *Liberation of France,* 143–153; Graeme Hayes, 'Resistancialism Revisited: Masculinity and National Identity in Claude Berri's *Lucie Aubrac* (1997)', *Studies in French Cinema,* 1/2 (2001), 108–117.

Some directors and members of the viewing public have been troubled by the ethical considerations of portraying the Holocaust realistically. Debates about the Holocaust on film, and about what it can and should depict, relate to debates about resistance and collaboration on film. Philosopher Theodor Adorno said: 'After Auschwitz to write a poem is barbaric.'[47] Holocaust survivor and intellectual Elie Wiesel was critical of attempts to recreate the experiences and fate of Jews in the Final Solution. He wrote: 'One does not imagine the unimaginable. And in particular, one does not show it on screen.'[48] Claude Lanzmann did not attempt to recreate the death camp in *Shoah* (1985) and has been disparaging of directors like Spielberg for attempting to do so. Lanzmann uses no footage or images from the 1940s. His film is firmly placed in the present. His goal was to explain how the killing took place. He was determined to find and interview those, including Jews like Abraham Bomba whom we discussed in Chapter 5, who had been 'enlisted to do the dirtiest work, guiding victims into the gas chambers, removing bodies from and cleaning the gas chambers after an execution, and cremating or otherwise disposing of the corpses'.[49] Though he collected interviews with individuals involved in rescue, Lanzmann left these out of his film because they did not contribute to the story of trauma and complicity that he wanted to tell.

Lanzmann is self-consciously ahistorical, as are many others for whom the memory of resistance and collaboration is not about the past, but about the present. Lanzmann speaks of the 'void' left by the death camps, to which he refers as '*non-lieux de mémoire*'.[50] The 'memory' of the Shoah must be lived in the present to retain its significance and sacredness, even if it entails traumatising people and even if, to elicit that response, the film must be contrived. Lanzmann has said that if he had come across film footage of gas chambers he would never have used it. In fact, he 'would have preferred to destroy it'.[51] Implicit in this statement is the belief that

---

[47] In Rosenstone, *History on Film/Film on History*, 135.

[48] In Rosenstone, *History on Film/Film on History*, 135.

[49] Aaron Kerner, *Film and the Holocaust: New Perspectives on Dramas, Documentaries, and Experimental Films* (New York: Continuum, 2011), 205.

[50] Raye Farr, 'Some Reflections on Claude Lanzmann's Approach to the Examination of the Holocaust', in Toby Haggith and Joanna Newman (eds), *Holocaust and the Moving Image: Representations in Film and Television since 1933* (London: Wallflower Press, 2005), 161–167, 164.

[51] Claude Lanzmann, quoted in David Rodowick (ed.), 'Seminar with Claude Lanzmann, 11 April 1990', *Yale French Studies*, 79 (1991), 82–99, 99.

there is a fine line between memorialisation and exploitation, regardless of filmmakers' intentions. There is also always the danger of violating the history of the Holocaust for an unethical (personal or commercial) end.

Issues raised in the memory wars relating to resistance and collaboration on film go beyond historical truth and the question of who was responsible for the Holocaust or why it came about. Questions about ownership of the past, honouring the memory of the deceased, and the commercial aesthetic (making good films that make money) are all intertwined in these debates. At the same time, the commercial aesthetic makes it more likely that certain topics will be privileged over others. Issues of gender and religion, if they are considered in relation to resistance and collaboration, are frequently treated in a superficial fashion. Films of varying quality, such as *Valkyrie* (2008), *Defiance* (2008), *L'Armée du crime* (2009), and *Inglourious Basterds* (2009) attest to the fact that the dominant filmic image of heroic masculine resistance has persisted over the decades and that the form of the suspenseful resistance film has not lost its appeal. With few exceptions – such as *Roma città aperta* – priests, members of religious orders, and the Catholic laity appear only fleetingly in such films. Thus, the medium teaches us little about what propelled believers or of the importance of faith in their lives. Furthermore, war has become the simple backdrop to the Holocaust narrative even though it was the very condition that made it possible. The disconnect between the highly theorised and complex explanations of the origins of and complicity in the Holocaust, and popular evocations of the Holocaust on film, is considerable. There is no reason to imagine that this chasm will be bridged in the near future, the critical success of a film like *Son of Saul* (2015) notwithstanding. As long as this remains the case, the memory wars will continue to be fought on the screen whereby the 'usual suspects' of resistance and collaboration are presented in different national settings.

The memory of resistance and collaboration in contemporary Europe

Public narratives of resistance and collaboration have always been politicised. This is true, not just of academic texts, but of all the other *lieux de mémoire*. Moreover, the various strands of public memory culture are entangled. All are connected in the common resistance/collaboration paradigm which is used by almost everybody to organise knowledge about the social history of World War II.

In many European countries, politicised debates about the nature of World War II remain prominent in public memory culture. In particular, the revival of populist nationalism across Europe resulted in attempts to challenge traditional narratives. This in turn provoked controversy, both within and between states. Prominent examples of countries where the memory of the war is still divisive include Belgium, Bosnia, Croatia, Hungary, Poland, Serbia, Slovakia, the Baltic states, and Russia. Here, we shall illustrate the point with two examples: Ukraine and Italy.

Memory politics in contemporary Ukraine

Politics in Ukraine have been fractured by 'memory wars' to a greater extent than in any other European country. The overthrow of President Viktor Yanukovych in February 2014, the subsequent Russian annexation of Crimea, and the outbreak of civil war in south-east Ukraine, were all directly related to fissures in public memory culture. Each of the main protagonists in the Ukrainian conflict was committed to a version of the past which was antagonistic to the narratives of rival actors.

The Ukrainian nationalists who seized power in 2014 conceptualised their project as the latest phase of an age-old struggle to achieve independence from Russian imperialism. Many of them were sympathetic to the memory of those Ukrainians who had fought against Soviet power in the 1940s, in particular the Organisation of Ukrainian Nationalists (OUN) and its armed wing, the Ukrainian Insurgent Army (UPA). They venerated Stepan Bandera, the leader of the OUN. Statues of Bandera were erected throughout western Ukraine and a major thoroughfare in Kiev was named after him, while torch-light parades were held on his birthday. During the 'Maidan' protest movement which toppled Yanukovych, demonstrators carried placards bearing Bandera's image and hung a giant portrait of him in the town hall.[52] In 2015 the Ukrainian parliament voted to make it illegal 'publicly to exhibit a disrespectful attitude' to the OUN, UPA, and other Ukrainian 'freedom fighters' of World War II.[53]

---

[52] 'Ukraine's Revolution and the Far Right', BBC News, 7 March 2014. Available at: www.bbc.com/news/world-europe-26468720 (accessed 20 December 2016).

[53] John-Paul Himka, 'Legislating Historical Truth: Ukraine's Laws of 9 April 2015', *Ab Imperio*, 21 April 2015.

Pro-Russian separatists in Ukraine told a very different story. In their view, the OUN, the UPA, and Bandera were traitors and collaborators, and the public rehabilitation of wartime Ukrainian nationalists was proof that the post-Yanukovych government was fascist in all but name. Among Russophiles who were hostile to the new regime in Kiev, the old narrative of World War II as a 'Great Patriotic War' against fascism was sacrosanct. This was also the view of the Russian government. The Russian authorities relentlessly denounced the historical revisionism of Kiev, while stressing more than ever before the achievements of the Red Army and Soviet partisans. Indeed, the memory of the 'Great Patriotic War' became the central plank of the Putin regime's Russian nationalism.[54]

However, the fragmentation of historical memory in Ukraine was more than a dispute between two opposing sides. Only a minority of Ukrainians expressed a positive attitude towards Bandera, the OUN, or the UPA.[55] In large parts of Ukraine there was still a deep attachment to old, Soviet-era traditions of commemorating the victories of the Red Army and the partisans. On the other hand, the majority, including most Russophone Ukrainians, were also opposed to the version of history used by the Putin regime to legitimise its military intervention. In other words, most people's understanding of the past was at odds with those of both the Kiev and the Moscow governments. The complicated nature of memory politics in Ukraine was often overlooked by foreign commentators who – in effect – imposed a simplistic resistance/collaboration binary onto a complex situation.

Memory politics in contemporary Italy

In the four decades after the end of World War II, politics in Italy was dominated by two political parties: the Christian Democrats (DC) and the Communist Party (PCI). Both parties claimed to be the heirs of the resistance. In the Christian Democratic tradition, the resistance was celebrated as

---

[54] Boris Dubin, 'Errinern als staatliche Veranstaltung: Geschichte und Herrschaft in Russland', *Osteuropa*, 58/6 (2008), 57–66; Igor Torbakov, 'History, Memory and National Identity: Understanding the Politics of History and Memory Wars in Post-Soviet Lands', *Demokratizatsiya*, 19/3 (2011), 209–232.

[55] 'Almost Half of Ukrainians have Negative Attitude to Bandera – Poll', *Interfax*, 5 May 2014. Available at: <www.interfax.com/newsinf.asp?pg=4&id=502455> (accessed 20 December 2016); Ivan Katchanovski, 'The Politics of World War II in Contemporary Ukraine', *Journal of Slavic Military Studies*, 27/2 (2014), 210–233.

a cross-class, patriotic movement against foreign occupation. By contrast, the PCI portrayed the resistance, not only as a movement of national liberation, but also as part of the continuing struggle for social justice against Italian elites. Competing versions of Italy's wartime history were articulated by historians, filmmakers, novelists, journalists, political activists, and politicians.[56]

In the 1980s, the dominant narratives of World War II in Italy were destabilised by political developments. The DC became mired in corruption scandals and the party dissolved itself in 1994. Meanwhile, the PCI suffered a serious decline in the 1980s and fragmented entirely after the collapse of the Soviet Bloc. As a result, the narratives that had dominated public memory culture since 1945 were weakened. A space opened up for an alternative, nationalist account of World War II which had thitherto been marginal, but which eventually became so popular that it provided a platform for the rise to power of Silvio Berlusconi and his populist right-wing party, Forza Italia.[57]

As always, the role of historians was of importance. Renzo De Felice and other scholars published a stream of books and articles that attacked the Communist 'myth' of the partisan resistance. They focused instead on the indiscriminate violence of the partisans and on the murder of alleged collaborators in the immediate post-war period. According to De Felice and his colleagues, the Italian republic had been constructed on this 'myth', which in turn had granted the Communists far too prominent a role in public life, and had seriously undermined the strength of Italian patriotism.[58]

Such views proved influential, not only in academic circles, but also with the Italian public. In 2003, journalist Giampaolo Pansa published a book entitled *Il Sangue dei vinti* (Blood of the Losers) which attacked the heroic idea of the Italian resistance movement and catalogued the alleged crimes of Communist partisans. The book was an immediate bestseller. In the first year after its publication, it sold 350,000 copies.[59]

---

[56] Andrea Cossu, 'Commemoration and Processes of Appropriation: The Italian Communist Party and the Italian Resistance (1943–48)', *Memory Studies*, 4/4 (2011), 386–400; Charles F. Delzell, 'The Italian Anti-Fascist Resistance in Retrospect: Three Decades of Historiography', *Journal of Modern History*, 47/1 (1975), 66–96; Philip Cooke, *The Legacy of the Italian Resistance* (Basingstoke: Palgrave Macmillan, 2011), Chapters 1–5.

[57] Art, 'Memory Politics in Western Europe'.

[58] Luca Baldissara, 'Auf dem Weg zu einer bipolaren Geschichtsschreibung? Der öffentliche Gebrauch der Resistenza in einer geschichtslosen Gegenwart', *Quellen und Forschungen aus italienischen Archiven und Bibliotheken*, 82 (2002), 590–637.

[59] Lowe, *Savage Continent*, 161–162.

Pansa was denounced, not just by the Italian Left, but also by scholars who pointed out that his methodology was slapdash and that his 'revelations' consisted of little more than a sensationalist montage of secondary texts.[60] Nonetheless, as a famous journalist backed by mass media, Pansa could reach a mass audience historians could not. Inspired by Pansa's book, the director Michele Soavi made a film, also called *Il Sangue dei vinti*, which conveyed the same message, and which likewise attracted controversy when it premiered at the Rome Film Festival in 2008.[61]

Another iconic moment in the public articulation of revisionist history was the screening, in 1994, of a television series called *Combat Film*. Using footage recorded by the U.S. Army during the war, *Combat Film* presented images of wartime suffering in such a way that the killings of collaborators by partisans, and even the execution of Mussolini, were equated with massacres by the Nazis. This shook Italians of liberal and left-wing inclinations. Barbara Spinelli wrote in *La Stampa*: 'the whole climate in Italy has altered. ... A ban has been removed, and a taboo has been broken. ... Fascism is now just an opinion like any other.'[62]

Right-wing politicians – and above all Berlusconi – were eager to bring this nationalist revision of Italian history into the political arena. At the same time as denigrating the resistance, they advocated what they regarded as a more 'balanced' view of the Fascist period in general, and of Mussolini in particular. In January 2013, Berlusconi provoked an uproar when he made a speech in which he claimed that Mussolini was not as bad as the history books would have us believe. All such attempts to normalise the Fascist past have been highly controversial.[63] In Italy, as in Ukraine and other European countries, the history of World War II – and in particular of resistance and collaboration – cast a long shadow.

---

[60] Massimo Storchi, 'Post-war Violence in Italy: A Struggle for Memory', *Modern Italy*, 12/2 (2007), 237–250.

[61] Camillo de Marco, '*Il Sangue dei vinti* Sparks Controversy', *Cineuropa*, 26 October 2008: cineuropa.org/nw.aspx?t=newsdetail&l=en&did=87426 (accessed 13 January 2017); Giacomo Lichtner, *Fascism in Italian Cinema since 1945: The Politics and Aesthetics of Memory* (Basingstoke: Palgrave, 2013), Chapter 2.

[62] Quoted in Guido Crainz, 'The Representation of Fascism and the Resistance in the Documentaries of Italian State Television', in R.J.B. Bosworth and Patrizia Dogliani (eds), *Italian Fascism: History, Memory and Representation* (Basingstoke: Palgrave Macmillan, 1999), 124–140, 136–137.

[63] Gareth Pritchard and Desislava Gancheva, 'Collaborator: No Longer a Dirty Word?', *History Today*, 64/12 (2014), 31–36.

Conclusion

Resistance and collaboration have been remembered and re-staged differently in different contexts. Memories can be stored in the public domain as well as privately, and then reshaped over time. Officially, the war has always been depicted as a struggle between good and evil. Resistance and collaboration had to be fashioned accordingly in collective memory. Privately, one's experience may have called that dichotomy into question. Normally, this was best left unsaid, especially in politically volatile or in politically repressive states.

The intense focus on resistance and collaboration in the public sphere allowed wider questions about the power of states in the war, and the alliances made to win it, to be swept under the carpet. Two very distinctive approaches to resistance and collaboration emerged on the continent. In the West, there were debates. Cultural product like film reflected, and in many cases sparked, such debates. In due course, a kind of consensus emerged in public life around three key elements: the celebration of resistance, the recognition that it was a minority activity, and contrition for the role of local populations in the Holocaust. The extent to which populist nationalism in Western Europe can challenge this consensus remains to be seen.

Memory politics in Communist countries developed along different lines. There was little reflection or public debate, and the identity of the heroes and villains of World War II became a matter of state dogma. The simplistic depiction of these cardboard-cut-out heroes and villains led to cynicism. Public memory culture in half of Europe was thereby infantilised by Communist bureaucrats whose goal was to construct a narrative that legitimised their power. Since Communism collapsed, the gap that opened up in public memory was largely filled by a nationalist version of the past which, while anti-Communist, demonstrated many of the same features of the old Communist narrative: it imposed rigid dichotomies, it focused on the victimisation of one's own people, and it was insensitive to the suffering of others. It was also intolerant of rival interpretations. The rise of nationalist history in former Communist countries demonstrated the ongoing capacity of elites to instrumentalise resistance and collaboration for political purposes.

Conclusion

In this book we have provided an overview of the development of the historiography of resistance and collaboration. In part, the evolution of the academic literature has been driven by the findings of generations of historians who have critiqued previous interpretations, often on the basis of new kinds of primary sources and innovative methodological approaches. One important trend over time has been a greater interest in the social history of resistance and collaboration. Another significant change has been the increasing importance of the Holocaust as it has been incorporated into our understanding of resistance and – more especially – of collaboration. Since the collapse of the Soviet Bloc, there has been a geographical shift in the focus of the literature. Though the ongoing contribution of the scholarship on France, Italy, Germany, and other Western European countries remains significant, there is an expanding body of pioneering work on the wartime experiences of people in Eastern and Southern Europe.

From the outset, historians of resistance and collaboration both influenced and were influenced by the political context in which they were writing. Two moments in the political history of post-war Europe were of particular importance. The first of these occurred in the 1960s and 1970s, when the more radical political climate of Western Europe led to a re-evaluation of patriotic myths and the creation of counter-myths. The second was the collapse of Communism, which opened up hitherto inaccessible archives and allowed scholars to ask of countries such as Poland, Ukraine, Russia, and the Yugoslav successor states the same kinds of questions that had been asked of wartime France, Italy, and Germany. The historiography of the Holocaust, in particular, has benefited from this development, and we can now see emerging a genuinely transnational history of genocide that seeks to resolve the tension between 'bottom-up' and 'top-down' approaches to the study of Hitler's empire. But conflicting interpretations of the role of local populations in the Holocaust have also led to tensions. In the scholarship of Germany and France, it has long been accepted that many thousands of local officials and 'ordinary' people cooperated in the persecution of Jews. In the historiography of wartime Hungary, Poland, Ukraine, and the Baltic states, the degree and character of local involvement are the subject of controversies that have spilled over into domestic politics and international relations.

One thing that has not changed in the historiography is the centrality of what we have called the resistance/collaboration paradigm. Even before the war was over, Hitler's European subjects were being classified as resisters, collaborators, or victims. This tendency became more pronounced during the immediate post-war period when states began to reward, punish, or compensate people on the basis of their wartime behaviour and experiences. Despite the many changes that have occurred in the historiography, historians ever since have used the binary concepts of resistance and collaboration as their main points of orientation.

We do not argue that the resistance/collaboration paradigm should be discarded. As descriptions of kinds of behaviour, both terms have their uses. Taking up arms to fight the Nazis was certainly a form of resistance, and taking up arms to fight for them was a form of collaboration. Rescuing Jews was resistance. Helping the Nazis to round them up and kill them was the opposite. The words resister and collaborator can also be applied without reservation to individuals like Jean Moulin and Vidkun Quisling, as we pointed out at the start of the book.

We should also be aware, however, that there are limitations to the resistance/collaboration paradigm. Like any form of organising knowledge about the past, it tends to highlight certain processes and phenomena, and conceal others. This is why so much behaviour that cannot easily be regarded as either resistance or collaboration is overlooked by historians, or mislabelled, or discussed purely within the context of a depoliticised history of everyday life. But even as a means of understanding resistance and collaboration, the paradigm has certain drawbacks. In particular, it tends to focus our attention on high-profile examples of resistance and collaboration. What is rarely acknowledged is that both collaboration and (more especially) resistance were social processes, the roots of which stretched deep into civil society.

Conclusion

The blanket application of the paradigm has also led to problems with the analysis of gender since, in the patriarchal societies of the 1940s, high-profile acts in the public sphere were more likely to be carried out by men. From the 1970s onwards there has been an attempt to incorporate gender as a category of analysis, but it has been applied asymmetrically. Historians' understanding of collaboration has been broadened to include female 'bystanders' and 'co-perpetrators'. Yet the image of the resister remains epically heroic and masculine. Another major problem with the resistance/collaboration paradigm is that it is teleological. Behaviour is interpreted as either resistant or collaborationist based on the degree to which it either facilitated or impeded the victory of the Allies, or the degree to which it facilitated or impeded the implementation of certain Nazi policies, especially the Holocaust. This is the case even when there is no demonstrable link between the behaviour in question and those outcomes.

If, then, we move beyond the resistance/collaboration paradigm, what might a new historiography of Hitler's empire look like? Above all, what we see are human beings and communities under enormous stress as a result of a total war being waged by a totalising dictatorship. How people responded to the extraordinary crisis that confronted them depended in part on what they brought with them into the war in terms of ideas in their heads and social relations in their communities. Pre-existing anti-Semitism in Poland influenced the way that non-Jewish Poles responded to the persecution of their Jewish neighbours. But, at the same time, deep Polish traditions of resistance to foreign occupation were a precondition for the widespread civil resistance that we discussed in Chapter 4.

On the other hand, there was little in people's responses to Nazi rule that was predetermined. The war as it was lived by Europeans was unpredictable and often destabilising. People who came from the same town, the same ethnic group, the same political and religious background often had divergent experiences. Their lives sometimes took radically different directions based on good or bad luck, on split-second decisions, or on the basis of decisions that, at the time, seemed only of minor significance. The contingencies of the experience of the war thus interacted in complex ways with pre-existing social structures and worldviews.

Yet, if we survey European society as a whole, we can identify some fairly clear patterns. Almost everywhere in Hitler's empire, normal civil administration broke down during the last three years of the war, in part as a result

Conclusion

of the stresses of total war, and in part as a result of the increasingly radical policies of the Nazis. Europeans under Nazi rule were increasingly dominated but less and less governed. What government there was became increasingly terroristic and arbitrary. Under these circumstances, a crucial factor that influenced people's behaviour was their definition of the border between 'us' and 'them'. In a country like Denmark, which possessed deep traditions of liberal democracy and a strong, inclusive sense of civic community, collaborators were socially and politically isolated and Jews were rescued. In other parts of Europe, where society was fragmented on ethnic, religious, and political lines, the brutality and arbitrariness of Nazi rule led to social collapse and the downward spiral of communal violence.

Despite the fact that so much has been written about World War II, examining these social processes has only just begun. If scholarship and public debate are to move beyond what has been achieved already, a shift of focus will be necessary. Hitherto, historians have been preoccupied with the concepts of resistance and collaboration. But there is still plenty of room for approaches to this history that place the lives of human beings and their communities at the centre of historical analysis. Thinking in terms of the social history of politics of Hitler's empire is one such approach. To understand why people behaved as they did, we must be able to see the situation as they saw it, in the light of their own lived experiences and the knowledge that was available to them at the time.

Suggestions for further reading

There is a substantial literature on resistance and collaboration in Hitler's empire. In the footnotes we have referred to a number of the key texts, but it is not possible for a book of this length to be comprehensive. Here we list some of the best examples of work on a range of topics that we have discussed. We have also included some of the older texts which have been important in the evolution of the historiography. Many of the books provide extensive bibliographies, which readers will find useful.

Arendt, Hannah, *The Origins of Totalitarianism* (New York: Harcourt, Brace, 1951).
Bartov, Omer, *The Eastern Front, 1941–45: German Troops and the Barbarisation of Warfare*, 2nd edn (Basingstoke: Palgrave, 2001).
Batinić, Jelena, *Gender, Revolution, and War: The Mobilization of Women in the Yugoslav Partisan Resistance during World War II* (Stanford, CA: Stanford University Press, 2015).
Behan, Tom, *The Long Awaited Moment: The Working Class and the Italian Communist Party in Milan, 1943–1948* (New York: Peter Lang, 1997).
Belco, Victoria C., *War, Massacre, and Recovery in Central Italy, 1943–1948* (Toronto: University of Toronto Press, 2010).
Berkhoff, Karel C., *Harvest of Despair: Life and Death in Ukraine under Nazi Rule* (Cambridge, MA: Belknap Press of Harvard University Press, 2004).
Browning, Christopher R., *Ordinary Men: Reserve Police Battalion 101 and the Final Solution in Poland* (New York: Aaron Asher, 1992).
Burleigh, Michael and Wippermann, Wolfgang, *The Racial State: Germany 1933–1945* (Cambridge: Cambridge University Press, 1991).

Cooke, Phillip and Shepherd, Ben (eds), *European Resistance in the Second World War* (Barnsley: Praetorian Press, 2013).

Dawidowicz, Lucy S., *The War against the Jews, 1933–1945* (New York: Holt, Rinehart and Winston, 1975).

Deák, István, *Europe on Trial: The Story of Collaboration, Resistance, and Retribution during World War II* (Boulder, CO: Westview Press, 2015).

Echternkamp, Jörg and Martens, Stefan (eds), *Experience and Memory: The Second World War in Europe* (New York: Berghahn, 2010).

Gildea, Robert, *Marianne in Chains: In Search of the German Occupation, 1940-1945* (London: Macmillan, 2002).

Gildea, Robert, Wieviorka, Olivier and Warring, Anette (eds), *Surviving Hitler and Mussolini: Daily Life in Occupied Europe* (Oxford: Berg, 2006).

Gross, Jan Tomasz, *Neighbors: The Destruction of the Jewish Community in Jedwabne, Poland* (Princeton, NJ: Princeton University Press, 2001).

Hæstrup, Jørgen, *European Resistance Movements, 1939–1945: A Complete History* (Westport, CT: Meckler, 1981).

Hilberg, Raul, *The Destruction of the European Jews* (Chicago, IL: Quadrangle Books, 1961, rev. edn, 3 vols, New York: Holmes & Meier, 1985).

Jackson, Julian, *France: The Dark Years 1940–1944* (Oxford: Oxford University Press, 2001).

Kalyvas, Stathis N., *The Logic of Violence in Civil War* (Cambridge: Cambridge University Press, 2006).

Kershaw, Ian, *Popular Opinion and Political Dissent in the Third Reich: Bavaria 1933–1945* (Oxford: Clarendon Press, 1983).

Koonz, Claudia, *Mothers in the Fatherland: Women, the Family, and Nazi Politics* (New York: St. Martin's Press, 1987).

Lower, Wendy, *Nazi Empire-Building and the Holocaust in Ukraine* (Chapel Hill, NC: University of North Carolina Press, 2005).

Lüdtke, Alf (ed.), *Everyday Life in Mass Dictatorship: Collusion and Evasion* (Basingstoke: Palgrave Macmillan, 2016).

Mazower, Mark, *Hitler's Empire: Nazi Rule in Occupied Europe* (London: Allen Lane, 2008).

Oliner, Samuel P. and Oliner, Pearl M., *The Altruistic Personality: Rescuers of Jews in Nazi Europe* (New York: Free Press, 1988).

Paxton, Robert O., *Vichy France: Old Guard and New Order, 1940–1944* (New York: Columbia University Press, 1972).

Suggestions for further reading

Rousso, Henry, *The Vichy Syndrome: History and Memory in France since 1944* (Cambridge, MA: Harvard University Press, 1991).
Schoenbaum, David, *Hitler's Social Revolution: Class and Status in Nazi Germany 1933–1939* (Garden City, NY: Doubleday, 1966).
Semelin, Jacques, *Unarmed against Hitler: Civilian Resistance in Europe, 1939–1943* (Westport, CT: Praeger, 1993).
Slaughter, Jane, *Women and the Italian Resistance, 1943–1945* (Denver, CO: Arden Press, 1997).
Snyder, Timothy, *Bloodlands: Europe between Hitler and Stalin* (New York: Basic Books, 2010).
Stone, Dan (ed.), *The Historiography of the Holocaust* (Basingstoke: Palgrave Macmillan, 2004).
Stone, Dan, *Histories of the Holocaust* (Oxford: Oxford University Press, 2010).
Wieviorka, Olivier, *The French Resistance* (Cambridge, MA: Belknap Press of Harvard University Press, 2016).

Index

For the reader's convenience, partisans, militias and other paramilitary formations are listed under the heading *armed bands*, individual historians mentioned in the main text under *historians*, film titles and directors under *film, television and theatre*, and Nazi organisations and concepts under *NSDAP* and *Nazi ideology* respectively.

Abetz, Otto   9
Adorno, Theodor   180
AK (Home Army) *see* armed bands
Albania   26, 52
Alltagsgeschichte see historiography of resistance and collaboration
Alsace-Lorraine   2, 8, 67, 151
   see also France
Amsterdam   21
Anouilh, Jean *see* film, television and theatre
anti-Communism   10, 29, 56, 57, 59, 62, 63, 67, 80, 107, 118, 141, 182, 186
anti-partisan warfare   13, 15, 35, 50, 56, 57, 59, 60, 64, 67, 93
   see also reprisals
anti-Semitism   10, 31, 105, 106–10, 111, 113, 116, 117, 129, 145, 146, 172, 189
Arājs, Viktors   56
Ardeatine Caves   13
armed bands   24, 50–72, 97, 111
   AK (Home Army)   20, 51, 52, 66
   Baltic states   56
   bandits   16, 24, 56–7, 64, 66, 70, 73
   Black Brigades   15, 57
   Bonny-Lafont Gang   11–12
   Chetniks   34, 35, 51, 52, 62, 66

Combat   52, 67
Communist   170, 174–5, 184–5
   see also Communists
EDES (National Republic Greek League)   52, 62–3
EKKA (National and Social Liberation)   52
ELAS (Greek People's Liberation Army)   20, 51, 52, 53, 57, 60, 63, 64
Forest Brothers   34, 71
FTP (Francs-tireurs et partisans)   52, 66
Garibaldi Brigades   53, 67
GL (People's Guard)   52
Italian   25, 54, 67
Jewish   53, 54, 121
Justice and Freedom   53
Légion Belge   52
Libération   52
Maquis   55, 114
Matteotti Brigades   53
Milice   15, 57, 59
Milorg   52
Mouvement National Royaliste   52
NLM (National Liberation Movement)   51, 52
NOV (People's Liberation Army)   20, 25, 50, 52, 53–4, 62, 67

Index

armed bands (*Continued*)
  NOW (National Military Organisation)   51, 52
  NSZ (National Armed Forces)   52
  Omakaitse   15
  Osoppo   67
  Partisans Armés   52
  Peasant Battalions (Bataliony Chłopskie)   52
  Republican National Guard   57
  Reserve Police Battalion 101   112–13
  Schutzmannschaften   15, 56, 59
  Security Battalions   15, 57, 60, 63, 64
  SNOF (Slav-Macedonian National Liberation Front)   53
  Soviet partisans   24, 25, 51, 52, 53, 57, 60, 70–1, 183
  Tartar militia   60–1
  UPA (Ukrainian Insurgent Army)   34, 51, 52, 62, 71, 182–3
  Ustaše   15, 56, 62, 91–2, 127
  'white-arm-banders'   56
Arrow Cross *see* fascist and collaborationist parties
'asocials'   107
  see also Nazi ideology
Athens   21
attentisme see historiography of resistance and collaboration
Aubrac, Lucie and Raymond   179
Auschwitz *see* concentration camps
Austria   1, 156

Baltic states and Balts   2, 5, 24, 34, 56, 57, 64, 69, 71, 182, 188
  see also Estonia; Latvia; Lithuania
Bandera, Stepan   35, 182–3
Barbie, Klaus   168
Bavaria   4, 154–5
  see also Germany
Bavaria Project *see* historiography of resistance and collaboration
Belarus   106
  see also Belorussia

Belgium and Belgians   2, 20, 21, 26, 52, 58, 60, 69, 151, 170, 182
  Flanders and Flemings   170
  Wallonia and Walloons   57, 170
Belorussia   2, 5, 53, 56, 57, 66, 122, 170
  see also Belarus
Berlin   140
Berlusconi, Silvio   184, 185
BHO (Berg-und Hüttenwerksgesellschaft)   6
Bielski, Tuvia   53, 122
Black Brigades *see* armed bands
black market   10–12, 77, 133, 151, 159
Blitz   100
Bohemia and Moravia *see* Czechoslovakia
Bomba, Abraham   120–1, 180
  see also film, television and theatre: *Shoah* (1985)
Bonny-Lafont Gang *see* armed bands
Bosnia and Bosnians   58, 66, 182
  see also Yugoslavia
Britain and the British   xx, 28, 58, 62, 63, 67, 70, 100, 159–60, 167, 179
'brown priests' *see* Catholic Church
Buchenwald *see* concentration camps
Bulgaria and Bulgarians   3, 4, 26, 57, 170

Cagoule   59
Canadians   67
Canisianum *see* Catholic Church
Carmelites *see* Catholic Church
Catholic Action *see* Catholic Church
Catholic Church   19–20, 138–62, 169, 175, 181
  'brown priests'   140
  Canisianum   156
  Carmelites   155–7
  Catholic Action   149
  Dames de Charité   152
  Jesuits   156
  Sisters of Notre-Dame de Sion   151–2

195

Catholic Church (*Continued*)
  Society of St Vincent de
    Paul   150–1
  youth associations   149–50, 153
Caucasus   58
Central Headquarters of the Partisan
  Movement   54, 69
Chambon-sur-Lignon   130
Channel Islands   65
Charlemagne Division *see* Waffen SS
Chechnya and Chechens   26, 58
Chirac, Jacques   168
Christian Democrats (DC)   183–4
churches, clergy and Christians   7, 12,
  29, 30, 39, 41, 45, 66, 76, 86, 97,
  111, 125, 130, 181
  Greek-Rite Orthodox   66
  Orthodox Church   7
  Protestant churches   130
  see also Catholic Church
  see also Jehovah's Witnesses
'clerical fascism'   141
Cold War   27, 32, 80
collaboration
  armed collaboration   15–16
  Catholic   139, 140–1, 144, 147, 153,
    160
  see also Catholic Church
  definitions   24–8, 37–8
  economic   17–18
  functional   18, 115
  see also commemoration of
    collaboration
  see also historiography of resistance
    and collaboration
collaborationism   22, 33, 45, 46,
  57, 60, 63, 75, 76, 77, 78, 88,
  91–2, 95, 103, 131, 168, 189
  anti-Semitism   107, 111
  Catholic Church   139, 140, 146,
    148, 162
  definition   15
  film   177–8
  Vichy   26–7, 59, 84, 129
collaborators (post-war)   26–7, 166–8,
  170, 188

Collegium Canisianum *see* Catholic
  Church: Canisianum
commemoration of
  collaboration   26–7, 163–8,
    170, 172–3, 176–9, 180, 182,
    185–6
commemoration of resistance   24–5,
  166–7, 168–71, 172–6, 178–9,
  180, 183–6
Communists   xvii, xviii, 10, 20, 26,
  32–3, 36, 53, 54, 90, 107, 116,
  170, 184, 186, 187
  Albania   52
  Belgium   20, 52
  Bulgaria   170
  Denmark   20
  France   20, 52, 66, 169–70
  Germany   12, 169
  Greece   20, 52, 62, 63, 64, 67
  Hungary   178
  Italy   20, 53, 57, 66, 67, 169, 183–5
  Netherlands   20, 169–70
  Poland   52, 175
  USSR   36, 51, 52, 130, 170
  Yugoslavia   20, 52, 62, 127, 168, 170
  see also armed bands
complicity and collective guilt   18–19,
  26–7, 35, 46–7, 82–5, 93, 100–1,
  104, 108, 110–17, 120–1, 131,
  133, 139–40, 159, 168, 186, 188
concentration camps (including
  transit camps, labour camps
  and death camps)   xiv (map),
  10, 12, 39, 42, 84, 92, 97, 99,
  106, 109, 111–12, 113, 114, 119,
  120–1, 122, 126, 154, 180
  Auschwitz   117, 123, 129, 180
  Buchenwald   33, 163
  Dachau   140, 154
  Drancy   128
  Theresienstadt   123–4
  Treblinka   120
Cossacks   58
counter-insurgency *see* anti-partisan
  warfare
Courcier, Huguette   153

Index

Cracow 179
crime 11–12, 39, 70, 133
  see also black market
Crimea 16, 26, 60–1, 182
Croat Peasant Party 127
Croatia and Croats 2, 3, 15, 34, 37, 56, 57, 66, 91, 127, 141, 148, 160–1, 168, 182
  see also Yugoslavia
culture wars 99–100
Czechoslovakia, Czechs and Slovaks 2, 26, 67, 91, 99, 141, 148, 166, 182
  see also Slovak Republic
  see also Sudetenland

Dachau *see* concentration camps
Dagestanis 58
Darnand, Joseph 59, 84
D-Day landings *see* Normandy
death camps *see* concentration camps
Demjanjuk, John 168
denazification 27
Denmark and Danes 2, 10, 16–17, 19, 20, 21, 26, 58, 60, 69, 126, 127–8, 190
denunciations 45, 47–8, 77, 83, 93–4, 166, 176
  see also informers
disabled people 12
doctors *see* medicine and medical personnel
Doriot, Jacques 15, 59, 84
Drancy *see* concentration camps

East Germany (GDR) 26, 33, 169
Eastern Front 55, 57, 87, 105, 108, 111, 119, 137
eastern troops (*Osttruppen*) *see* Wehrmacht
Eichmann, Adolf 30, 168
Einsatzgruppen *see* NSDAP: SS (Schutzstaffel)
ELAS (Greek People's Liberation Army) *see* armed bands
Endlösung see Final Solution (*Endlösung*)
Entgrenzung see historiography of resistance and collaboration

Estonia and Estonians 10, 15, 58
  see also Baltic states and Balts
ethnic cleansing 26
eugenics 106–7
  see also Nazi ideology
'euthanasia' campaign 29, 87, 147

fascist and collaborationist parties
  Arrow Cross (Hungary) 15
  National Gathering (Norway) 15, 91
  National Socialist Movement (Netherlands) 15, 91
  PPF (French Popular Party) 15, 59
Fascists (Italy) xviii, 27, 80, 85, 89, 137, 146, 159, 178, 185
film, television and theatre 76–7, 85, 89, 99, 124, 163, 170–1, 172–81, 184–6
  Anouilh, Jean, *Antigone* (1944) 96
  L'Armée des ombres (Army of Shadows, 1969) 176
  L'Armée du crime (2009) 181
  La Bataille du rail (Battle of the Railways, 1946) 175
  Bertolucci, Bernardo 178
  Casablanca (1942) 174
  Le Chagrin et la pitié (The Sorrow and the Pity, 1969) 176–7
  Charlotte Grey (2001) 173
  Combat Film (1994) 185
  The Conformist (1970) 178
  Curtiz, Michael 174
  Defiance (2008) 53, 122, 181
  Les Femmes de l'ombre (Female Agents, 2008) 173
  The Guns of Navarone (1961) 173
  The Heroes of Telemark (1965) 173
  Holocaust (1978) 170–1
  Inglourious Basterds (2009) 181
  Kanał (1957) 175
  This Land is Mine (1943) 174
  Lacombe Lucien (1974) 177–8
  Lanzmann, Claude 120–1, 180–1
  Lucie Aubrac (1997) 173, 179
  Malle, Louis 177
  Melville, Jean-Pierre 176

film, television and theatre (*Continued*)
  Mephisto (1981)   178
  Ophüls, Marcel   176–7
  Office de Radio-Télévision
    Française   176
  Pokolenie (A Generation, 1955)
    175
  Popiół i diament (Ashes and
    Diamonds, 1958)   175
  Renoir, Jean   174
  Roma città aperta (Rome, Open City,
    1945)   175, 181
  Rossellini, Roberto   175
  Il Sangue dei vinti (2008)   185
  Schindler's List (1993)   179, 180
  Spielberg, Steven   179, 180
  Szabó, István   178
  Shoah (1985)   120–1, 180
  Soavi, Michele   185
  Son of Saul (2015)   181
  Valkyrie (2008)   181
  Un Village français (2009–17)   171
  Wajda, Andrzej   175
Final Solution (*Endlösung*)   106, 108,
  109, 110, 113, 180
  see also Holocaust
Finland   3, 4
food   xviii, 10–11, 24, 54–5, 56–7, 60,
  70, 75, 120, 125, 133, 135, 150,
  155
  see also black market
forced labour   6, 13–14, 17, 21, 55,
  94–5, 100, 121, 154–5
  see also STO
Forest Brothers *see* armed bands
Forza Italia   184
France and the French   10, 14, 77–8,
  126, 134, 154
  administration   xiii (map), 8–9, 16
  'ambiguities' 95–7, 98, 102
  Catholic Church   147, 148–53,
    155–7, 158–9
  collaboration   18, 25–7, 57, 30,
    36–7, 46, 52, 58, 59, 84, 91, 166,
    167, 168
  Communists   20, 169–70

film and television   171, 173, 175,
    176–8, 179
  Holocaust   110–11, 127, 128–30,
    114, 188
  memory culture   169–70
  resistance   21, 28, 24, 40, 46, 48, 52,
    55, 65, 66, 67, 69, 75–6, 84, 99,
    101–2, 169–70
  see also Vichy
Frank, Hans   2, 5
Friuli   67

Galen, Clemens August von   29, 147
Galicia   38, 59, 66, 117
gassing, gas chambers   108, 120, 121,
  180
Gauleiter   5
Gaulle, Charles de   28, 101, 103, 159,
  175, 177
GDR (German Democratic Republic)
  see East Germany
gender   xvi, 22, 25, 29–30, 40–1, 45,
  46–9, 53–4, 70–2, 78, 86, 91–7,
  100, 101, 133–4, 135, 137,
  142–4, 149, 151–3, 161, 166,
  169, 173, 176, 181, 189
Generalgouvernement   2, 5
  see also Poland and Poles
genocide   35, 88, 105, 108, 111, 112,
  113, 115, 116, 119, 120, 126,
  130, 187–8
  see also Holocaust
German Labour Front (DAF) *see*
  NSDAP
German Women's Welfare (DFW) *see*
  NSDAP
Germans, ethnic (non-Reich)   10,
  58, 66
Germany and Germans   11, 12, 14,
  56, 92–4, 97–8, 106–9, 119,
  154–5, 168
  administration   xi (map), 4–5
  Catholic Church   139–40, 146–7,
    154–5, 156
  film   172, 178

Germany and Germans (*Continued*)
  Holocaust   109, 112–13, 118–19, 172, 188
  resistance   20, 39, 40–1, 65, 92–4
  society   85–8, 89–90, 92–4
  totalitarianism   xvii, 79–83, 84–5, 90, 109
  young people   12, 39, 97, 168–9
  see also East Germany
  see also West Germany
Gesellschaft für deutsche Sprache (Society for the German Language)   171
  see also West Germany
Gestapo   37, 47, 80, 83, 93–4, 163
Gleichschaltung see Nazi ideology
Goebbels, Joseph   9, 109
Goering, Hermann   5, 14
Great Patriotic War   183
Great War *see* World War I
Greece and Greeks   2, 4, 11, 15, 20, 24, 52, 53, 54, 57, 60, 61, 62–3, 64, 67, 69, 73, 137–8
Greek-Rite Orthodox Church *see* churches, clergy and Christians
Grenoble   151–2

Habsburg Empire   38
Heydrich, Reinhard   2, 116
Hilfswillige (*Hiwis*) *see* Wehrmacht
Himmler, Heinrich   5, 7, 9, 58
historians and other academics
  Alano, Jomarie   71
  Andrieu, Claire   48
  Arendt, Hannah   90, 113
  Armstrong, John   68
  Aron, Robert   28
  Azéma, Jean-Pierre   29
  Bartov, Omer   137, 138
  Batinić, Jelena   71
  Battaglia, Roberto   69
  Behan, Tom   137, 138
  Belco, Victoria   137, 138
  Bergen, Doris   144
  Bhabha, Homi   165
  Bracher, Karl Dietrich   80, 86

  Broszat, Martin   29, 40–1, 42, 81, 109
  Browning, Christopher   112–13
  Bourtman, Ilya   167
  Burleigh, Michael   87
  Capdevila, Luc   166
  Cooke, Phillip   65
  Dahrendorf, Ralf   86
  Dallin, Alexander   69
  Dean, Martin   117
  De Felice, Renzo   184
  Delaney, John   154–5
  Diamond, Hanna   71
  Dietrich, Donald   146
  Evans, Richard   29
  Foot, M.R.D.   69
  Fulbrook, Mary   92
  Fuller, J.F.C.   68
  Furst, Juliane   71, 169
  Gellately, Robert   47, 83
  Gerlach, Christian   125
  Gildea, Robert   23
  Goldhagen, Daniel   31, 113
  Gottlieb, Roger   39
  Grenkovich, Leonid   68
  Gross, Jan   111, 117
  Grunberger, Richard   86
  Gutman, Yisrael   20
  Hæstrup, Jørgen   69–70
  Halbwachs, Maurice   163–4
  Harvey, Elizabeth   47
  Hawes, Stephen   65
  Herf, Jeffrey   86
  Hilberg, Raul   30–1, 112
  Hildebrand, Klaus   80, 86
  Hill, Alexander   68
  Himka, John-Paul   73
  Hofer, Walter   40
  Housden, Martyn   43–4
  Johnson, Eric   83
  Kalyvas, Stathis   73, 137–8
  Kershaw, Ian   29, 41, 42, 83, 86–7, 136, 137
  Koonz, Claudia   47, 83
  Kucherenko, Olga   37–8
  Laborie, Pierre   29

historians and other academics (*Continued*)
Lagrou, Pieter 136, 169
Lambert, Peter 85, 94
Liddell Hart, Basil 68
Lower, Wendy 138
Marcot, François 48
Mason, Tim 29
Mazower, Mark 73
Michel, Henri 69
Mommsen, Hans 109
Moore, Bob 65
Naimark, Norman 115
Nora, Pierre 164, 165
Northrop, Douglas xx
Oliner, Samuel 151
Pansa, Giampaolo 184–5
Pätzold, Kurt 109
Paxton, Robert 18, 29, 30, 36–7, 84
Peukert, Detlev 29, 42–3, 86, 136, 137, 152
Phayer, Michael 142
Ponomarenko, P.K. 69
Poznanski, Renée 128
Rings, Werner 42, 124
Rochet, Bénédicte 99
Rousso, Henry 29, 173
Sahlins, Peter 165
Saunders, Thomas 87
Schleunes, Karl 109
Schoenbaum, David 85–6
Schwartz, Paula 71
Semelin, Jacques 75
Shepherd, Ben 65
Slaughter, Jane 71
Snyder, Timothy 94, 107, 125–6, 128
Stone, Dan 115, 118
Tebinka, Jacek 39, 69
Vošahlíková, Pavla 99
Wachsmann, Nikolaus 84, 92
Warring, Anette 23
Weiss, Fabrice 99
White, Ralph 65
Wieviorka, Olivier 23, 39, 69
Wippermann, Wolfgang 87

Woodhouse, Christopher (Monty) 69
historiography of resistance and collaboration xv–xx, 45–9, 134–5, 187–90
agency inflation 88–95, 115
Alltagsgeschichte 81
attentisme 77–8, 100, 123
Bavaria Project 81
Communist 25, 26, 32–5, 68, 167, 169–70, 183–5, 186
diaspora 34, 35
East-Central Europe and the Balkans 25, 26, 32–7, 68, 94, 165, 166, 167, 169, 182–3, 186, 187–8
Entgrenzung 136
lieux de mémoire 164–6, 170–2, 180, 181
memory studies 163–5
Western Europe xix, 28–32, 69, 77–88, 95–7, 98, 100–2, 124, 165, 166, 172–3, 176–7, 184–6, 187–8
historiography of the Holocaust xix, 30–1, 108–19, 124, 131, 138, 165, 172, 187–8
Hitler, Adolf xx, 4, 5, 6, 7, 8, 20, 30, 83, 89, 106, 108, 109, 110, 118
Hitler's empire (administration) x–xiv (maps), 1–9
HJ (Hitler Youth) *see* NSDAP
Holocaust 4, 30–1, 35, 42, 49, 56, 59, 78, 84, 88, 89, 105–31, 134, 144, 158, 168, 171, 172, 179–81, 186, 189
see also Jews: persecution of
see also historiography of the Holocaust
Holodomor 126
homosexuals 12, 107
Horthy, Miklós 35
Höss, Rudolf 117
Hungary and Hungarians 2, 3, 4, 15, 26, 34, 66, 118, 178, 182, 188

Index

Independent State of Croatia (NDH)
   see Croatia
Indians 67
informers 60, 83, 93–4, 176
   see also denunciations
Innsbruck, Carmel of 156
   see also Catholic Church
internet 164, 171–2
Isonzo, River 67
Italian Social Republic (Salò
    Republic) 2, 57
   see also Italy
Italy and Italians xviii, 3–4, 5, 15, 40,
    57, 62, 137, 139, 159–60
  armed bands 24, 25, 50–1, 53, 54,
    66, 67, 69
  collaboration 26, 27, 91, 166
  Communists 20, 66, 67
  film 175, 178
  memory culture 168, 169, 183–5
  totalitarianism xviii, 79, 80, 82, 88–9

Jehovah's Witnesses 12, 21
Jesuits *see* Catholic Church
Jewish ghettoes 42, 92, 120, 121, 122
  Lodz Ghetto 16, 122
  Vilna Ghetto 122
  Warsaw Ghetto 10–11, 122
  Warsaw Ghetto Uprising 121, 122, 124
   see also Jews: resistance
Jewish kapos 120
Jews
  emigration 119
  persecution 7, 10, 12, 15, 21, 45,
    56, 59, 77, 83, 84, 85, 95, 97–8,
    105, 108, 111, 114, 119, 123,
    127, 128, 130, 144–7, 158–9,
    188, 189
   see also Holocaust
  rescue 21, 31, 39, 45, 124–5, 127–
    30, 131, 142, 144, 145–6, 151–2,
    158, 159, 162, 180, 188, 190
  resistance 20, 42, 53, 54, 66, 97,
    119, 121–4
   see also armed bands (Jewish)
John Paul II (Karol Wojtyła) 77, 146

Jong, Johannes de 158
Joyce, William (Lord Haw-Haw) 167
Judenräte (Jewish councils) 16, 120

kapos *see* Jewish kapos
Kazakhs 58
Keneally, Thomas, *Schindler's Ark*
    (1982) 179
Koch, Erich 2, 7
Krasnodar trial 167
Kristallnacht see *Reichskristallnacht*
Kyrgyz 58

labour camps *see* concentration camps
Latvia and Latvians 56, 58
   see also Baltic states and Balts
Laval, Pierre 28, 167
Legion of French Volunteers against
    Bolshevism *see* Wehrmacht
Lemkin, Raphael 119–20
Levi, Primo 123
Ley, Robert 89
Lisieux, Carmel of 155–7
   see also Catholic Church
literature and literary activities 76,
    96, 123, 124, 163, 164, 184
Lithuania and Lithuanians 34, 56, 66
   see also Baltic states and Balts
Lodz Ghetto *see* Jewish ghettoes
Lohse, Hinrich 2
looting 14, 56–7, 60–1, 63, 70
Luxembourg 2, 26
Lviv 5, 59
Lyon 21

Macedonia 53, 66
   see also Yugoslavia
Maidan protest movement 182
massacres and pogroms xviii, 13, 56,
    59, 60, 88, 93, 106, 107, 109,
    111–12, 116, 117, 118–19, 125
   see also reprisals
   see also Jews: persecution
medicine and medical personnel 71,
    75, 87

Mein Kampf 108
men and masculinity *see* gender
Mendès-France, Pierre 177
Mihailović, Dragoljub (Draža) 35, 167
Milice *see* armed bands
militia *see* armed bands
Molotov-Ribbentrop Pact 38, 106
Montenegro 66
 see also Yugoslavia
Moulin, Jean 37, 188
Munich 168
music and musicians 19, 76, 85, 97–8, 123–4
 Chevalier, Maurice 98
 Furtwängler, Kurt 97–8
 Herz-Sommer, Alice 124
 Hot Club, Paris 97
 jazz and jazz clubs 97
 Karajan, Herbert von 97–8
 Messiaen, Olivier 97
 Piaf, Edith 98
 Reinhardt, Django 97
 Swing Youth 97
Muslims 16, 58
Mussert, Anton 15
Mussolini, Benito 3, 8, 57, 67, 88–9, 185

Nachtigall (Nightingale Battalion) *see* Wehrmacht
Nantes 21
National Gathering (Norway) *see* fascist and collaborationist parties
National Socialist Movement (Netherlands) *see* fascist and collaborationist parties
Nazi ideology 9–10, 40–1, 58, 86–90, 95, 106, 109, 115, 116–17, 118, 133, 135, 137, 178
 Endlösung see Final Solution
 Gleichschaltung 89
 Volksgemeinschaft 89, 106
Nazis *see* NSDAP
NDH (Independent State of Croatia) *see* Croatia
Nedić, Milan 3

Netherlands and the Dutch 2, 10, 11, 18, 20, 26, 58, 91, 158, 162, 167, 169–70
New Zealanders 67
Nordland Division *see* Waffen-SS
Normandy 13, 102, 134, 153
 see also France and the French
North Africa 54
Norway and Norwegians 2, 10, 15, 26, 52, 58, 91, 100, 167
Notre-Dame de Paris 103, 159
NOV (People's Liberation Army) *see* armed bands
NSDAP (National Socialist German Workers Party) xviii, 15, 80, 85–7, 109, 115, 146, 179
 DAF (German Labour Front) 5, 89, 94
 DFW (German Women's Welfare) 5
 HJ (Hitler Youth) 5, 12
 KdF (Strength Through Joy) 5
 SA (Sturmabteilung) 5
 SS (Schutzstaffel) 5, 6, 8, 9, 80, 92, 95, 106, 107, 109
 SS: Einsatzgruppen 107, 109, 111, 116, 118
Nuremberg Laws 108
 see also anti-Semitism
Nuremberg trials 108, 117, 168
 see also denazification

Odessa 37–8
Office of the Four-Year Plan 5
Omakaitse *see* armed bands
Oradour-sur-Glane 13
OSS (Office of Strategic Services) 54
Ostministerium (East Ministry) 6, 7
OUN (Organisation of Ukrainian Nationalists) 51, 59, 182–3

Papon, Maurice 168
paramilitarisation 61–72, 133
 see also armed bands
Paris 21, 66, 84, 96, 103, 128–9, 149, 150–1, 152, 154, 157, 158–9

partisans *see* armed bands
Partisans (Yugoslavia) *see* armed bands: NOV
Pavelić, Ante 3, 126–7
PCI *see* Communists: Italy
peasants and farmers 6, 11, 24, 56–7, 61, 71, 75, 77, 85, 125, 160, 175
Pétain, Philippe 3, 8, 25, 28, 98, 103, 128, 150, 167
Pius XII 66, 139, 142, 144, 145–6, 157, 158
Poland and Poles 2, 17, 34, 38, 59, 66, 92, 126, 127, 134, 175, 182, 188, 189
  armed bands 20, 50, 52, 53, 54, 66, 67
  resistance 24, 65, 76–7, 189
  Polish Underground State 76–7
  forced labour 95, 154–5
  Holocaust 106, 109, 112–13, 114, 117
  Catholic Church 140, 145–6, 151, 154–5
  see also Generalgouvernement
popes *see* John-Paul II *and* Pius XII
police 21, 50, 84, 93, 111, 128–9, 155
POWs (prisoners-of-war) and POW camps 7, 10, 13, 53, 56–7, 58, 67, 97, 151, 152, 154, 159–60, 161
PPF (French Popular Party) *see* fascist and collaborationist parties
prisons 12–13, 26–7, 39, 84, 92, 167
propaganda 8–9, 82, 89, 124
prostitution 95
  see also forced labour
Protestant churches *see* churches; clergy and Christians
Putin, Vladimir 36, 183

Quisling, Vidkun 15, 37, 167, 188

rape 95
Red Army 13, 35, 51, 53, 58, 68, 69, 70, 106, 183
refugees 129

Reichskommissare (Nazi civilian governors) 2, 5
Reichskristallnacht 108, 109
  see also Jews: persecution
Renault, Louis 17–18
reprisals 24, 51, 60, 93, 101, 120, 185
Republican National Guard *see* armed bands
resistance
  active (*Widerstand*) 19–22, 41, 70, 72, 75, 77, 88, 101, 122, 129, 131
  armed *see* armed bands
  Catholic 143–4, 147, 151, 153, 159, 162
  see also Catholic Church
  cultural 21, 123–4
  definitions 27, 38–44
  economic 20–1
  escape lines 48, 152
  passive (*Resistenz*) 19, 40–1, 42, 70, 76, 82, 100, 101, 129, 131
  political 20, 74, 93
  religious 21
  see also commemoration of resistance
  see also historiography of resistance and collaboration
resisters (post-war) 24–5, 168–9, 188
Ribbentrop, Joachim von 9
ROA (Russian Army of Liberation) 7, 58
Roma 10, 12
Romania 3, 4, 5, 26
Rosenberg, Alfred 6, 7
Rumkowski, Chaim 16
Russia and Russians 57, 58, 59, 67, 167, 170, 182
Russian Army of Liberation *see* ROA
Russian Federation 36, 69, 182, 183
Russian Revolution 107

SA (Sturmabteilung) *see* NSDAP
Salò Republic *see* Italian Social Republic
Sauckel, Fritz 6, 7, 9
Schindler, Oskar 179
Scholl, Hans and Sophie 168–9

schools, teachers and universities 7, 29, 75, 76, 89, 92, 99–100, 124, 125, 174, 179
Schutzmannschaften *see* armed bands
Security Battalions *see* armed bands
Serbia and Serbs 2, 3, 34, 35, 56, 66, 127, 128, 182
  see also Yugoslavia
Seyss-Inquart, Arthur 2
Sheptyts'kyi, Andrei 66
Shoah 105, 146, 165, 180
  see also Holocaust
Shoah Foundation 179
Shukhevych, Roman 35, 59, 62
Sippenhaft 93
slave labour 6, 7
  see also forced labour
Slovak Republic 2, 3, 91
  see also Czechoslovakia
Slovenia and Slovenes 2, 66, 67
  see also Yugoslavia
social history of politics xix, 135–8, 157, 158, 161–2, 190
socialists 12, 52, 53
Society of St Vincent de Paul *see* Catholic Church
SOE (Special Operations Executive) 34, 54, 55, 63, 69
Sokols 99
Sonderkommandos (special detachments) 120
Soviet Union *see* USSR
Spain and Spaniards 57, 66
Spanish Civil War 51
Speer, Albert 9
Spinelli, Barbara 185
SS (Schutzstaffel) *see* NSDAP
Stalingrad 54, 106, 167
Stauffenberg, Claus von 20, 24, 29
Stepinac, Alojzije 160–1
STO (*Service du Travail Obligatoire*) 9, 55
  see also forced labour
Stuck, Franz 154
Strasbourg 151
  see also Alsace-Lorraine

Strength Through Joy (KdF) *see* NSDAP
strikes 20–1
Stülpnagel, Carl-Heinrich von 8
Sudeten Germans 26, 166
  see also Czechoslovakia
  see also Germans, ethnic (non-Reich)
Suhard, Emmanuel 158–9
Sweden 128
Switzerland 152, 156, 159, 176
Szálasi, Ferenc 3, 15

Tatars 10, 16, 26, 60–1
teachers *see* schools, teachers and universities
television *see* film, television and theatre
Terboven, Josef 2
theatre *see* film, television and theatre
Thérèse of Lisieux (St) 155–6
Theresienstadt *see* concentration camps
Tiso, Jozef 3, 35
Tito (Josip Broz) 67, 114
Todt Organisation 5, 18
torture 93, 140
total war xviii, 61, 87, 88, 106, 119, 125, 137, 150, 162, 190
totalitarianism and totalitarian theory xviii, 35, 61, 79–81, 84, 86–90, 94–5, 109, 113, 115, 117, 147, 162
Touvier, Paul 168
trade unions 12, 20–1
Treblinka *see* concentration camps

Ukraine and Ukrainians (post-independence) 69, 182–3
Ukraine and Ukrainians (pre-independence) 2, 5, 17, 24, 32, 35, 37–8, 56, 58, 59, 62, 63, 64, 69, 71, 117–18, 126, 130, 188
  see also USSR
United States and Americans 25, 67, 69, 79, 120, 170, 171, 179, 185

universities *see* schools, teachers and universities
UPA (Ukrainian Insurgent Army) *see* armed bands
U.S. Army Military Intelligence Corps 69
USSR 2, 4, 38, 56, 62, 67, 105, 107, 116, 126, 134, 167, 182
   Holocaust 105, 106, 107, 116, 125
   occupied territories xii (map), 5–8, 16, 17, 18, 24, 25, 53, 54–5
   partisans 24, 25, 51, 52, 53, 54–5, 69, 169
   totalitarianism xx, 79, 80
   see also Ukraine and Ukrainians (pre-independence)
Ustaše (Croatia) *see* armed bands
Uzbeks 58

Versailles Treaty 1
Vichy 2, 3, 8, 25–6, 28, 30, 40, 84, 91, 98, 99, 103, 110–11, 114, 128–9, 150, 168, 173, 177
   see also France
Vilna Ghetto *see* Jewish ghettoes
Vlasov, Andrei 7
Volhynia 66, 117
Volksgemeinschaft see Nazi ideology

Waffen-SS 8, 15, 50, 58, 65
   Charlemagne Division 58
   Nordland Division 58
Wannsee Conference 108, 110
Warsaw 20, 21, 120
Warsaw Ghetto *see* Jewish ghettoes

Wehrmacht 2, 5, 7, 8, 15, 17, 18, 30, 31, 38–9, 50, 53, 57, 58, 65, 67, 95, 107, 118, 130, 137, 144
   eastern troops (*Osttruppen*) 58
   Hilfswillige (*Hiwis*) 15, 57–8
   Legion of French Volunteers against Bolshevism 59
   Nachtigall (Nightingale Battalion) 59
West Germany (Federal Republic of Germany) 27, 28–9, 46, 79, 168–9, 170–1, 172, 176
White Rose resistance group 168–9
Wiesel, Elie 180
women and women's history *see* gender
Wojtyła, Karol *see* John Paul II
World War I 126

Yanukovych, Viktor 182
young people and children 12, 30, 39, 82, 86, 91, 92, 96, 97, 99–100, 129, 149, 150, 152, 153, 168–9, 174, 175, 177
Yugoslavia 2, 4, 20, 24, 25, 26, 33–4, 52, 53, 54, 56, 62, 63, 67, 68, 91, 114, 126–7, 161, 167, 170
   see also Bosnia and Bosnians
   see also Croatia and Croats
   see also Macedonia
   see also Montenegro
   see also Serbia and Serbs
   see also Slovenia and Slovenes

Zionism 122

www.ingramcontent.com/pod-product-compliance
Ingram Content Group UK Ltd.
Pitfield, Milton Keynes, MK11 3LW, UK
UKHW021909220326
469204UK00009B/274